DEMARKETING

We all understand the basic principles underpinning marketing activity: to identify unfulfilled needs and desires and boost demand for the solutions a product is offering. The mantra is always "sell more". Demarketing tries for the very opposite. Why would a company actively try to decrease demand?

There are many good reasons to do so: a firm cannot supply large enough quantities, or wants to limit supply to a region of narrow profit margin. Or, crucially, to discourage undesirable customers: those that could be bad for brand reputation or, in the case of the finance sector, high risk. Demarketing can yield effective solutions to these issues, effectively curtailing demand yet (crucially) not destroying it. Nevertheless, the fundamental negativity of demarketing strategies often causes organizations to hide them from view and, as a result, they are rarely studied.

This then is the first book to cast light on the secretive, counterintuitive world of demarketing, deconstructing its mysteries and demonstrating how to incorporate them into a profit-driven marketing plan. A selection of thought leaders in strategic marketing mix theory with illustrative global cases, providing insight into how these strategies have been employed in practice and measuring their successes and failures. It's a must-read for any student or researcher that wants to think differently about marketing.

Nigel Bradley was Senior Lecturer in Marketing at the University of Westminster, UK.

Jim Blythe is Professor of Marketing at Westminster University and Visiting Professor at Plymouth Business School, UK.

DEMARKETING

Edited by
Nigel Bradley and Jim Blythe

Routledge
Taylor & Francis Group

LONDON AND NEW YORK

First published 2014
by Routledge
2 Park Square, Milton Park, Abingdon, Oxon OX14 4RN

and by Routledge
711 Third Avenue, New York, NY 10017

Routledge is an imprint of the Taylor & Francis Group, an informa business

© 2014 Nigel Bradley and Jim Blythe

British Library Cataloguing in Publication Data
A catalogue record for this book is available from the British Library

Library of Congress Cataloging in Publication Data
Demarketing / edited by Nigel Bradley and Jim Blythe.
  p. cm
  Includes bibliographical references and index.
  1. Marketing–Management. 2. Marketing. I. Bradley, Nigel, 1958- II. Blythe, Jim.
  HF5415.13.D3697 2013
  658.8–dc23
          2013015515

ISBN: 978-0-415-81647-2 (hbk)
ISBN: 978-0-415-81648-9 (pbk)
ISBN: 978-0-203-59120-8 (ebk)

Typeset in Bembo
by Taylor & Francis Books

MIX
Paper from
responsible sources
FSC
www.fsc.org   FSC® C013604

Printed and bound in Great Britain by
CPI Group (UK) Ltd, Croydon, CR0 4YY

Sadly, Nigel Bradley passed away shortly before completing this book. His was the initial idea, and he was the driving force behind it right up to the day before his sad demise. He will be remembered for his kindness, courage, and his rigorous intellect – he will be missed.

To my friend and colleague Nigel, whose courage and integrity will always be with me.

CONTENTS

LIST OF TABLES AND FIGURES

Tables

Figures

Box

ACKNOWLEDGMENTS

This book is something of a departure for both of us. We both teach marketing, and have both been practitioners and consultants, but the main thing people always want us to address is ways of increasing business. In this book, we are looking at ways in which marketers sometimes decrease business – and the reasons why this happens.

In an edited book of this nature, a lot of things have to come together – the overall planning is one thing, but taking a disciplined and academically rigorous approach to the actual writing is critical. We would therefore especially like to thank our contributors, who have taken on the challenge of explaining various aspects of demarketing – this has been an education for both of us, even though we already thought we understood the subject quite well.

We also want to acknowledge the many organizations, commercial and otherwise, who have been so generous in helping with the case study material. For these individuals and organizations, there is no immediately obvious benefit in helping with an academic publication, so their help has been especially appreciated.

At Routledge, we would like to thank Amy Laurens for giving us the chance to produce this book, and Rosie Baron for her patience and persistence in ensuring that we kept to the deadlines, kept within the law, and created something publishable.

Finally, we would like to thank our wives and families, especially of course Alison and Sue, for bearing with us through the process and putting up with our occasional panic attacks. We couldn't have done it without you.

CONTRIBUTORS

Paul Baines is Professor of Political Marketing, Cranfield School of Management and Programme Director, MSc in Management. Over the last fifteen years, Paul's research has particularly focused on political marketing, public opinion and propaganda. Paul's latest books include *Political Marketing* (Sage Publications, 2011), with Sir Robert Worcester, Roger Mortimore and Mark Gill, *Explaining Cameron's Coalition* (Biteback Publishing, 2011) and a 4-volume book set on *Propaganda* with Nicholas O'Shaughnessy (Sage Publications, 2013). Paul's consultancy includes experience working with UK government departments on communication research projects as well as small and large private enterprises on market research/marketing planning. He operates his own strategic marketing/research consultancy, Baines Associates Limited.

Jim Blythe is Professor of Marketing at Westminster University and Visiting Professor at Plymouth Business School, UK.

Clive Boddy is now Professor of Leadership and Organisational Behaviour at Middlesex University Business School in London, where he was previously an Associate Professor in Marketing. Prior to academia, he co-founded a multi-national market research company with offices throughout the Far East. He is currently researching the impact of Corporate Psychopaths on business, marketing, employees, corporate ethics and the global financial crisis. Clive regularly presents at marketing and management conferences around the world and publishes papers on ethics, marketing morals, research techniques and psychopathic management in journals including *The Marketing Review*, the *International Journal of Market Research* and the *Journal of Business Ethics*. He is the author of the book *Corporate Psychopaths: Organisational Destroyers* and the well-known paper called 'The Corporate Psychopaths Theory of the Global Financial Crisis'. He is a Fellow of the Chartered Institute of Marketing, a Fellow of the Association for Tertiary Education Management and a Fellow of the Australian Institute of Management.

Nigel Bradley was Senior Lecturer in Marketing at the University of Westminster, UK.

Robin Croft joined Bedfordshire Business School in 2010, having previously held teaching posts at Glamorgan and Lincoln Universities. He has a lifelong interest in interpersonal communication, having gained a first degree in languages. Robin has written extensively on word of mouth, political marketing, arts marketing, and more recently on technology and social media – an area which has led to appearances on TV and radio. He has published more than 70 conference papers and journal articles since joining academic life from industry in 1993. He is a graduate of the universities of Oxford and Salford, and is a prolific amateur photographer and saxophonist.

Jillian Dawes Farquhar is Professor of Marketing Strategy at the University of Bedfordshire, where she also directs the doctoral programme in the Business School. Previous employment has included Reader at Oxford Brookes and positions at Northampton and Manchester Metropolitan Universities. She is visiting professor at the universities of Pusan in Korea and Salerno in Italy. Author of books, book chapters and international journal papers and a former journal editor, Jillian has long contributed to research in marketing strategies in services and particularly financial services. Recent work has taken her in the direction of research methods, specifically case study research.

Nadio Granata is a Chartered Marketer and Company Director. Until recently he was a Senior Lecturer in Marketing at the University of Huddersfield where he was a lead academic in practical-based research projects. He has been involved in numerous place marketing initiatives and is currently consulting with Rugby Borough Council on their preparations for the Rugby World Cup 2015.

Nigel Jones has worked in defence and security for over 25 years as practitioner and academic. He is particularly interested in sociotechnical factors affecting communications and human behaviour. This he developed in an Army career that saw operational deployments in the Balkans and Middle East. He leads several courses on cyber, operational planning and communications at Cranfield Defence and Security, located at the Defence Academy of the United Kingdom. Prior to joining Cranfield, Nigel led a security and research team at QinetiQ PLC where he was also Director of the UK Government's Cyber Security Knowledge Transfer Network. This was a Technology Strategy Board initiative, bringing academic, public and private sector parties together to work on contemporary security challenges. His research and writing focuses on the effective application of social science in problem solving and communication.

Theresa A. Kirchner, PhD, MBCP, MBCI, is Assistant Professor of Management with the School of Business, Hampton University. Her background includes over twenty years of work with nonprofit boards of directors as well as extensive for-profit corporate executive experience. Her research interests include strategic management/marketing and organizational business continuity and resiliency management. Her publications have appeared in *International Journal of Nonprofit and Voluntary Sector Marketing*, *Journal of the Academy of Business and Economics*, *Disaster Recovery Journal*, *Arts Marketing: An International Journal* and *European Journal of Management*.

Nnamdi O. Madichie, PhD, is Associate Professor of Marketing at the University of Sharjah (UAE) as well as Visiting Research Fellow at the Royal Docks Business School, University of East London, UK. Prior to his current position, he was Senior Lecturer and Programme Leader for both the BA (Hons) Marketing and BA (Hons) Business Studies at the University of East London (2003–2008). He has developed both teaching and research interests in consumer behaviour in various contexts – spanning both places (UK, Middle East, Africa and South Asia) and spaces (sports, retail and shopping malls), having published papers on consumer behaviour in sports in the Middle East, self-service in petrol stations and online shopping. Nnamdi Madichie is currently Editor-in-Chief of the *African Journal of Business and Economic Research* (AJBER) as well as MENA Regional Editor for both *Management Decision* and *Foresight* journals in the Emerald Portfolio. He can be contacted at: nmadichie@sharjah.ac.ae.

María Pilar Martínez-Ruiz is Associate Professor of Marketing at Marketing Department, University of Castilla-La Mancha, Spain. Her research interests fall in the areas of retailing, pricing and marketing communications. Professor Martínez-Ruiz has published in *European Journal of Marketing*, *Journal of Retailing and Consumer Services*, *Journal of the Operational Research Society*, *International Journal of Market Research*, *Tourism Management*, *Decision Support Systems*, and other journals. She co-chaired the Track on Retailing and Pricing at the 2012 AMA Summer Marketing Educators' Conference.

Sally McKechnie is Associate Professor in Marketing at Nottingham University Business School, Member of the Academy of Marketing Science, Academy of Marketing and Member of the Chartered Institute of Marketing. She is also a Governor of the History of Advertising Trust. Prior to returning to academia, she held marketing positions in the exhibitions and direct marketing industries. She also held a teaching company associateship at the University of Strathclyde. She is a member of the editorial boards of the *Journal of Customer Behaviour* and the *International Journal of Bank Marketing*, and has published in a number of journals including the *European Journal of Marketing*, *Journal of Business Research*, *Journal of Marketing Management*, *Journal of Product and Brand Management*, *International Journal of Retail Distribution and Management*, *Journal of Consumer Behaviour*, *International Journal of Advertising* and *Journal of Customer Behaviour*. Her research interests continue to be in the areas of consumer behaviour and marketing communications, with a particular interest in consumption issues.

Dominic Medway is Professor of Marketing at Manchester Business School, UK. He is Head of the Marketing, Operations Management and Service Systems (MOMS) Division.

Heather Skinner is Reader in Marketing at the University of South Wales' Business School, and a National Teaching Fellow. Heather has 27 papers published in peer-reviewed journals, she has authored three book chapters, and presented 53 refereed papers at international and national conferences. Her publications reflect the four main themes of her research: Place Marketing & Branding; Services, Sports and Non-profit Marketing, and Marketing Research; Marketing Communications and Education.

(Daisy) Jing Tan currently works as a lecturer in marketing at the University of Wolverhampton. She was formerly a Quintin Hogg Scholar at the University of Westminster, where she received her PhD degree. She researches on e-commerce, digital marketing, social media and industrial marketing. Her work has appeared in 3-star journal *Information & Management*. Dr Tan has also presented her work at conferences at both national and international levels.

Gary Warnaby is Professor of Marketing in the School of Materials at the University of Manchester. His research interests focus on the marketing of places and retailing. Results of this research have been published in various academic journals in both the management and geography disciplines, including *Environment and Planning A, Journal of Business Research, Journal of Marketing Management, Marketing Theory, Consumption Markets & Culture, European Journal of Marketing, Area, Cities and Local Economy.* He is co-author of *Relationship Marketing: A Consumer Experience Approach*, co-editor of *Perspectives on Public Relations Research*, and has contributed to numerous edited books.

Steve Welsh is a Senior Manager in a UK law-enforcement agency dealing with serious organized crime. He heads the agency's Behavioural Science & Futures team. Previously he was a Detective Superintendent with the National Crime Squad (NCS). He was originally a police officer serving in the Metropolitan Police Service, completing over 30 years' service, mainly as a detective specializing in combating organized crime. Steve was part of the multi-agency team that produced the National Intelligence Model for UK Law Enforcement. He led for UK law enforcement in the Home Office project that planned UK adoption of cross border surveillance within the EU on behalf of ACPO and ACPOS. He chairs the Global Futures Forum's Community of Interest on Transnational Organised Crime. His team provides regular horizon scanning on organized crime to ministers as well as policy and law-enforcement partners via the National Security Council.

David Wyles studied town planning before becoming a chartered town planner with Kirklees Council in 1974. In 1984, he was appointed Kirklees' first tourism officer, developing the Pennine Yorkshire brand with Calderdale Council, which was runner up in the English Tourist Board's 'England for Excellence' awards.

In 1994, David joined the Council's Partnership Service, supporting joint partnership developments including the McAlpine (now John Smith) stadium, Kingsgate shopping centre and town centre regeneration projects. In 1999, this role was extended to take on town centre management responsibilities for

Huddersfield, establishing one of the largest town centre companies in England and becoming 'Town Centre Manager of the Year' in 1993. David later managed teams dealing with town and village centre regeneration, markets and town centre management across the district before taking early retirement in 2010.

David has written about the architecture of Huddersfield and contributed to a wide number of publications and radio and television features.

1

DEMARKETING

An overview of the antecedents and current status of the discipline

Nigel Bradley and Jim Blythe

Introduction

Demarketing can be defined as the deliberate attempt by marketers to reduce demand for a product by using the same tools and techniques as are normally used to increase demand. At first, this appears to be a contradiction: to the lay person, and indeed to many marketers, the purpose of marketing is to increase demand, whether from the same group of customers or from new customers recruited to the firm's loyal group of regular users. The emphasis in segmentation theory is always on satisfying the needs of a specific group of customers, presumably all with similar characteristics, but the frame of this picture is too small – it fails to show the far greater number of customers who are being excluded. Demarketing seeks to reduce demand for a product, sometimes overall, sometimes from 'undesirable' customers, and sometimes at specific times. This is the flipside of segmentation.

This chapter provides an overview of the antecedents and current status of demarketing derived from published works. It explains how demarketing has evolved; although marketing has successfully encouraged and satisfied demand, mass production has caused environmental damage and there is a general recognition that humanity cannot keep increasing its consumption of natural resources. This paradox led to various responses including appeals to practise sustainability and responsible marketing. After the turn of the century, scientific arguments were brought to a wider public in an easy-to-understand way, and thus people began to re-examine consumption and production, not only from the viewpoint of environmental sustainability but also from the viewpoint of practical, efficient marketing.

The beginnings of demarketing

In their pioneering article, Kotler and Levy (1971) described three different types of demarketing:

1. General demarketing, which is required when a company wants to shrink the level of total demand.

2. Selective demarketing, which is required when a company wants to discourage the demand coming from certain customer classes.
3. Ostensible demarketing, which involves the appearance of trying to discourage demand as a device for actually increasing it.

A fourth type, unintentional demarketing, is also important: it was mentioned in a negative way as an effort to increase demand, resulting actually in driving customers away.

Kotler and Levy gave several examples, including the following:

- Eastman Kodak introduced its Instamatic camera in the early 1960s and found itself facing runaway demand. A few years passed before Kodak achieved enough capacity to handle demand.
- Wilkinson Sword introduced its new stainless steel blade in the early 1960s and was besieged by regular and new dealers for supplies, not all of whom could be satisfied.
- Anheuser-Busch underestimated the rate of growth in demand for its popular Budweiser beer and found itself in the late 1960s having to ration supplies to its better dealers and markets while it was making a crash effort to expand its plants.
- Savings and loan associations in 1970–1971 faced an oversupply of savings relative to their ability to invest the funds and sought means to discourage the savings customers. They were willing to encourage small accounts, but refused large depositors.

According to Kotler and Levy, these cases represent temporary shortages in supply for which demand must be adjusted. They suggest using the classic tools of marketing to reduce demand, in the following ways:

- Curtail advertising expenditures for the product, modifying the content of the messages.
- Reduce sales promotion expenditures, investing less in trade exhibits, point-of-purchase displays, catalogue space, and so on.
- Cut back salesmen's selling time on the product and their entertainment budgets, asking them to concentrate on other products, spend more time in service and intelligence work, and learn to say *no* in a way that customers find acceptable.
- Increase the price and other conditions of sale to the advantage of the marketing company. (This may include eliminating freight allowances, trade discounts, and so on.)
- Add to the time and expense necessary for the buyer to procure the product or service – what might be called his 'effort and psychological costs' – as a means of discouraging demand.
- Reduce product quality or content, either to encourage deconsuming or to make more of the product available and thus demarket at a slower rate.
- Curtail the number of distribution outlets, using the product shortage as an opportunity to eliminate undesirable dealers and/or customers.

For the purposes of this book, we have expanded Kotler and Levy's original four types of demarketing into a total of six types, as follows:

1. Synchromarketing. Synchromarketing involves looking at the overall market for the product, and trying to manipulate it so that sales occur at times which synchronize with the firm's production scheduling. The aim may be to 'redistribute' existing sales (that are already at optimum levels) so that they occur at times, or in places, that the supplier prefers. Thus, for example, organizations that have highly seasonal sales (which make inefficient use of resources) may want to increase non-seasonal sales. Synchromarketing might be achieved by differential pricing, or by cutting advertising at times of peak demand, or perhaps by simply limiting availability at peak times.

2. Counter-marketing. This is a deliberate attempt to counteract a pressure to buy, and is often undertaken as part of a public health campaign to reduce consumption of drugs, tobacco or alcohol. It is usually a public-sector activity (but is occasionally undertaken by the private sector, where some uses of a product are damaging the corporate image). There may be an objective of stopping consumption completely.

3. General demarketing. This is an attempt to reduce overall demand across the board, and might be undertaken if demand is simply too high. Kotler and Levy give the example of a small restaurant where demand exceeds capacity, resulting in large groups of people hanging around in the hope of benefiting from a cancellation. These groups might affect the restaurant's ambience, so management would clearly want to demarket the restaurant to the point where capacity matches demand.

4. Selective demarketing. This involves discouraging demand from certain customer classes. For example, a hotel might want to discourage disruptive guests, or an insurance company might want to discourage people who are most likely to make a claim. Clearly, differential pricing can be used to achieve the right outcome, but in some cases that will not be enough – the insurance company might want to discourage people from even applying for a policy. This requires some extremely subtle promotional policies.

5. Ostensible demarketing. This involves creating the appearance of trying to discourage demand as a device for actually increasing it. Sometimes a company will want to appear as if it wants to lose customers so that demand increases – for example, a company that claims that there is a limited supply of a product, or that it is exclusive, might therefore increase people's desire to be one of the 'chosen few' who are allowed to buy. In other cases, companies have threatened to withdraw products because sales are low, thus generating publicity that increases sales.

6. Unintentional demarketing. There have been many botched attempts to increase sales: unintentional demarketing is marketing that goes a step further, resulting in lost sales rather than gains.

Demarketing and the environment

During the first part of the twenty-first century, demarketing has become more common, as environmental issues have increased in importance and as companies have had to become more careful in directing their limited resources.

The 1970s are remembered by many people for oil shortages, recession and inflation. It is against this background that new strands of thought about marketing emerged. We saw non-profit and social marketing developing as a result of a greater sense of social responsibility. Kotler and Levy (1971) defined demarketing, and Corporate Social Responsibility (CSR) emerged. In 1973, Dr Schumacher, a former adviser to the British National Coal Board, published his book *Small is Beautiful*, in which he stressed that decentralized business activities should be encouraged; such decentralism opposes globalization (Schumacher 1973). He felt that the workplace should be dignified and meaningful and that the world's natural resources must be considered. The book was pivotal in changing people's thinking, and has been republished many times since, the latest edition in 2011. These notions have been echoed in many initiatives that grew from his ideas. One pioneer of this wave of responsible marketing was George Fisk (1973, 1974), who identified both the consumer and supplier of products as accountable for effects on the environment. There were of course many other voices. In the 1980s, we saw the emergence of Services Marketing and also the first wave of green marketing. CSR Reports started with the ice cream producer Ben & Jerry's, whose financial report was supplemented by a wider view on the environmental impact of the corporation. In 1987, a document prepared by the World Commission on Environment and Development defined sustainable development as meeting 'the needs of the present without compromising the ability of future generations to meet their own need', this became known as the Brundtland Report and was another step towards widespread thinking on sustainability in everyday activity (WCED 1987).

The view that the human race was (and is) consuming far too much was becoming a threat to traditional marketing thinking, which had assumed that the greatest good would be obtained if people's material standard of living were to be maximized. The new thinking was that the greatest good would be obtained by ensuring that marketing was sustainable, so that the natural environment could cope with supplying raw materials and absorbing waste products.

In 1989, a manmade disaster came in the form of the Exxon Valdez oil spill. Over 10 million gallons of crude oil was lost into the sea and this killed fish, birds and other forms of life. It is one of the most damaging environmental disasters created by humankind. This and other 'misdeeds' by corporations led to greater policing of conduct, but, more importantly, to a sense of responsibility from the organizations themselves.

In the early 1990s, two marketing authors assembled their knowledge and views into two key books, both of which were called *Green Marketing*. They were Ken Peattie (1992) in the United Kingdom and Jacquelyn Ottman (1993) in the United States of America. Green marketing seeks to meet consumer needs with minimum damage to the environment, recognizing that consumers also have a need to live in a healthy world, and corporations cannot long survive if they simply destroy everything they touch. During the same decade, the phrase 'triple bottom-line' was coined by John Elkington (1994) in his article 'Towards the sustainable corporation'. This is easily remembered as People, Planet and Profits, and recognized that profit alone cannot be the only aim for a corporation. Without responsibility towards people and to the planet on which they live, corporations cannot survive. It was effectively a tangible step towards social, environmental and monetary accountability on the balance sheet.

During the second decade of the twenty first century, over-consumption has again been under attack, this time as the main factor in obesity. Marketers have come under fire for promoting sugary drinks, fatty fast foods and unhealthy ready meals: the rise in binge drinking has also led to accusations that corporations encourage over-indulgence in alcohol consumption.

The thrust towards sustainable business inevitably led to a greater emphasis on controlling (directing) demand rather than maximizing it. At the same time, greater competitive pressures and tighter financial constraints pushed firms more and more towards selectivity in targeting market segments.

Demarketing and social responsibility

Another driver for demarketing has been a rise in social responsibility, especially among government departments that seek to control or prevent consumption of some products. The most obvious demarketing campaigns have been the anti-smoking campaigns carried out by governments in most countries, but other demarketing campaigns have been initiated by charities and even commercial organizations. These have been mainly in the counter-marketing or general demarketing areas – reducing or eliminating demand for a product category – but some have been selective, for example campaigns aimed at reducing salt intake for people with high blood pressure.

The effect of these campaigns has been a tendency for manufacturers to follow suit – distillers now commonly say 'Enjoy our brand responsibly' in their advertising. This may be an example of ostensible demarketing – pretending to encourage people to drink less as a way of reassuring them that the brand is a good, honest one to buy – or it may simply be a measure of corporate responsibility.

Firms may also use selective demarketing to improve the safety of staff and other customers. For example, railway operators use billboard advertising to warn passengers that unruly behaviour will result in expulsion from the trains, and potentially a ban on travelling on the railways in future. Football fans travelling to away matches often find that they are provided with outdated (and much less comfortable) rolling stock, and are herded by police through barriers. Selective demarketing might involve a simple refusal to do business with an undesirable market segment, as happens when car hire companies refuse to hire to young drivers, or when an insurance company raises the premiums on people who live in areas with high car crime rates.

Marketing mistakes

There are so many examples of marketing errors that have led to losing business that it is difficult to know where to begin. Firms introduce products that flop, or produce advertising campaigns that damage the firm's image, or mishandle their PR campaigns to the extent that people shun the business and its products.

Unintentional demarketing implies that a deliberate act on the part of the marketers led to an unexpected or unwanted consequence – a reduction in sales. A simple failure to act (for example, neglecting to promote a brand) is not sufficient to amount to demarketing. Likewise, a new product launch that fails to cover the costs of development should not be classified as demarketing. Sales promotions such as the infamous Hoover debacle of the 1990s (in which Hoover offered free airline tickets to anyone who bought a Hoover appliance) also do not count, even though the company lost money dramatically and had to be bailed out by the US parent company, because there was no loss of demand for the products – quite the reverse, in fact. In such cases, the marketing has succeeded in what it set out to do, namely increase demand, even if it is ill-advised in that it failed to deliver increased profits.

The attempt by Netflix to enter the digital streaming market in 2011 was certainly unintentional demarketing. Up until then, Netflix had operated a mail-order DVD rental service, and were turning over $16bn a year. They launched their Qwikster download service as an easy alternative to mail-order. Unfortunately, having both systems in place made the system more complex, and also more expensive for subscribers – the company failed to give existing subscribers the new system for free, and thus lost 800,000 subscribers and 77 per cent of the company's share value in only four months (CNET 2012). This was an impressive example of unintentional demarketing – the company even failed to notice that the name Qwikster already belonged to a Twitter account holder, which effectively barred Netflix from using Twitter.

Although not every example of unintentional demarketing is as extreme as the Netflix example, it is extremely common for marketers to make mistakes. By its nature, marketing is a creative profession, and therefore past experience is only of limited help in meeting new circumstances: therefore, each campaign, however carefully planned, carries with it the risk of meeting with the unexpected.

Drawing the boundaries

The boundaries between the different types of demarketing can be somewhat blurred. Counter-marketing and general demarketing can look very similar, also selective demarketing and synchromarketing can seem to overlap. For example, a counter-marketing campaign to stop consumption of, say, illegal drugs will (at best) probably only reduce demand overall, which is of course what general demarketing sets out to do. Synchromarketing aims at reducing demand at peak times, but, in the case of (say) package holidays, the rise in prices seen during school holidays may seem more like selective demarketing aimed at families.

Ostensible demarketing (in which companies appear to want to reduce demand, but actually aim for the opposite) may well backfire and become unintentional demarketing, and may in any case be very hard to distinguish from other forms of demarketing since it is the intention that makes the difference, not the action.

Of course, this is often true of other aspects of marketing – prices may be regarded as sales promotions sometimes, or as marketing communications (conveying an image of quality or value for money, for example). Since demarketing is still an area that has received relatively little thought or attention, these anomalies may well be addressed in the future.

References

CNET 2012 (accessed February 2013): http://news.cnet.com/8301–1023_3-57468798-93/netflixs-lost-year-the-inside-story-of-the-price-hike-train-wreck/?part=rss&subj=news&tag=title

Elkington, John (1994): Towards the sustainable corporation: Win-Win-Win business strategies for sustainable development. *California Management Review*. Winter, 36 (2) p. 90.

Fisk, George (1973): Criteria for a theory of responsible consumption. *Journal of Marketing* 37 (April) pp. 24–31.

——(1974): *Marketing and the Ecological Crisis* (New York: Harper and Row).

Kotler, P. and Levy, S. J. (1971): Demarketing, yes, demarketing. *Harvard Business Review* 49 (6) pp. 74–80.

Ottman, J. (1993): *Green Marketing* (Lincolnwood Ill: NTC Business Books).

Peattie, K. (1999[1992]): *Green Marketing* (London: M&E Handbooks).

Schumacher, E. F. (2011): *Small is Beautiful: A study of economics as if people mattered* (New York: Vintage Publishing).

World Commission on Environment and Development (WCED) (1987): *The Brundtland Report: Our common future* (New York: United Nations).

2

SYNCHROMARKETING

María Pilar Martínez-Ruiz

Introduction

Traditionally, it has been assumed that a professional marketer focuses principally on the task of creating and maintaining demand for certain goods and services. As pointed out by Kotler (1973), and subsequently revisited by the same author 20 years later (Kotler, 1993), this is only a limited perspective regarding the different marketing challenges faced by organizations. From a broader point of view, marketing management can be understood to be a question of regulating the level, timing and character of demand for one or more products of an organization. In general, a company's desired level of demand is considered to be based on profit optimization: that is to say, sales maximization subject to a profit constraint, satisfying the current or desired level of supply or some other type of analysis (Kotler, 1973).

As Kotler (1973) suggests, one of the challenges refers to the fact that it is common for many organizations to find that their demand experiences excessive seasonality. This can be so extreme that it may vary from day to day, or even from hour to hour, causing problems of excess or absence of demand. Transportation services are an example of this. Thus, it is not surprising to find that at peak times there may be a shortage of vehicles providing certain services, whilst at off-peak times there may be a number of empty vehicles. A further example is that of museums, which receive the majority of their visitors at weekends and, therefore, the current level of demand may be below, equal to, or above the desired level of demand. These are some examples of what is known as irregular demand.

In the specific problem posited of irregular demand, the explicit task of marketing management is not simply to build demand, but rather to regulate the level, timing and character of demand for an organization's product in terms of its objectives at the time. This view applies to all organizations where marketing management involves the marketing question of synchronizing demand, formally known as synchromarketing (Kotler, 1973). Therefore, it encompasses the management of fluctuating but otherwise normal and expected demand (in terms of average demand and supply). This would be a particular demarketing type, encompassing the marketing task of trying to resolve irregular demand, by trying principally to bring the movements of demand and supply into better synchronization.

This is precisely the subject of this chapter, which will illustrate the main applications of synchromarketing. In the following section, the concept of synchromarketing will be reviewed, after which the main types of synchromarketing, as well as some illustrative examples, will be given.

The concept of synchromarketing

An organization may often be very satisfied with its average level of demand, but quite dissatisfied, however, with its temporal pattern. For example, some seasons may be marked by demand surging far beyond supply capacity, and other seasons may be marked by a wasteful underutilization of the organization's supply capacity. From this point of view, irregular demand was first defined by Kotler (1973, p. 46) as: 'a state in which the current timing pattern of demand is marked by seasonal or volatile fluctuations that depart from the timing pattern of supply'.

In this respect, many examples of irregular demand can be cited, either from tangible product categories or from services. For example, frozen dairy products can be considered as one of the grocery categories with the clearest seasonal sales pattern. No doubt summer is the most important season for eating ice cream and other related products. This pattern is very prominent in countries such as the USA, despite certain regional differences. As a matter of fact, every year USA production starts up in March and April to fill retail and foodservice pipelines in the late spring and early summer. June is the highest production month of the year, but it remains strong through August to satisfy summer demand, while it declines at the end of the year (Roeder, 2012a). This seasonal pattern is so manifest in this market that there is even a National Ice Cream Month as well as a National Ice Cream Day, which were designated by President Reagan in 1984 as July and the third Sunday of the month, respectively. He even called on all people of the United States to observe these events with 'appropriate ceremonies and activities' (Roeder, 2012b).

Another good example of irregular demand, this time for services, can be found in the tourism sector of most European countries. Especially in Mediterranean countries associated with an image of 'sun and sand destination', demand for tourism services is highly seasonal and bargains are hard to find in July and August, which clearly represent these countries' peak holiday periods. This seasonal pattern can also be found regarding weekdays, as usually hotels are under-booked at this time, whereas they are overbooked at weekends.

A less common version of the irregular demand situation is where supply, despite being available, fluctuates in a perverse way in relation to demand (Kotler, 1973). That is to say, although supply and demand are both available, they move in opposite directions. As Kotler (1973) suggests, this would be the case, for example, of a kind of fruit that ripened in winter but that people desired in summer. In this case, the marketer has the option of attempting:

- to alter the demand pattern to fit the common supply pattern;
- to alter the supply pattern to fit the natural demand pattern;
- to alter both supply and demand to some degree.

Bearing this in mind, it is important to highlight how synchromarketing is a particular kind of demarketing, encompassing the marketing task of trying to resolve irregular demand by trying to bring the movements of demand and supply into better synchronization. Several marketing actions can be taken to achieve this goal. As a matter of fact, marketing can promote new uses and desires for the product in the off-season. For example, in the previously mentioned example of ice creams and other frozen dairy products, advertising can demonstrate how these products can be also consumed in other seasons besides summer, as manufacturers in the industry have in fact attempted. Regarding the example of tourism services, operators in the sector can charge a higher price in the peak season and a lower one in the off-season. This strategy is heavily used in practice in the sale of different seasonal services such as flight and hotel reservations and package holidays. Moreover, the marketer can advertise more heavily in the off-season than in the peak season.

As Kotler (1973) points out, after these actions, synchronization between supply and demand can be readily achieved, in some cases, through simple switches in advertising or promotion. Nevertheless, in other cases, synchronization may be achieved, if at all, only after years of continuous efforts to modify habits, patterns and desires. This latter view is consistent with Zeithaml and Zeithaml (1984) who argue that synchromarketing is one of the different strategic actions that companies should design in order to modify the organizational context, rather than a mere tactical reaction in response to existing conditions. In fact, using Galbraith's three-part framework, these authors consider smoothing as one of the possible environmental management strategies aimed at solving irregular demand. In this way, they seek to provide a strategic perspective through which marketing theory can develop the more entrepreneurial and proactive orientation needed. They also suggest that, in appropriate conditions, this strategy might be used together with other environmental management strategies in an integrated programme of environmental management.

In the next section, a review of the main types of synchromarketing will be presented, providing some examples of each type for illustrative purposes.

Types of synchromarketing

As previously mentioned, Kotler (1973) highlighted the importance of the relationship between marketing and different demand states by defining eight states based on the level of actual versus desired demand. Irregular demand is one of those states, in which the current pattern of demand is marked by seasonal or volatile fluctuations that depart from the supply pattern. According to Kotler (1973), each of these demand states gives rise to a specific marketing approach that aims to balance actual with desired demand. Hence, he highlighted that a more in-depth analysis of the demand was required, depending on the organization's particular circumstances, which in turn encouraged greater efforts and the ability to adapt to the demand situation.

This work was of such great importance that it inspired other later key research, such as the study of Dumwright and Vernon (1984). In their investigation, the authors developed an analytical framework for the healthcare industry in which four different types of synchromarketing were identified. These categories emerged from the complex, specific situation they described regarding the healthcare industries, where the general synchromarketing concept suggested by Kotler (1973) appeared to be too simplistic.

Despite having been developed in the area of a specific industry, almost 30 years later these categories represent interesting insights for different industries and are more necessary and current than ever. For this reason, given their relevance, these four categories will be described below, providing examples in each case. Before that, it is important to point out how the first three types of synchromarketing to be explained deal with demand as given, and make up a continuum ranging from simplistic techniques for shifting demand to shifting supply through the strategic alteration of resources. However, the fourth type of synchromarketing is, to a certain degree, different, in the sense that it involves a conscious effort to alter the environment.

Synchromarketing Type 1

This type of synchromarketing encompasses a wide variety of techniques aimed at smoothing demand to fit the existing structure of capital, personnel, finance and, in general, all organizational resources. Therefore, this is used to discourage demand for the product or service when a situation of excess exists. This can be achieved either by:

- offering sales promotions during off-peak seasons;
- advertising the benefits of purchasing products/services during off-peak seasons; or
- a combination of both.

A specific example of the first technique mentioned can be found in sales promotion campaigns targeted at either trade or end consumers. One example of promotions directed at trade can be found in Daimler Trucks 'Top Marques' programme aimed at the Daimler Trucks dealer programme by Mercedes-Benz Australia. This programme was launched after Australia's truck market declined at the end of 2011 by 5 per cent compared to 2010 and an overall 27 per cent below 2007. With the programme objective of increasing Mercedes-Benz Truck sales and market share in 2011 during a period of long-term market sales decline, cost-effectively selling Aged Stock vehicles and increasing staff knowledge of the product, the Daimler Trucks 'Top Marques' programme was designed to train the sales team to be more effective in selling

Aged Stock and to reward them for selling specified truck inventory. The programme targeted the Sales and Sales Management Personnel within the Daimler Trucks dealer channel, representing the Freightliner and Mercedes-Benz brands. The campaign included a sales incentive and an e-Learning reward, which was communicated by email to all sales staff. Text messaging was used to orientate the time-sensitive information. Programme engagement was impressive and achieved significant results, with sales increasing by 9 per cent in 2011 over 2010, while overall market sales decreased by 9 per cent in 2011. Daimler Trucks' market share grew from 2.66 per cent in 2010 to 3.68 per cent in 2011 (Circle of Excellence, 2012).

An example of promotions aimed at end consumers can be found in the numerous tourism service companies whose objective is to encourage demand during off-peak seasons. This is why, especially from October to January when the holiday season has finished and the off-peak months begin, several tourism operators try to stimulate demand by luring customers by implementing interesting sales promotions during those dates: e.g. direct price deals and 2 for 1 packages in a lot of tourism services (e.g. in packages, flights and hotel reservations). This is a common practice for theme parks such as Disneyland Paris, which often offer several value activities on sale for the winter season. Among these offers, free days and nights can be found, as well as the possibility for children under 12 to stay and play free in the park.

An example of the second kind of technique is observed in those companies that advertise how travelling during winter can provide travellers with extra advantages, such as the possibility of finding the places quieter, less crowded, more available and with better service. In August 2010, Bath Tourism Plus launched a new campaign to promote winter breaks in Bath entitled 'Winter Highlights'. The campaign included a brand-new brochure and a website packed with diverse ideas aiming at increasing the visits of both individuals and groups to the city of Bath between September and March. In particular, the campaign sought to offer a series of suggestions for visiting Bath during winter, highlighting it as an ideal place to beat the winter blues. For this reason, they used ideas such as associations of Bath with pre-Christmas breaks; relaxing retreats; a spa destination for the New Year, etc. The 'Winter Highlights' brochure and website provided a guide to Bath including information on shopping, festivals, events and details of the Christmas Market. In addition, there were ideas on spa breaks and suggestions for celebrating Valentine's Day. Along with this brochure, coach and tour operators were given valuable information including how to get to Bath, details of attractions and accommodation options (http://visitbath.co.uk, 2010).

Finally, a combination of both previous techniques can be found in http://visitparis-cultureguide.parisinfo.com/en (2012). During the winter sales (usually from early January to mid-February), the Tourist Office in Paris puts together a specially customized programme advertising markets and activities during that period. The lure is not only focused on bargains, but also explains how visitors can find many discounts on hotels and restaurants, etc. But, in addition, themed and guided tours depending on different types of shopping advantages are provided to allow visitors to conveniently make the most of their time in Paris, depending on their particular orientations: luxury, fashion, creativity, bohemian chic, eco-ethnic, etc. These latter actions contribute to increasing information about the options that best fit the person's desires, thus reducing the time spent in the evaluation of the chosen alternatives.

Synchromarketing Type 2

This encompasses efforts to shift demand as described in Type 1, as well as attempts to alter supply through a short-term adjustment of products and services. A Type 2 adjustment involves the alteration, or improvement, of programmes and facilities within the constraints of the existing organizational structure and budget. Characteristically, changes of this nature do not require the approval of governing boards or regulatory agencies.

An interesting example of this can be found in the tourism strategies followed by several sun and sand destinations in Spain. As a matter of fact, Ibiza is popularly known not only for being a typical sun and sand destination, but also for being one of the most prominent clubbing destinations in the world. However, a repositioning of the destination image is required from late September to the beginning of October onwards, when temperatures begin to fall. During the winter months, the marketing strategies of this destination are more oriented towards other types of visits, such as cultural tourism. In this way, from approximately October to April, the image of Ibiza is reoriented by advertising other types of tourism resources and activities, such as visits to museums, exhibitions, natural and historical monuments; interaction with the locals and the community; different types of sport; mushroom picking, etc. Although most hotels and clubs are closed, other types of accommodation are open to accommodate tourists with other necessities, more in line with other kinds of tourism, such as cultural tourism, hippy tourism, etc. For further information, visit, for example, the Official Tourism Site of Ibiza.

Synchromarketing Type 3

This involves long-range strategic planning to alter the permanent resource base, including capital, personnel and financial resources. It means rearranging the product mix, or the range of services offered, to match existing demand patterns. It is similar to Type 2, but, in this case, the remodelling is intended to be permanent and to be dedicated to the new purpose in the long run. This is due to the fact that the demand decreases in the long run, and there is no way to recover the lost demand.

A good example of this can be found in the new distillery that the Bacardi Company is currently building for its Bombay Sapphire brand in the UK. In particular, the Bacardi Company is currently transforming the historic Laverstoke Mill (Hampshire), 60 miles from London, into an art design gin distillery and visitor centre. This began in February 2012, when the company obtained planning permission for the multi-million-pound restoration of Laverstoke Mill, which once housed England's most significant paper-making facility. In fact, it was devoted to manufacturing high-quality paper for making bank notes for India and the British Empire.

As a site historically renowned for the highest levels of quality and crafts-manship, it carried a natural synergy in line with the values of the Bombay Sapphire brand, and so was selected to reopen its doors to a public wanting to discover more about the iconic spirit. At the moment, Bombay Sapphire has started by introducing the team working on the Laverstoke Mill restoration and the experts striving to complete this project to the highest levels of design, functionality and sustainability for autumn 2013.

The visionary London design studio Heatherwick Studio, creators of the Olympic Cauldron, will be the leading designers in the Laverstoke Mill restoration project. The studio's ambition for the design restores and complements the heritage of the site's buildings and grounds, whilst introducing a new structure that will act as a showcase for the Bombay Sapphire brand. The highlight of the complex will be the 'glass house', which will be home to the ten botanical plants used to make the spirit and act as a symbol of the brand's careful, skilful and imaginative approach to gin making (for further information, visit http://www.laverstokemill.co.uk/).

Synchromarketing Type 4

This implies that the organization refuses to accept the environment as given, but rather engages in active efforts to alter its relevant environment or extend it. This means that the efforts made by the company enable them to change consumers' opinions. Thus, this type of synchromarketing involves an institutional effort involving not only the desired environmental outcomes, but also their strategic impact on the organization. In this type of synchromarketing, the expansion of the company's market (either from local to regional, regional to national or even from national to international) is contemplated. This could involve re-evaluation of the target markets in order to find more viable ones to add to or replace current markets. This may also involve focusing on the perception of the brand identity and conducting or studying surveys of consumer behaviour in relation to existing products/services and also studying quarterly portfolios of the competition.

For example, the Irish clothing retailer Primark is expanding rapidly overseas, while at the same time continuing to cater for the needs of consumers at home as well. The recent growth of revenues reported by the company was boosted by an increase in sales at Primark, as German and Spanish customers turned to the chain that has captivated British youth for a decade (*The Times*, 2012). The company has carried out such a large European market expansion that today, as well as operating in Ireland, it is also present in Austria, Belgium, Germany, Portugal, Spain, the Netherlands and the United Kingdom.

Another way of achieving this type of synchromarketing is by means of forming associations with other representatives or prestigious entities, such as research centres and schools, which will contribute to increasing the reputation and, in turn, customers. As an example, Carrefour group has introduced a major social and ethical approach, for which it is implementing diverse cooperative agreements with different entities. Currently, the company offers a wide range of Carrefour sustainability products aimed at meeting high quality and safety standards, sold at a reasonable price and for every pocket. This can be achieved through its relations with suppliers and farmers: by building sustainable relations with suppliers and promoting fair and socially responsible trade. Moreover, the group is also trying to integrate into the local economy by, among other actions, encouraging employment and local sourcing, integrating into the local economy and managing solidarity and sponsorship actions. Thus, it is necessary to perform cooperative agreements in order to synchronize the mix, the level and periodicity of the goods and/or services provided.

To end this section, Table 2.1 summarizes the main aspects of each of the previous kinds of synchromarketing types.

TABLE 2.1 Summary of main synchromarketing types

Type	Description	Objective	Actions to be taken
1	Techniques oriented to smoothing demand in order to fit the current structure of the organizational resources.	To discourage excess of existing demand.	– Sales promotions during off-peak seasons; – Advertising during off-peak seasons; – A combination of both.
2	Efforts to shift demand into off-peak seasons, as well as attempts to alter supply through a short-term adjustment of products and services.	The alteration, or improvement, of programmes and facilities within the constraints of the existing organizational structure and budget.	Enhance alternative goods/ services uses for short periods of time.
3	Long-range strategic planning to alter the permanent resource base.	The rearranging of the product mix or the range of services offered to match existing demand patterns.	Enhance alternative goods/ services uses for the long run (no looking back).
4	Active efforts by the organization to alter its relevant environment or to extend it.	To change consumers' opinions.	– Market expansion (e.g. local to regional; regional to national; national to international); – Cooperative agreements with other entities and institutions to enhance market share via reputation.

Source: Own source, based on Dumwright and Vernon (1984)

Implications for organizations

Implications for management-decision processes

By making demand management a core part of any sourcing, manufacturing and service strategy is critical for creating a lasting competitive advantage, as there are connections between superior supply chain performance and financial success. It is not, therefore, surprising that leading companies have found that efforts to synchronize demand, procurement and production can be transformed into above-average results in, among other benefits, inventory turns, cost of goods sold and return on assets.

However, an organization attempting to design and carry out any effort or technique to synchronize demand has to take into account different types of implications that are very relevant for organizational management-decision processes. Bearing these ideas in mind, this section is devoted to analysing the main implications for management-decision policies of companies dealing with irregular demand, distinguishing between implications for companies producing physical goods and those producing services.

Implications for companies producing tangible goods

One of the main challenges for organizations with irregular demand refers to the difficulty in predicting their inventory policies. This should be taken into account by marketers of physical goods who can hold inventories to buffer fluctuations in supply demand, while it should not be forgotten that services are acts or processes and, therefore, difficult or impossible to inventory.

There is no doubt that demand forecasts play an important role in all industries of tangible goods. As a matter of fact, the greater the ability of an organization of this type to share demand signals directly between customers and suppliers, the greater the increase in financial and operational excellence. Working on streamlining these connections brings greater transparency throughout the supply chain and, over time, better response times from suppliers, thus making inventory turns faster and, therefore, a higher return on assets.

Nevertheless, since future demand is, to a greater or lesser extent, uncertain, a marketer has to rely on forecasts when making order decisions. To take order decisions correctly, marketers tend to rely on quantitative forecast models. Such models usually assume that relationships from the past also hold true in the future and that some kind of demand pattern can be observed. However, in real life, situations may arise where demand differs from its regular pattern, as in those situations mentioned in the preceding sections. Therefore, it is not surprising that it becomes especially complicated for companies to develop a model that forecasts under conditions of irregular demand. Especially in the recent competitive environment, where manufacturing companies operate in very unstable sectors, managing irregular demand patterns is an increasingly frequent but complex issue.

The complexity of dealing with these kinds of demand patterns lies in finding the best trade-off between the negative effects related to high storage levels, such as a high amount of space and resources for keeping large warehouse areas, high holding costs, high risks and costs due to item obsolescence, and negative effects related to low storage levels, such as lost demand and customers. In this respect, it is important to take into account the fact that big organizations equipped with major facilities are the ones that need to pay more attention to these issues, whilst small and medium-sized (SME) companies, with fewer facilities of this type, can adapt more flexibly to changing conditions.

When dealing with irregular and sporadic demand patterns, some of the relevant issues commonly discussed refer to demand forecasting in future periods, as well as the utilization of demand forecasting obtained for managing stocks. Gamberini *et al.* (2010) present an interesting review in this research line. Based on the work of these authors, Table 2.2 summarizes some of the main approaches to modelling the previously mentioned problems, which are mainly applied to the context of manufacturing companies.

As seen in Table 2.2, Croston (1972) is one of the most relevant researchers in this line, as he was one of the first explicitly to recognize the need to take into account intermittent demand patterns by specifically modelling and implementing the subsequent information in the management-decision process by companies. This work inspired many later studies that emerged from this line of research and it was common from that moment onwards to consider the need to model irregular fluctuations of demand.

Implications for companies producing services

Demand fluctuations in service firms are also a problem of major concern for marketers of these firms. Since ability to supply a service is in large part a function of personnel constraints, the challenge in confronting fluctuations of service demands is more related to personnel in these types of industries, as Krentler (1988) points out.

In fact, the most feasible approach for implementing synchromarketing in services is to operate with a staff size sufficient for low-demand periods and then add temporary or part-time staff when demand increases. This is one of the most important issues for service marketers, which involves taking on the ability to hire and train properly. In fact, hiring extra part-time employees is one of the two most common strategies used to cope with fluctuations in demand, the other being cross-training employees to perform other tasks.

A second important issue is how to control the quality of the intangible product. As intangible services are heterogeneous, the potential for variability in the performance of services is high. This feature of services results in difficulties with respect to standardization and quality control. The need to establish and maintain at least a minimum level of quality for products – taking into account consumer expectations – has long been recognized as a key to successful product strategy. Quality control can be monitored, to some extent, by paying

TABLE 2.2 Summary of main modelling approaches

Research	Objective	Description
Croston (1972) (successively improved by Rao, 1973)	Forecasting of irregular and sporadic demand.	He started from the assumption that single exponential smoothing, even if frequently used for forecasting in inventory control systems, achieves inappropriate results when applied to intermittent demand patterns. He considers the consumers' past series of orders with demand occurrences generated by a Bernoulli process and with demand sizes (when not null) following a normal distribution. Then, he separately applies a single exponential smoothing to non-null demand sizes and inter-demand intervals. Finally, he combines them.
Johnston and Boylan (1996)	Analysis of demand patterns with the order arrival process modelled as a Poisson stream.	Supposing a negative exponential distribution to represent inter-order arrivals, the authors propose a model for estimating the variance of demand and use it in a forecasting demand approach. The performance is tested by considering a wide variety of operative conditions (i.e. many different average inter-demand intervals, negative exponential, Erlang and rectangular as distributions of order size).
Segerstedt (2000)	The proposal of an alternative Croston's approach modification, adopted in sporadic demand inventory control.	This author derives his alternative Croston's approach modification by coupling it to the computation of probability of stock shortage, supposing demand following an Erlang distribution.
Syntetos and Boylan (2001)	The explanation for the detection of a mistake in Croston's mathematical derivation of the expected estimate of demand per time period. This leads the authors to propose an alternative approach.	The alternative approach that they propose is based again on the concept of forecasting demand from its constituent events.

TABLE 2.2 (continued)

Research	Objective	Description
Willemain *et al.* (2004)	Their objective is to forecast the cumulative distribution of demand over a fixed period of production time using a new type of time-series bootstrap.	In their model, the hypothesis of demand independence between subsequent time periods is disregarded and the existence of autocorrelation is considered.
Syntetos *et al.* (2005)	A proposal to categorize the demand patterns by following an alternative procedure.	Several steps are proposed in this alternative procedure: firstly, analysing the optimal performance areas of several forecasting methods and then categorizing the demand patterns in accordance with the results obtained. Although, on the one hand, these pioneering steps in the direction of demand-pattern categorizing are very interesting, on the other, the study by Syntetos *et al.* (2005) is based on assumptions not always confirmed by real-life data (e.g. demand occurring as a Bernoulli process or independence of demand values).
Syntetos and Boylan (2005)	They improve Croston's original estimator of mean demand by introducing a factor equal to $(1-\alpha/2)$.	By including a factor equal to $(1-\alpha/2)$ applied to Croston's original estimator of mean demand, with α equal to the smoothing parameter in use for updating the inter-demand intervals, they attempt to obtain a theoretically unbiased estimator. The derivation of the new estimator is based on Croston's assumptions of a stationary, identical, independently distributed series of demand sizes and demand intervals, geometrically distributed inter-demand intervals and independence of demand sizes and intervals.

Source: Adapted from Gamberini *et al.* (2010)

careful attention to the organization's personnel (particularly, contact personnel). By emphasizing selection, training and education in marketing concepts and communication skills, a company can count on personnel to maintain a consistent level of service quality.

However, these two latter issues and their specific treatment are logically inconsistent when viewed in the wider context of the service market's overall strategy. On the one hand, careful selection, training and education of personnel take time and cost money. Marketers faced with an immediate but temporary period of over-demand are most probably unable or unwilling to expend such efforts on extra part-time employees. Thus, the service marketer who responds to over-demand periods by hiring temporary help is likely to be toying dangerously with the quality control level of the product.

On the other hand, poor service quality experienced by a customer during peak demand periods is very likely to have long-term repercussions for the organizations in obvious ways, such as loss of patronage, negative word-of-mouth communications, etc. This would be the case, for instance, for retail stores experiencing seasonal fluctuations. If these stores rely heavily on part-time help, pressing them into service with minimal training can result in inadequate responses to customers in diverse aspects, such as incorrectly answering enquiries or dealing with inventory issues, etc.

Therefore, the variability in the quality provided to the customer largely depends on the individual with whom the customer interacts. In this way, if customers deal with a new employee, they may experience some frustration and form a negative attitude towards the institution, which will affect future choices of stores in which to shop.

Service marketers can implement different strategies other than just hiring temporary employees to overcome the problems of fluctuating demand. Krentler (1988) highlights two main categories of approaches for high-demand periods: strategies to increase supply and strategies to reduce demand. Table 2.3 summarizes these main approaches.

Although these strategies do not generally cause the aforementioned problems of quality control, they may cause other types of problems.

Potential negative implications

One of the doubts regarding synchromarketing techniques is that some of them may generate unnecessary demand, which could contribute to wasting the organization's resources. Specifically, some sales promotions activities may generate more consumer demand than is really desired in order to attain normal working of the organization. This could occur as a consequence of a fundamental reason: that, despite the fact that the aim of sales promotions is to increase product/service recognition among the desired target consumers, which would give rise to efficiency in the demand for the said goods/service, what could happen is that more consumers other than the desired target ones for the company know the product/service via such promotions and, therefore, once they know

TABLE 2.3 Summary of main alternative approaches

Increasing supply strategies	Use differential scheduling of existing employees during peak times.	This can include both hourly and longer-term adjustments.
	Have employees work overtime.	Employees' schedules can be increased so that more employees are on the job at peak hours of the day or peak days of the week. Vacations can even be prohibited during peak times of the year.
		Despite some potential inconveniences, this strategy provides the firm with increased capacity from trained and qualified personnel.
	Subcontract work to others.	If carefully chosen, contractees can provide high levels of quality without the need for extensive training.
	Cross-train employees to perform other tasks.	The training process can be accomplished during slack periods, in itself providing a solution to 'filling time' during seasonal downturns. This approach has the added benefit of uncovering expanded potential and employees.
	Increase customer self-service.	By identifying what tasks can easily and adequately be accomplished by consumers, the firm frees up personnel to focus on the provision of services requiring their attention.
	Improve service production efficiency.	A careful analysis of the service firm's physical layout, for instance, may lead to rearranging for increased efficiency. Moving stock closer to the customer service area may save the personnel work, thus improving their efficiency and increasing production capacity. Order processing may be streamlined, again with the result of increasing efficiency.
	Use of capacity-sharing technologies.	For example, surfing and skiing firms sharing a building, each occupying it for the corresponding six months, is an example of creative capacity sharing.

(continued on next page)

TABLE 2.3 (continued)

Increasing supply strategies	Use differential scheduling of existing employees during peak times.	This can include both hourly and longer-term adjustments.
Decreasing demand strategies	Let work fall behind.	For example, if a service is normally performed in a week, taking three weeks at peak seasons may convince consumers to wait until another time or to seek service elsewhere.
	Attend to regular customers and allow others to wait.	Peak periods can require the service firm to discriminate between customers. Focusing attention first on regular customers who support the firm in times of low demand may be a logical decision for the overworked organization.
	Turn away business.	This may be a preferred option to the alternative of providing consumers with poor-quality services. A customer who is turned away because of over-demand may leave with a more positive long-term view of the firm than the individual provided with a service of questionable quality.
	Educate customers to use services available during non-peak times.	This may be the most positive of the demarketing approaches.
	Offer incentives to customers using services during non-peak times.	Promotions encouraging retail patrons to shop during less crowded times are solutions that not only deal with the firm's current over-demand problem, but also work to resolve under-demand situations that firms will face in the future.

Source: Krentler (1988)

them, begin to demand them. This outcome would thus result in inefficiency and a waste of the company's resources, given that the greatest expected demand of the desired consumers would not have been achieved. Further, this latter phenomenon could contribute to increasing the negative results of irregular demand, emphasizing consumer demand in those periods in which there was already excess demand *per se*.

To prevent these negative results occurring, those responsible for managing the organization should be fully trained and aware of all the principles and applications of synchromarketing. Their knowledge of the subject must be maintained and increased over time, if possible with continuous training programmes, which enable them continually to update their know-how, by, for example, attending seminars, workshops, conferences, etc.

Social implications

Bearing in mind the different types of synchromarketing, especially the fourth type, it is possible to argue that synchromarketing is related to the concept of social marketing. The truth is that social marketing can be understood as marketing that implies different socially beneficial ideas and causes. One principal aspect that relates this type of synchromarketing to social marketing is that it enables us to exercise an influence over people so that they are more inclined to accept new behaviour, which involves changes in attitude and conduct. These changes would be observed in the conduct both of workers and employers, who would have to modify their working habits in order to be more open to changing their guidelines and perceptions with regard to the new conditions for rendering their services. These changes might even involve wide-ranging alterations to a sector or organization, as well as to the power and authority structures that are established in the organization: something that, however, could entail a reduction in the costs of the services rendered.

The fourth type of synchromarketing would not be the only one related to social marketing. To a greater or lesser extent, the rest of the types of synchromarketing would also involve the concept of social marketing. The truth is that to design and implement sales promotions or advertising during off-peak periods or devote installations to other uses and/or applications at other times of the year, for example, might require changes in the behaviour of all the stakeholders involved in the organization, as well as possibly resulting in unexpected behavioural changes.

For all these reasons, it is necessary for those responsible for managing the organization to be able not only to predict as far as possible the potential results that could be observed in the objectively measurable performance variables of the organization, such as sales, market share or profitability, but also to anticipate the results that in the long term might be generated with the different stakeholders of the organization, both internally (employees, directors, etc.) and externally (suppliers, customers and consumer associations). Needless to say, one has to bear in mind that we would be dealing with results that, although more difficult to measure, might have an influence on the key variables for the long-term success of the business, such as image or reputation of the organization.

There is no doubt that both the concept of synchromarketing and all the techniques it entails have functionally broadened the marketing perspective. Nowadays, the expanded role of marketing in society could be said to consist of putting supply and demand on the same level and providing the necessary information bases so that those responsible in the organization for marketing, together with the consumers, can make the correct decisions. Thus, marketing managers should not be satisfied with merely creating and maintaining demand, but rather they should take on the task of regulating the level, timing and nature of the demand in order to obtain profits in local, regional, national and, even, international markets.

References

Circle of Excellence (2012). "Dealer distributor program. Daimler Trucks 'Top Marques'", http://www.incentivemarketing.org/associations/2592/files/Daimler%20Trucks%20Dealer%20Distributor%20Program.pdf

Croston, J. D. (1972). Forecasting and stock control for intermittent demands. *Operational Research Quarterly*, 23, 289–303.

Dumwright, M. E. and Vernon, I. R. (1984). Synchromarketing: A new concept for hospital administrators. *Journal of Health Care Marketing*, 4 (2), 45–50.

http://visitparis-cultureguide.parisinfo.com (2012). *Winter Sales in Paris*, available at http://visit paris-cultureguide.parisinfo.com/en/markets-and-activities/winter-sales-in-paris-e-763792

http://www.laverstokemill.co.uk (2012). 'Welcome to Laverstoke Mill – The home of imagination', available at http://www.laverstokemill.co.uk/

Johnston, F. R. and Boylan, J. E. (1996). Forecasting for items with intermittent demand. *Journal of the Operational Research Society*, 47, 113–21.

Kotler, P. (1973). The major tasks of marketing management. *Journal of Marketing*, 37 (October), 42–49.

——(1993). The major tasks of marketing management. Eight different types of demand situations dictate marketing strategy. *Marketing Management*, 2 (3), 52–56.

Krentler, K. A. (1988). Maintaining quality control during the "crunch" in service firms. *The Journal of Services Marketing*, 2 (1), 71–74.

Official Tourism Site of Ibiza (2012). Available at http://www.ibiza.travel/en/

Roeder, J. (2012a). *Ice cream sales and trends*, International Dairy Foods Association, available at http://www.idfa.org/news – views/media-kits/ice-cream/ice-cream-sales-and-trends/

Roeder, J. (2012b). *July is national ice cream month*, International Dairy Foods Association, available at http://www.idfa.org/news – views/media-kits/ice-cream/july-is-national-ice-cream-mon/

Segerstedt, A. (2000). *Forecasting Slow-Moving Items and Ordinary Items – A modification of Croston's idea*. Working paper, Industrial Logistics, Luleå University of Technology.

Syntetos, A. A. and Boylan, J. E. (2001). On the bias of intermittent demand estimates. *International Journal of Production Economics*, 71, 457–66.

Syntetos, A. A. and Boylan, J. E. (2005). The accuracy of intermittent demand estimates. *International Journal of Forecasting*, 21, 303–14.

Syntetos, A. A., Boylan, J. E. and Croston, J. D. (2005). On the categorization of demand patterns. *Journal of the Operational Research Society*, 56, 495–503.

The Times (2012). "Europeans join the queue for Primark's expanding fashions", available at http://www.thetimes.co.uk/tto/business/industries/retailing/article3592278.ece

Visitbath.co.uk (2010). 'Bath Tourism Plus launches new campaign to promote winter breaks', http://visitbath.co.uk/media/press-releases/2010/8/11/bath-tourism-plus-launches-new-campaign-to-promote-winter-breaks-a386

Willemain, T. R., Smart, C. N. and Schwarz, H. F. (2004). A new approach to forecasting intermittent demand for service parts inventories. *International Journal of Forecasting*, 20, 375–87.

Zeithaml, C. P. and Zeithaml, V. A. (1984). Environmental management: Revising the marketing perspective. *Journal of Marketing*, 48 (Spring), 46–53.

3

SYNCHROMARKETING

Demarketing places

Gary Warnaby and Dominic Medway

Introduction: defining place demarketing

In the specific context of places, demarketing has been defined as 'activities aimed at *deflecting* interest, visitors and/or investment from a particular place' (Medway and Warnaby, 2008, p. 644). In many ways, it can be regarded as the mirror image of more conventional place marketing, where, in an increasingly competitive spatial environment, the prime focus is on the *attraction* of interest/ visitors/investment, and on communicating the benefits of the attributes/facilities/ attractions of a particular place to identified target audiences.

Consequently, conventional place marketing is characterized by an explicit and overt accentuation of the positive, even when the claims made for a place may not be totally warranted (see Burgess, 1982). For example, many places trumpet their accessibility, arising by virtue of favourable location – Ward (1998) notes that the terms 'hub' and 'gateway' are common tropes in place marketing messages, even for locations that could best be described as peripheral. A crucial element of place marketing activity is, therefore, the creation – and management – of an attractive place image, through the selective appropriation of place product elements relevant and attractive to particular audiences, and their subsequent commodification in appropriate media. Indeed, when the issue of *negative* place image is discussed in the academic literature, the focus is usually on the identification of effective strategies for image *improvement* (see, for example, Avraham, 2000, 2004; Avraham and Ketter, 2008; Kotler *et al.*, 1993, 1999).

The implication, therefore, is that a negative place image is undesirable *per se*. However, there are situations where accentuating the negative – for whatever reason – can be an appropriate place marketing strategy. This chapter considers the motivations behind this and some of the strategies that individual places can adopt in order to demarket themselves, with particular emphasis on synchro-marketing. The chapter starts by briefly summarizing different types of place demarketing strategies and the factors that might motivate their adoption, before moving on to consider synchromarketing in more detail, via case studies of two very different places in the United Kingdom: (1) the island of St Kilda, the remotest part of the British Isles, west of the Western Isles archipelago; and

(2) London, a world city that attracts millions of visitors annually, but that during the period of the 2012 Olympic Games sought to dissuade certain groups of place users because of concerns relating to the ability of the city's transport infrastructure to cope with increased demand.

A place demarketing typology

In their discussion of demarketing in a specific place context, Medway and Warnaby (2008) and Medway et al. (2011) distinguish between passive and active forms of demarketing. Passive place demarketing is a process that is manifest in many different contexts and is arguably implicit in the processes of segmentation, targeting and positioning, which can be applied to places as much as to any other 'product' that is offered for acquisition, use or consumption to different types of consumers. Thus, by emphasizing certain place product attributes to market a location to certain customer segments (perhaps arising from the need to prioritize scarce marketing or other place resources), it may automatically follow that other elements (which might be attractive to other groups) are de-emphasized. Thus, cities, towns or holiday resorts that market themselves as party destinations for young, single people (perhaps on stag and hen party celebrations) may, in doing so, discourage visits by families and older people who may prefer a less raucous location for their holidays.

Medway and Warnaby argue that passive place demarketing can be both *general* and *specific*. *General* passive demarketing may be an appropriate strategy where a place need not actively encourage visitors due to the fact that it has what Kotler et al. (1999, p. 52) term an already 'overly attractive image'. Thus, for example, people will come to a city such as Venice whatever happens because of its unique attributes and associations, and those responsible for marketing such places do not need to be particularly proactive in order to be successful. With regard to *specific* passive demarketing, by deliberately emphasizing certain place attributes to market a location to certain types of individuals or organizations, it may automatically follow that other elements that may attract alternative types of individuals or organizations are *de facto* demarketed, as is the case with some locations favoured by the stag and hen parties mentioned above.

However, a more *active* demarketing of individual places may also occur. Following Kotler and Levy (1971), who in their original exploration of the concept suggested that demarketing may often be a temporary strategy, Medway and Warnaby (2008) suggest that active demarketing may typically take place over a discrete time window, often to manage and/or attempt to avert or reduce the impact of a crisis situation, or other time-limited event. Thus, during the UK Foot and Mouth crisis in 2001, many central and local government agencies actively demarketed the countryside. The effectiveness of this activity was manifest in the enormous uphill struggle of re-marketing the countryside post-crisis, when it became increasingly clear how adversely rural economies had been affected (for further details, see, for example, Franks et al., 2003; Ward et al., 2004). Similarly, the messages emanating from the organizing body of the London

2012 Olympics before the event, relating to possible transport and other infrastructure challenges within the city, dissuaded many non-Olympic visitors. This had some significant implications for more general tourism and economic activity in the city that were widely reported in the media at the time (and which will be discussed in more detail later).

Medway and Warnaby also identify another form of active demarketing – *informational place demarketing* – which may be implemented by agencies internal or external to particular places. An example of this would be the way that various national governments provide ongoing advice to their citizens about which locations they should not travel to. This may be the result of specific events such as natural disasters or terrorist activity, but equally such advisory notices may be ongoing, arising from more general political instability in an area that is anticipated to continue into the foreseeable future.

Indeed, the issue of temporality is important here, and this could be regarded as a major criterion in determining the specific nature of place demarketing activities, in the sense that such activity may be a one-off, more *ad hoc* strategy to deal with a specific set of circumstances that have a discrete timescale, or alternatively an ongoing situation that requires some form of longer-term strategy to accommodate its wider implications. If these situations could be considered as the extremes of a temporal continuum impacting on place demarketing strategies, then somewhere in the middle might be the need for *periodic* demarketing activity. This may arise, for example, from structural demand issues, such as the inherent seasonality of tourist visitation in some locations, which may necessitate some form of active and/or passive demarketing at certain times of the year. In many ways, this resonates with demand management issues implicit in the marketing of services, where service characteristics such as inseparability (of demand and supply) and possible capacity limitations of service providers may mean that measures to try to even out demand (in order to cope, given finite supply-side resources) may have to be taken.

Place demarketing motives

Another factor influencing the specific nature of any place demarketing activity in an individual location will be the motives impelling demarketing. Linking to some of the issues mentioned above, Medway *et al.* (2011) identify four different place demarketing motivations, relating to: sustainability; market segmentation and targeting; reducing the effects of seasonality; and crisis prevention/management.

One reason why tourist places in particular have implemented demarketing strategies is to make their place 'product' more sustainable in terms of managing visitor numbers to help ensure a lesser but regular supply of visitors that does not place an undue strain on the infrastructure of the location (especially if because of factors such as 'world heritage site' designation this supporting infrastructure is unable to be expanded). Whilst some places would inevitably benefit financially from more visitors, there is recognition of the potential adverse effects on the visitor's experience of the place if numbers are not regulated in some way.

As indicated above, another reason for places using demarketing links back to the basic marketing principles of segmentation and positioning, namely that, by targeting a particular favoured type of place consumer, other segments are the subject of (either active or passive) demarketing activity. One rationale for this approach might be to target those customers that are higher spenders in order to achieve economic objectives, or alternatively those consumers who are more sympathetic to the values of the place (perhaps in terms of environmentalism etc., or who are more likely to treat — and behave within — the place with due respect to its heritage, culture and traditions).

Linking back to the issues of demand management in a services context as mentioned, a third motivation for place demarketing might be an attempt to spread visitor numbers and therefore reduce negative impacts of seasonality. Thus, an aim might be to market locations that are commonly perceived as being only summer destinations to places that can be visited all year round. This may have significant implications for the portrayal of the place in marketing communications activities, which could involve active demarketing to summer visitors (perhaps by mentioning overcrowding, etc.), but also employing more conventional marketing messages (with the usual accentuation of the positive) for other periods. For many tourism destinations, extending the 'visiting season' could also have obvious benefits for the local economy.

Lastly, demarketing could also be a powerful tool for managing or preventing a crisis. Sometimes, this kind of demarketing activity may be 'reactive' in its response to a crisis that is already occurring on the ground that has to be dealt with in the best way possible. However, Medway *et al.* (2011) suggest that there is evidence that place demarketing can also be used in a more proactive way to *prevent* as well as to manage a crisis, analogous to the notion of contingency planning. This could occur in terms of deflecting possible acts of public disorder at large public events, such as demonstrations and rallies. For example, if there are concerns about a large influx of protestors expected to come to a specific location, then messages about the level of police presence and other precautionary measures might be communicated in advance so as to try to dissuade any troublemakers from attending.

Synchromarketing strategies for places

Synchromarketing — in a more conventional marketing context, defined as redistributing existing sales (which are already at an optimum level) so that they occur at times, or in places, that the supplier prefers — has an obvious resonance in this particular place context. When considering synchromarketing strategies for places, the spatial and temporal aspects referred to in the above definition provide a useful starting point. Before outlining some possible place synchromarketing strategies, it must be noted that these spatial and temporal dimensions are not mutually exclusive, and in this specific context could perhaps be better thought of as axes on a graph that will give an indication of strategic orientation rather than a definitive either/or choice. Thus, if synchromarketing focuses on re-routing demand to a location and time of the supplier's choosing, place synchromarketing strategies could involve *restricting access* to a particular location, on a permanent or time-limited basis, which could be used in conjunction with the active promotion of alternative locations – what could be termed *diversionary place demarketing*.

Medway et al. (2011) make the point that if access is restricted in some way then place consumers may have little choice in the matter and are forced to comply with predetermined restriction guidelines. Linking to the temporal dimension above, these restrictions could be permanent, or (more likely) temporary, relating to seasonal patterns of user visitation and demand. Thus, for some tourist destinations, access may only be restricted at certain times of peak demand. Such restrictions may be manifest in terms of timed visitation systems (using timed tickets that allow access to the place) in order to regulate user numbers. This approach could take the form of what could be termed *time-limited* ticketing, whereby visitors have a finite time period within which to experience the destination (and must leave at the end of the period), or, alternatively, a *time-banded* system could ensure visitors arrive at a certain time (but does not determine the actual duration of their visit).

Taken to its extreme, entrance to a place may be totally forbidden, as was the case in the UK countryside during the Foot and Mouth disease outbreak in 2001. This approach is not without its potential problems. Medway et al. state that restricting access – particularly via more draconian measures – can be contentious, and the conflicting interests of different place stakeholders may need to be accommodated and managed effectively if this policy is to be successful. An obvious source of potential conflict is those independent businesses proximate to and/or associated with overly popular tourist attractions/destinations that may depend on visitors to the main attraction for revenue and profits. Obviously, any demarketing strategy will directly impact on them and they may resist any activities in pursuit of that strategy.

Acknowledging the view that restricting access may constitute synchromarketing in temporal terms only, it can be used in conjunction with a spatially oriented approach. Thus, in situations where a place cannot cope with demand, it might also engage in activities involving the promotion and marketing, or redirection, of tourist visitors to an alternative place offer. This could be termed *diversionary place demarketing*: in other words, consistent with the above definition of synchromarketing, attempting to redistribute demand to alternative places. Medway et al. note that such demarketing by the promotion of another place, or suggestion of alternatives, has been used by one English city-centre management scheme in a small historic city to deflect the visitor pressures of organized parties of Continental children who pose problems for the city centre. Consequently, attempts have been made to demarket the city by promoting other nearby places of interest such as zoos that are more suited to this age group than an historic city, and also communicate the fact that a full-day visit to this particular city is not needed.

Another demarketing approach identified by Medway and Warnaby (2008) that has synchromarketing connotations is *informational place demarketing*, defined in terms of providing information about a place, such as the guidance issued by governmental agencies (e.g. the British Commonwealth and Foreign Office in the UK) providing a realistic assessment of the potential dangers of travelling to particular places. Inevitably, such efforts can only be advisory and the decision to go to a place remains the prerogative of the individual. However, with the provision of accurate judgements regarding potential risk (as opposed to the usual place marketing hyperbole), an informed decision as to whether to visit a place can be made by the individual concerned, and some potential visitors may be deterred as a consequence.

This notion of informed decisions as to whether to visit a place is also manifested in what might be termed *admonitory place demarketing*. Whilst many places might not be so dangerous as to warrant Commonwealth and Foreign Office travel advice, there might be issues relating to the place that potential visitors have to be made aware of if they are to get the full benefit from any visit, or indeed, be able to get to the place at all because certain preconditions have to be met for any visit. Thus, admonitory place demarketing serves to warn potential visitors about any precondition affecting visitation and/or specific rules and behavioural standards that have to be adhered to in the place. Such admonitory stipulations may again serve to dissuade and deter some visitors. For example, there have been calls to curb visitation to numerous heritage sites in the UK because of the potential risk to their sustainability. For example, Thorpe and Davies (2009) highlight the problems created by the growing international appeal of Highgate Cemetery in London, which in 2009 was included in a list of the city's top 100 tourist attractions announced by Mayor Boris Johnson, and which was the setting for American author Audrey Niffenegger's recent book *Her Fearful Symmetry*. They quote the chairman of the Friends of Highgate Cemetery as stating:

> *We are now told that this is the most important cemetery in Europe and there are more people coming to see it than ever before … but it is a busy burial ground, too, and we want to make sure that every family with a grave can visit in peace. This is a sacred place.*

Thus, some tourists are being turned away from the cemetery, the older, more historic part of which can only be viewed in the company of a trained guide. Similar strategies are also applicable to the island of St Kilda, which is discussed in more detail below.

As noted above, these strategies are not mutually exclusive, and a specific place could deploy a combination of strategies to demarket the place in order to achieve whatever objectives have been set. The next part of this chapter outlines various activities that could be described as synchromarketing in two very different places in the UK.

St Kilda

The example of demarketing in the context of St Kilda – the remotest part of the United Kingdom – is primarily motivated by sustainability issues, and the demarketing strategies adopted could be seen as a combination of the informational and admonitory, as outlined above. This case study begins with a brief discussion of context relating to remote places (especially those designated as World Heritage Sites – WHS), before moving to set the scene for St Kilda, and then, more specifically, discussing those actions that could be described as aimed at demarketing the islands in an effort to maintain their unique character.

General context

St Kilda is an exemplar of remote heritage sites, especially those with WHS designation. The appeal of such sites to tourists and other visitors can lead to potential problems in terms of maintaining sustainability, consequently requiring protection of those attributes of the place that are of unique natural and/or cultural value, and that warrant the initial WHS designation. Gilmore *et al* (2007) highlight that the prime objective of WHS designation is indeed the preservation of the natural, built and/or socio-economic resources within the designated area.

Whilst WHS designation is not intended as a tourism marketing device, Gilmore *et al.* (2007) emphasize that it represents an international top brand in tourism terms, with tour operators using WHS to promote an area. The competing pressures, which inevitably impact on the sustainability of sites in such situations, are perhaps inevitable. Gilmore *et al.* (2007) view these pressures in terms of *environmental* and *socio-economic* perspectives. On one hand, the environmental perspective encourages protection, conservation, restriction (i.e. of access to, and activities allowed within, the site) and isolation (in order to protect the area from excessive visitation), whereas the socio-economic perspective explicitly encourages visitors, growth, revenue (i.e. from visitation) and also interaction and engagement with visitors. This latter perspective may be of particular importance to WHS in developing countries and/or peripheral areas, where otherwise there may only be limited opportunities for economic development. In such situations leveraging the potential of WHS designation might be the most obvious means by which such development might occur. Hall notes that:

> World Heritage Site (WHS) listing usually carries with it enormous expectation. At first glance these expectations often focus on the extent to which listing is meant to bring in extra tourists to the site or attract more government and agency support for the maintenance of the site's values. However, on closer inspection it is apparent that there are many other implications of WHS listing, including potentially changed access and use of the site, new regulatory structures, and changed economic flows.
>
> *(2006, p. 21)*

Thus, the implications of WHS designation can be widespread and various, and tensions are often evident, as can be seen in relation to St Kilda, as discussed below.

St Kilda – description and background

St Kilda is a remote Atlantic island group that lies 41 miles (64km) west of the Western Isles of Scotland, and about 110 miles west of the Scottish mainland. It consists of four small islands:

> Hirta – the largest of the four islands (1,575 acres), with two bays – Glen Bay and Village Bay, the latter being the focus of human habitation in documented history;
> Dun – a small island separated from Hirta to the western side of Village Bay by a narrow channel, only 50 yards wide;
> Soay – the second largest island, lying to the north-west of Hirta, with a land area of 244 acres and surrounded on all sides by steep cliffs;
> Boreray – lies four miles to the north of Hirta, consisting of 189 acres surrounded by a wall of rock which varies in height from 300–301,245 feet above sea level.
>
> *(National Trust for Scotland – NTS, 2003; Steel, 2011)*

In addition to the four islands, there are numerous sea stacs, the three biggest ones being Levenish (south-east of Hirta), Stac Lee and Stac an Amin (close to Boreray). The total land mass of the islands and these three stacs is 2111.8 acres (854.6 hectares) (NTS, 2003).

Given its location, St Kilda is extremely prone to strong winds and bad weather. Steel notes that '[for] at least eight months of the year, St Kilda, whose annual rainfall is about fifty inches, is subjected to frequent and severe storms' (2011, p. 29). Such conditions have obvious implications for access and indeed exacerbate the perception of the islands' remoteness. This, in turn, has served to fuel their mystique, a factor that has long resonated for many. For example, Steel quotes one newspaper correspondent from the mid-nineteenth century as follows:

> It seems almost beyond credence that such an interesting little colony, such an exclusive commonwealth exists as part of this busy kingdom. Beyond the whirl of commercial life, untroubled by politics, completely isolated from the rest of the world, the St. Kildan lives his simple life.
>
> *(2011, p. 26)*

Notwithstanding the harsh climate and the privations associated with life on Hirta, St Kilda was occupied, almost continually, for over 2000 years. The lifestyle of the native population and the traditional economy of the islands, described in detail in Tom Steel's (2011 [1975, 1988]) book *The Life and Death of St Kilda*, was uniquely adapted to the conditions they faced, and their isolation from life outside their small home was pervasive. However, as Steel (2011, p. 31) notes, 'St Kilda's reputation as the most isolated spot in the United Kingdom was quick to become widespread', and as time progressed there was greater contact with the mainland, although poor weather conditions meant that the islands were frequently cut off from outside contact for extended periods.

In the mid-nineteenth century, the invention of the steamship reduced St Kilda's isolation and there developed a tourist trade whereby for the first time the general public could make the voyage to St Kilda in reasonable comfort. However, weather conditions meant that a landing on Hirta was frequently impossible because of heavy seas, although this, according to Steel, merely 'added to the allure of the place' (2011, p. 125). The advent of tourism inevitably changed the lifestyle of the inhabitants and the economy of the island, and, as contact with the wider world became more extensive, their self-sufficiency lessened – as Steel notes:

> The influx of tourists undermined the economy of the island. Their money led to a decline in productivity and in the people's interest in the traditional way of life on Hirta. With money obtained from tourists the islanders could purchase all the grain and foodstuffs required to maintain a dwindling population. But an economy based on tourism places too great an emphasis upon wind and seas, the two elements upon which the St Kildans had never relied. Within forty years of tourism, life on St Kilda became impossible.
>
> *(ibid, p. 135)*

In 1930, the last native St Kildans were evacuated from Hirta and in the following year the islands were sold. The new owner, the 5th Marquis of Bute, ran the islands as an unoccupied bird sanctuary, and, when he died, he bequeathed St Kilda to the National Trust for Scotland, to be held inalienably, and the islands were formally acquired in 1957. Since then, there has been a military radar tracking station present on Hirta, and all the islands and stacs comprising St Kilda designated a National Nature Reserve, leased to and managed by Scottish Natural Heritage (SNH). Since the 1930 evacuation, St Kilda has had no permanent inhabitants, although since 1957 Hirta has had a temporary and/ or seasonal population involved in the military activities, and latterly National Trust for Scotland and SNH staff and also scientific researchers. There is also an annual St Kilda Work Party programme, whereby volunteers spend two weeks on the islands carrying out conservation work with free time to explore (NTS, 2003). St Kilda also receives other tourist visitors, drawn by the continuing mystique of the islands.

Since 1986, St Kilda has been designated as a WHS in recognition of its natural heritage, principally the cliffs and seabird colonies it supports. In 2004, this designation was extended to include the marine environment and cultural landscape, and St Kilda remains the only site in the UK to hold such 'Dual Heritage Status'. The increased profile of St Kilda has seen an increase in visitation. From 1986 to 2002, annual visitation ranged from just under 1,000 to a peak of 1,958 in 1997 (NTS, 2003). However, this figure had risen to more than 4,000 in 2010 (Steel, 2011).

Demarketing St Kilda?

Such increased visitation inevitably places strains on the maintenance of the vision and guiding principles of the Management Plan for St Kilda (produced as a consequence of WHS designation), which focuses on conservation, minimal intervention and sensitive public access and interpretation of the site (see NTS, 2003). Thorpe and Davies (2009, p. 19) quote a representative from NTS as saying, 'We've never actively promoted St Kilda for the reason that it is so heavily designated and fragile'. However, for those interested in St Kilda – and it retains the ability to captivate people because of its historic and ongoing mystique (see Jamie, 2012, for an evocative description of the continuing 'pull' of St Kilda) – there is a website (www.kilda.org.uk), which has proved to be very popular.

However, on the website, which indeed, provides much useful information about St Kilda in an attempt to satisfy the curious, there is little of the usual tourism marketing hyperbole that is aimed at attracting visitors. The first sentence (highlighted in bold type) of the 'Visiting St Kilda' page states:

> Getting to St Kilda is not easy, but those who are persistent can find a variety of ways to achieve their goal.

The site goes on to give various points of advice to potential visitors to Hirta in order to ensure that their activities make as little impact on the site as possible. Thus, for example, all visitors must contact the St Kilda Ranger on arrival, and visitors can only come ashore by tender or dinghy (to avoid the introduction of rats and other predators). The absence of public toilet facilities on the island is also emphasized. Also highlighted is the fact that all the elements of the historic built environment on the island are protected by law as Scheduled Ancient Monuments and should not be abused. The advice also warns visitors about the need to respect wildlife, and the fact that certain birds are very protective of their nests and will dive-bomb or hit visitors who venture too close.

Other advice warns of the potential dangers, and warns that visitors have to take responsibility for their own actions, as the following excerpts from the 'Access Leaflet' to St Kilda illustrate:

> **Weather systems can change rapidly and can be severe, even in summer. Plan ahead and be properly equipped.**
>
> Gale force winds are experienced for 20 per cent of the year. Low temperatures and cloud can prevail for days, even in the warmest months. Ensure that you have appropriate wind- and waterproof clothing and stout footwear for slippery vegetated slopes. If travelling out with Village Bay carry, and be able to use, a map, compass and whistle, and please leave a route card with the Ranger. If you have arranged to remain on the islands overnight you should have adequate provisions for several days in case you are stranded owing to weather conditions.

St Kilda has high cliffs and slippery slopes and is remote from rescue services and medical care. Be self-reliant and take care.

After rain or heavy mists, grassy slopes can be very slippery – be aware of your surroundings. Waterproof trousers can greatly accelerate a fall! Wind gusting at cliff tops and skua attacks can catch you unawares. There is no mobile phone reception on the islands and the coastguard helicopter is based remotely. Know your own abilities and seek guidance from people who know the landscape.

(NTS, n/d)

This combination of informational and admonitory place demarketing serves to provide a realistic and plain-speaking picture of St Kilda, so that visitors who find themselves in trouble, or indeed stranded, on Hirta cannot claim that they had not been warned!

London and the 2012 Olympics

This second case study considers a very different type of place, namely the UK capital city of London, which is one of the great world cities. Place demarketing activities are also evident here, albeit motivated by different factors than those for St Kilda. This case, which takes as its specific context the 2012 Summer Olympics held in the city, focuses on synchromarketing activities primarily aimed at crisis prevention/management, and the specific strategies discussed here could be regarded as a combination of informational and diversionary place demarketing.

General context

For many, the 2012 Summer Olympics (officially the Games of the XXX Olympiad) – or more commonly known as London 2012 – need little introduction. These events – including the 2012 Summer Paralympics, which began just over two weeks after the closing ceremony of the main Olympics – were an integral element of a celebrated summer of sport in the UK that was centred on the capital city. Inevitably, the scale of these activities necessitated a massive logistical operation, which provided many challenges for those responsible for administering the city and managing its infrastructure.

In particular, concerns were expressed about the ability of the city's transport system to cope with the expected influx of visitors, competitors, officials and representatives from the world's media. The International Olympic Committee's (IOC) initial evaluation of London's bid to host the Games identified transport issues as potential problems, but concluded that with regard to this aspect of infrastructure:

> During the bid process, substantial London rail transport infrastructure investments have been clearly confirmed, guaranteed and accelerated.

Provided that this proposed programme of public transport improvements is fully delivered on schedule before 2012 and the extensive Olympic Route Network is implemented, the Commission believes that London would be capable of coping with Games-time traffic and that Olympic and Paralympic transport requirements would be met.

(IOC, 2005, p. 78)

Indeed, in preparation for the Games, there were numerous transport infrastructure projects that were initiated, upgraded or accelerated in order to enable the city to cope with the anticipated influx of visitors. The various organizations responsible for this – including the Olympic Delivery Authority (ODA), Transport for London (TfL), Network Rail, central government and numerous contractors – invested billions of pounds in improvement schemes. These included:

- investing £125 million to treble capacity and increase accessibility at Stratford Regional Station (the nearest station to the main venues);
- a new East London Line, linking 21 stations from Dalston in east London to West Croydon and Crystal Palace in the south;
- increasing the capacity and frequency of services on the London overground North London Line, which connects Richmond and Clapham in south-west London to Stratford via north London;
- the extension of Docklands Light Railway by 2.6km under the River Thames, to provide an important north–south link for spectators.

In addition to these infrastructural improvements, there was significant investment to increase capacity of transport services generally, and to run additional services during the Games period (i.e. earlier in the morning and later in the evening).

Notwithstanding all these developments, as one ODA publication stated:

… the huge number of spectators, combined with the usual high number of tourists and people using the transport system, means that London will still be significantly busier than normal (that is, the same times on the equivalent dates in 2010).

Stations and lines across London will be particularly busy at peak competition and peak commuter times. For example, during the Games at peak times, King's Cross St Pancras, Waterloo and London Bridge stations will all be much busier than normal.

Transport, travel routes, deliveries/collections and freight operations could be affected throughout London and around venues elsewhere in the UK.

(ODA, 2010, p. 4)

A key task therefore was to ensure that, during the period when the Games occurred, life for residents in the city could continue as normally as possible, especially in terms of getting to and from work and also ensuring as far as possible that business performance was not adversely affected. Here, the emphasis was to ensure that Londoners were fully informed about the timing and location of potential transport disruption so that contingency plans could be put in place – both personal and business-related. Part of this was also 'diversionary' in an attempt to manage/reduce demand on an already intensively used transport infrastructure, even before all the additional Games-related usage over the summer.

'Keep on Running'

The emphasis of this strand of the London 2012 communications campaign was to inform local businesses of the location and duration of potential problems, so that they could accommodate this into their operations during the period of the Games, and to 'Keep on Running' as normally as possible.

The locations of these potential transport problems – 'travel hotspots' – had been identified well in advance of the Games, particularly those routes that linked central London with venues and major interchange stations. A 'Map of affected areas' across the capital was widely disseminated and, in addition, detailed maps of specific districts/areas were available online, with information on how roads and public transport would be affected. In order to maximize efficiency of travel, Games spectators were encouraged to use certain stations and the lines that serve them to get to and from competition venues. Local businesses were explicitly advised to avoid these stations and routes, especially during peak competition times (identified in advance).

Businesses were encouraged to carry out assessment impacts well in advance and also to develop contingencies regarding four main areas, as appropriate: staff travel to and from work, travel for customers and other visitors, deliveries/collections and other suppliers, and also any business-related travel occurring during the period. Moreover, a range of potential solutions was identified from which businesses could develop appropriate coping strategies in order to ensure as far as possible a continuance of normal operations (see ODA, 2010). Such solutions were analogous with demarketing in general, such as avoiding travel wherever possible, as well as synchromarketing more specifically. Here, for example, businesses were encouraged to 'manage essential journeys' in terms of rescheduling trips to avoid busy periods, re-routing trips to avoid busy locations, and using less busy modes of transport. Businesses were also encouraged to allow their employees to work from home where appropriate, or temporarily relocate employees to other workplaces. Another strand was to encourage what was somewhat euphemistically termed 'active travel' – in other words, not using public transport but walking or cycling for all or part of their journey.

'Get Ahead of the Games'

Linked to this was a parallel campaign with the strapline 'Get Ahead of the Games', which essentially encouraged Londoners to think in advance about how they would be able to move around the city during the Games period.

A Transport for London press release quoted the London Mayor, Boris Johnson, as stating:

> Our roads and public transport services are going to be excessively busy, and journeys may take longer than usual. So it's vital that businesses and Londoners don't adopt a 'wait and see' approach and play their part in putting on a fantastic Olympics.
>
> *(TfL, 2012a)*

This message was disseminated across the city in various ways, most notably an announcement from Boris Johnson was broadcast in tube trains and across the transport network, which, in itself, generated a lot of media coverage arising from Johnson's already extensive media celebrity. His recorded message was:

> Hi folks! This is the Mayor here. This is the greatest moment in the life of London for 50 years. We're welcoming more than a million people a day to our city and there is going to be huge pressure on the transport network. Don't get caught out. Get online and plan your journey at GetAheadoftheGames.com.
>
> *(Daily Telegraph, 2012)*

The message was reiterated in a poster campaign around the city, especially focused on the transport network itself.

Moreover, social media were used to provide a fast way to get up-to-date travel information to travellers in the city by means of Twitter, posting tweets from @TfLTravelAlerts and also via the interactive Get Ahead of the Games website. By the end of the Games period, the website had received 4.7 million visits, and there were nearly 63,000 followers on Twitter (TfL, 2012b).

In terms of the success of these initiatives, the Get Ahead of the Games website states:

> We know from your feedback that many spectators, regular transport and road users across the UK used the travel information and advice we provided.
>
> In London alone, around a third of you changed your regular journeys on public transport to avoid the busiest times and places, mostly by changing the time of travel or the route taken. Motorists avoided driving near the Olympic and Paralympic Route networks with traffic levels in central London reduced by around 15%.
>
> This meant that London's transport networks were able to operate smoothly while carrying record numbers of passengers. During the Olympics over 62 million journeys were made on the Tube – up 35% on normal levels.
>
> Transport for London, the Mayor of London, National Rail, the Department of Transport, Highways Agency and other partners will continue to work together and build on valuable lessons learnt during the Games, including better travel information and advice.
>
> *(TfL, 2012b)*

Conclusion

The nature of places as 'products' to be marketed, and the often finite nature of place resources that may limit the ability to cope with visitor demand, can lead to situations where demarketing is an appropriate strategy. This chapter has outlined different motivations for – and approaches to – place demarketing, with particular emphasis on synchromarketing. In this context, synchromarketing involves trying to redistribute visitation and other place usage, so that a place is able to cope (either in terms of infrastructure, or in order to ensure the sustainability of the characteristics and attributes that attract visitation in the first place). As can be seen from the two case studies discussed above, such activities can be applicable to very different types of place. Indeed, it may be the case that almost any place, at some point in time (given a particular combination of circumstances), may have to engage in some form of demarketing.

References

Avraham, E. (2000) Cities and their news media images, *Cities*, vol. 17 No 5, pp. 363–70.

——(2004) Media strategies for improving an unfavourable city image, *Cities*, vol. 21 No. 6, pp. 471–79.

Avraham, E. and Ketter, E. (2008) *Media Strategies for Marketing Places in Crisis: Improving the image of cities*, Countries and Tourist Destinations. Oxford: Elsevier/Butterworth Heinemann.

Burgess, J. (1982) Selling places: Environmental images for the executive, *Regional Studies*, vol. 16 No 1, pp. 1–17.

Daily Telegraph (2012) *London 2012 Olympics: Recorded message from Boris Johnson to warn commuters of travel chaos*. Available at http://www.telegraph.co.uk/sport/olympics/9371897/London-2012-Olympics-recorded-message-from-Boris-Johnson-to-warn-commuters-of-travel-chaos.html. Accessed 28 September 2012.

Franks, J., Lowe, P., Phillipson, J. and Scott, C. (2003) The impact of foot and mouth disease on farm businesses in Cumbria, *Land Use Policy*, vol. 20 No 2, pp. 159–68.

Gilmore, A., Carson, D. and Ascenção, M. (2007) Sustainable tourism marketing at a World Heritage Site, *Journal of Strategic Marketing*, vol. 15 No 2 and 3, pp. 253–64.

Hall, C. M. (2006) Implementing the World Heritage Convention: What Happens After Listing? In A. Leask and A. Fyall (Eds) *Managing World Heritage Sites*. Oxford: Butterworth-Heinemann, pp. 20–34.

International Olympic Committee (2005) *Report of the IOC Evaluation Commission for the Games of the XXX Olympiad in 2012*. Lausanne: IOC.

Jamie, K. (2012) 'Three ways of looking at St Kilda', in K. Jamie, *Sightlines*. London: Sort Of Books, pp. 130–63.

Kotler, P. and Levy, S. J. (1971) Demarketing, yes, demarketing, *Harvard Business Review*, Nov/Dec, pp. 74–80.

Kotler, P., Haider, D. H. and Rein, I. (1993) *Marketing Places: Attracting investment, industry, and tourism to cities, states and nations*. The Free Press, New York.

Kotler, P., Asplund, C., Rein, I. and Haider, D. (1999) *Marketing Places Europe: Attracting investments, industries, and visitors to European cities, communities, regions and nations*. Financial Times Prentice Hall, Harlow.

Medway, D. and Warnaby, G. (2008) Alternative perspectives on marketing and the place brand, *European Journal of Marketing*, vol. 42 No 5 and 6, pp. 641–53.

Medway, D., Warnaby, G. and Dharni, S. (2011) Demarketing places: Rationales and strategies, *Journal of Marketing Management*, 42 (1–2), pp. 124–42.

National Trust for Scotland (2003) *St Kilda World Heritage Site Management Pan 2003–8*. Available at http://www.kilda.org.uk/StKildaManagementPlan.pdf. Accessed 27 September 2012.

National Trust for Scotland (n/d) *St Kilda – A guide to access*. Available at http://www.kilda.org.uk/St%20Kilda%20Guide%20to%20access.pdf. Accessed 27 September 2012.

Olympic Delivery Authority (2010) *Keep on Running – Keep your business running smoothly during the 2012 Games*. London: ODA.

Steel, T. (2011) *The Life and Death of St Kilda: The moving story of a vanished island community*. London: Harper Press.

Thorpe, V. and Davies C. (2009) Calls to Curb Heritage Site Tourism, *The Observer*, 26 April, p. 19.

Transport for London (2012a) *Get Ahead of the Games* – Press Release 4 July. Available at www.tfl.gov.uk/corporate/media/newscentre/metro/24613.aspx#. Accessed 14 September 2012.

——(2012b) *Thank you for Getting Ahead of the Games*. Available at www.getaheadofthegames.com. Accessed 14 September 2012.

Ward, N., Donaldson, A. and Lowe, P. (2004) Policy framing and learning the lessons from the UK's foot and mouth disease crisis, *Environment and Planning C*, vol. 22 No 2, pp. 291–306.

Ward, S. V. (1998) *Selling Places: The marketing and promotion of towns and cities 1850–2000*. London: E. and F.N. Spon.

4

COUNTERMARKETING IN A WICKED PROBLEM CONTEXT – THE CASE OF COCAINE

Nigel Jones, Paul Baines and Steve Welsh

Introduction

In this chapter, we examine the cocaine supply problem from the perspective of wickedness, not in a moral sense but as a problem that seems intractable. We review the complexity of attempting to demarket cocaine by influencing the demand and supply sides at play. In doing so, we seek to introduce frameworks that can help policy makers and planners navigate the complexity of the phenomenon in such a way that tangible behavioural outcomes might be identified and pursued. We do not prescribe what precise interventions and policy should result, not least because further research needs to be undertaken at the local level into the effectiveness of existing interventions and into the user community and their motivations in order to allow them to be precisely segmented. Rather, we hope to help the planner and policy maker span the analysis gap between the apparent complexity of the strategic picture and local thinking about specific interventions that needs to take place. We advocate the lens of a wicked problem, the utility of soft systems thinking and the structure of social marketing as a way of moving from the strategic picture to the local. We begin by defining wicked problems in the context of cocaine supply and demand. We then discuss the origins of cocaine use and the global nature of cocaine distribution and supply so that the interconnected dynamics of the problem can be established. A review of the literature on cocaine use and its causes is undertaken as we introduce soft systems and social marketing perspectives. Finally, we derive a set of principles that we think will be important in the development of policy and future cocaine demarketing interventions in the UK and elsewhere.

Wicked problems

There are few discussions involving cocaine use and anti-drug policy that do not illustrate its complex nature. The complexity of the cocaine problem space accounts for the many lenses through which it is studied, including law enforcement, social marketing, medicine, health and psychiatry, sociology and psychology, economics and policy studies, to name a few. Whilst this makes for a data-rich environment on which to plan interventions, it poses the problem of identifying the operable variables to leverage or address. It makes the public policy context a contested space with controversial debates over victims and priorities. Moreover, the complexity involved makes engagement in and between government and communities challenging. It can appear like a problem that cannot be tied down and for which coherent and targeted solutions seem beyond grasp. To intervene in one area is to create another somewhere else; to close down a crack house here is to open another one there: the so-called 'squeezing of the balloon'. The problem is exacerbated by innovative and competitive gangs providing new business models and services. Indeed, the problem is wicked in every sense of the term (see Rittel and Webber, 1973). Part of the reason for the complexity is that it incorporates so many stakeholders, each of which could be a target for a demarketing intervention. These include: the cultivator; manufacturer (chemist); the importers (smugglers, mules, money-launderers) and distributors (investors, major dealers); the dealers (regional, crack house suppliers, delivery service operators); the security men; the accountant; the sellers (street sellers and 'runners'); lookouts and other middlemen; and, finally, the user (Johnson and Golub, 2007).

Therefore, in seeking to define a demarketing intervention, three frameworks are worth noting that help our understanding of complex and unbounded problems and how interventions might emerge. First is the notion of wicked problems; second is systems thinking, specifically soft systems; and third is social marketing. We consider each of these below.

The (wicked) problem of reducing cocaine consumption

Rittel and Webber (1973) defined wicked problems, particularly social problems, through a number of characteristics, as opposed to the 'tame' problems of science and engineering. Their characteristics are listed below together with a comment on how that characteristic may be interpreted in the case of cocaine:

1. There is no definitive formulation of a wicked problem. In the context of cocaine, the problem itself is difficult to tie down as, in trying to formulate it, it opens up more questions or problem features. For example, if drug use is a consequence of economic or social stress, do the problems of economic stress need to be addressed – and what are the underpinning structures that drive the stressors?
2. Wicked problems have no stopping rule. As the problem cannot be formulated, the solution cannot be formulated. The only way of stopping dealing with the problem is when resources run out. Consequently, drug use is likely to have a persistent presence in society and dealing with it is limited by our motivation and resources.

3. Solutions to wicked problems are not true or false, but good or bad. The judgements of many groups involved will differ, so proposed solutions are likely to be better or worse, more satisfying or good enough.

4. There is no immediate and no ultimate test of a solution to a wicked problem. Consequences of the solution are difficult to evaluate until the repercussions have completely run out. The consequences of interventions in cocaine behaviours may take some time to surface and be realized.

5. Every solution to a wicked problem is a 'one-shot operation'; because there is no opportunity to learn by trial and error, every attempt counts significantly. An intervention 'leaves traces that cannot be undone'. For example, the consequences of legalizing or proscribing a drug have knock-on consequences that must be addressed.

6. Wicked problems do not have an enumerable (or an exhaustively describable) set of potential solutions, nor is there a well-described set of permissible operations that may be incorporated into the plan. There is no exhaustible list of approaches that might be adopted.

7. Every wicked problem is essentially unique. Addressing the issue in one context may not provide a template solution to other contexts. In terms of cocaine, a number of papers have commented that the crack cocaine epidemic from the United States was predicted to follow the same pattern in the UK, yet they found heterogeneity in user profiles, as variations were related to unique social structures and historical context (Green et al., 1994; Hammersley and Ditton, 1994; Power et al., 1995).

8. Every wicked problem can be considered to be a symptom of another problem.

9. The existence of a discrepancy representing a wicked problem can be explained in numerous ways. The choice of explanation determines the nature of the problem's resolution. In the context of cocaine, how we attribute what we observe shapes our intervention, and there are many ways in which cocaine-related behaviours are attributed.

10. The planner has no right to be wrong. Planners are liable for the consequences of the actions that they generate and have important social consequences.

To elaborate these issues further, the next section provides an overview of the cocaine problem.

The origins of cocaine use

Cocaine is processed from the leaf of the coca plant (Erythroxylum Coca), which grows easily in the high-altitude regions of South America, in such countries as Colombia, Bolivia, Peru and Brazil. The plant has also been grown in other regions, for example, Taiwan, Java, India and parts of Africa. In South America, native Indians have been accustomed to chewing its leaves for hundreds of years either for religious ceremonies or to counteract the effects of fatigue. The leaves of the plant in its traditional form comprise only about 2 per cent active stimulant, so this habit has not tended to generate significant health or social issues but is rendered unlawful under international conventions on narcotic drugs. Bolivia is seeking an exemption for this 'traditional' practice to re-enter the UN Single Convention on Narcotic Drugs, 1961, which is proving contentious among current signatory states. About 120 years ago, a technique was developed to extract cocaine hydrochloride from the leaf for use as an effective local anaesthetic. Its use proliferated in health and quasi-health products such as tonics and then into popular commercial products including drinks, for example, Coca Cola (an ingredient until 1903). With widespread use, its addictive properties became apparent, and safer synthetic alternatives were developed for use as anaesthetics. However, its attraction as a stimulant did not diminish and its consumption persisted increasingly despite its criminal status. This persisting use found favour in wealthy social circles in North America and Western Europe (Stockley, 1992: 77). The definitions of traditional, healthy, detrimental and recreational uses are contested.

As a powerful stimulant, the drug produces a pronounced sensation of wellbeing, euphoria and excitement, heightening activity. It has an invigorating effect that reduces the onset of the effects of tiredness and assists the user to resist the need to sleep. However, misuse of cocaine can often lead to a psychological dependence, which is developed as the body acquires a natural tolerance to consumption. The European Monitoring Centre for Drugs & Drug Addiction (EMCDDA) Annual Report (2012: 65) concludes 'the health consequences of cocaine use are likely to be underestimated', citing the unspecific or chronic nature of pathologies arising from long-term use. Certainly, regular use may be associated with cardiovascular, neurological and psychiatric problems, irrespective of whether it is snorted or not. Use accelerates the development of coronary artery disease and may be the trigger for acute cardiovascular conditions (HASC, 2012: 9). Large doses of cocaine may cause sleeplessness, hallucinations, tremors and convulsions. Paranoid delusions may occur, which can progress to aggressive and violent behaviour. Overdosing on cocaine induces heart and breathing malfunctions, frequently proving fatal (a characteristic used in the Scottish 'Know the Score' campaign – see later). The harm footprint of cocaine in respect of the health of the consumer is clouded in part due to the frequency that it is often taken in conjunction with other illicit substances (a 'polydrug' mix) or with other substances such as alcohol, which have their own health implications (Gossop *et al.*, 2006). Bulking and cutting agents, used to adulterate cocaine, also present their own health problems and expand the problem space to include variations, innovations and diverse supply and trafficking chains, all with varying degrees of legality.

Cocaine distribution and supply

Nowadays, illicit cocaine emanates almost exclusively from South America. The majority of the UK's cocaine supply originates from Colombia, although data compiled by the UN suggests that Peru and Bolivia ebb and flow in significance, correlated to the existing challenges of illicit cultivation and processing in

Colombia at any time. The major decline in cocaine production in Colombia from 2006 to 2010 has been balanced by increased production in Peru and Bolivia (UNODC, 2012: 12). Production and trafficking of cocaine is a perpetual 'arms race' between the evolving capabilities and capacities of the counter-narcotics effort run by the UK and other countries' governments and those of the traffickers. Illicit coca crops tend to be grown in 'ungoverned space' or areas of low governance. The availability of such space (by nature or through conflict) in South America results in the 'squeezing the balloon' issue: when cultivation is progressively constrained by a government's successful measures in one state, the deficit in crops is addressed by increased production in other nearby states. In South America and Africa, the terrain promotes porous borders aiding traffickers in moving consignments between states. Access to the sea routes into both the Pacific and Atlantic also assists cocaine trafficking. Success by military and law-enforcement agencies against these maritime routes has led to the displacement of cocaine trafficking to the Gulf of Mexico, leading to the destabilizing and bloody current conflict in Mexico where one trafficking crime group competes with another, whilst resisting and attacking the government's attempts to disrupt the lucrative trade. Similarly, success in maritime interdiction against consignments concealed in vessels dispatched to Europe and Africa led to the traffickers loading cocaine into aircraft and establishing an air bridge into West Africa from South America. West Africa's emergence as a transit state has also been accompanied by increasing levels of cocaine consumption in that region (UNODC, 2012: 27). Traffickers have also exploited semi-submersible craft in the Pacific but the Atlantic swell seems to have precluded this mode of transport from consignments dispatched from the eastern seaboard. The global nature of the problem makes meaningful, coordinated intervention itself a complex problem.

Another key dimension is containerized shipping. Although, according to UNODC (2012), only 2 per cent of container movements are inspected worldwide, in 1999, the World Customs Organization reported that 64 per cent of cocaine seizures related to concealment in maritime containers. More recently in 2010, 80 per cent of cocaine seized entering Spain came from containers. Speculative inspections of containers do not tend to take place due to the commercial pressure on ports to implement 'just in time logistics' and bring in as many containers as possible to achieve economies of scale and maximize profits. There is often an overriding concern in countries not to displace commercial container operators to maritime hubs in other states. Only countries with the greatest attraction as large, lucrative markets, e.g. the USA, are able to impose greater control over containerized imports than weaker economies, which can, if necessary, be accessed conveniently from ports in neighbouring states. This economic pressure taken with the volume of traffic and balanced against available enforcement resources means that most inspections are now by necessity intelligence-led. This in turn promotes a 'cat and mouse' contest with law-enforcement intelligence seeking to identify the nature and routings of traffic containing cocaine consignments and cataloguing any tell-tale anomalies or indicators that aid the task. The illicit traffickers constantly seek novel concealments and routings and to design out any tell-tale anomalies. The activity is therefore situated within another economic system with links across multiple legitimate activities.

Adulteration adds another dimension to criminal flexibility and resilience in the trafficking and supplying of cocaine. Recently, Colombian producers have added Levamisol, an animal worming treatment, to augment effect. However, the recent trend for increasing preference for Active Pharmaceutical Ingredients (APIs) to use as 'bulking' or 'cutting' agents to increase mass and extend profits has proved to be more significant. APIs with properties that mimic those of cocaine are selected because these chemicals allow greater adulteration with less prospect of purchaser awareness or detection of the extent to which the cocaine has been diluted. This has extended across most, if not all, links in the supply chain where profit is taken. This is evidenced by the demand from traffickers selling the drug at these various stages for hydraulic presses and packaging resources so that consignments may be adulterated or 'cut' and then repackaged to appear to remain in the same branded kilo packages in which it left the producer. 'Caveat emptor' (buyer beware) would seem to be prudent advice for purchasers at all stages in the cocaine supply chain. Cocaine 'cut' prior to importation will often prove to contain high levels of phenacetin, a pharmaceutical ingredient, suspected in the past of having carcinogenic properties and therefore is no longer popular for legal use. However, once cocaine enters the UK, the favoured 'cutting agent' API, is benzocaine. Recently, tonnes of benzocaine, often contained in 20-kilo barrels, has been a popular and overt import into the UK. The volume imported far exceeds that necessary to satisfy the demand for legal use. The manner and the form in which the API is imported also generally renders the product unsuitable and unsellable for any such legal use, e.g. in terms of provenance and certainty of sterile condition. Countermeasures instituted in the UK against the overt import of large shipments of APIs, obviously destined for diversion into drug supply, has led to the APIs being increasingly smuggled into the UK via mis-description and other methods. UNODC analysis suggests that cocaine is heavily cut after importation into the UK (UNODC, 2012: 48). Essentially, a lot of UK cocaine users face the prospect of actually buying benzocaine laced with as little as 10 per cent to 20 per cent cocaine. An information asymmetry exists that gives the advantage to the dealer over the user.

Adulteration using APIs affords the trafficker and supplier some resilience to success from law enforcement with the potential to increase adulteration when supplies of cocaine are leaner with less likelihood that the customer will realize. There is similar use of APIs in cutting 'crack cocaine', e.g. phenacetin remains bonded to the 'rock' during the processing of cocaine into 'crack', whilst most other adulterants are 'burnt off', which has hitherto rendered crack more dependable in terms of purity. Therefore, while the 'street level' sale price of a wrap of 'cocaine' to a user may remain relatively inelastic, the amount of cocaine actually present is likely to be increasingly elastic to wholesale supply conditions. The significance may be gauged by the finding that there has been a decline in cocaine production but no fall in global consumption (UNODC, 2012: 35). But APIs also have their own significant health issues and side effects to factor into the overall risk posed by 'cocaine' deals in which API predominates. Along with the cocaine itself, precursor chemicals used in the production process are controlled and monitored, e.g. potassium permanganate, a chemical reagent. This has led to efforts by criminals to circumvent restrictions by identifying and exploiting viable unregulated pre-precursor chemicals to produce the necessary precursors.

The cocaine market is assessed by UNODC to be the most globalized of all the illicit drug markets (UNODC, 2012: 69). In recent years, the European market has grown, whilst that in North America has declined. However, since 2008/09, there have been some indications of a downturn in consumption, settling in the high consumption states in Europe, including the UK. This also applies to the young adult category of 15 to 34 years (UNODC, 2012: 32). The UK is one of Europe's largest markets for cocaine. The Advisory Council on the Misuse of Drugs (ACMD) estimates that 25 to 30 tonnes of adulterated and unadulterated cocaine is needed each year to satisfy demand in the UK (HASC, 2012: 21). In terms of illicit drugs in the UK, cocaine continues to be the second most used illicit drug in the UK after cannabis, used by around 2.1 per cent of those aged between 16 and 59 years old (NSMC, 2012); 8.8 per cent of 16–59-year-olds report lifetime use of cocaine (UK Focal Point on Drugs, 2010); and there was estimated to be 188,697 crack cocaine users in England alone in 2008/09 (UK Focal Point on Drugs, 2010).

There are various routes by which cocaine arrives in Europe and the UK. Important hub countries are Spain and the Netherlands, whilst West African states continue to serve as transit countries. However, the transatlantic maritime route to Europe continues to be very significant, often via hub countries in the Caribbean. London, Liverpool and Birmingham are key distribution nodes for cocaine entering the UK and drugs are often routed via England for markets in Wales, Scotland and Northern Ireland. According to the Scottish Serious Crime and Drugs Enforcement Agency (SCDEA), crime groups active in Scotland are increasing direct importation north of the border (UK Focal Point Report for 2011, 2012: 152–53).

Seizures of cocaine in the UK soared in the mid- to late 1980s and continued upwards in the 1990s. Analysis of British Crime Survey data demonstrates that the only illicit drug whose prevalence of use has increased significantly in the UK for the period since 1996 has been cocaine, although, since 2008 to 2009, there has been some levelling out and indications of a slight downturn in consumption (UK Focal Point Report for 2011, 2012: 43). Of prime concern is that the expansion of the market over the past two decades has in part occurred with an increase in young people consuming the drug.

In terms of cocaine reaching the user in the UK, the 'Kevin Bacon' social network theory on degrees of separation appears to prove valid in sourcing cocaine. The British Crime Survey data suggests 75 per cent of persons consuming drugs in the preceding year had sourced the drug either (a) from a friend or family member (54 per cent), or (b) from someone else they knew (21 per cent). Only

22 per cent reported sourcing the drug from anyone with less social connection, e.g. a 'contact' or 'dealer' primarily accessed for supply. The most common environment for the act of supply/purchase was someone else's house (38 per cent) or the user's own home (21 per cent). Of the respondents, 12 per cent stated that they last acquired illicit drugs at a party, club or rave, 10 per cent stated it had last occurred on the street, park or other open area, and 9 per cent replied that it was in a bar or club (UK Focal Point Report for 2011, 2012: 153). This picture does not specifically deal with cocaine supply and consumption but its prevalence as a drug of abuse makes it likely to be indicative.

In terms of environmental impact, the illicit crop cultivation for cocaine production and the associated processing has had a pronounced effect. The Home Affairs Select Committee (HASC) in its recent report on UK Drug Policy quotes *The Ecologist* in that by 2009 cocaine production effectively destroyed an area the size of Wales in the Amazonian rainforest. It has also been estimated that, due to the overall logistics of cultivation and production, four metres of rainforest are cleared for every gramme of cocaine produced (HASC, 2012: 20).

As well as being the most globalized of the drugs markets, cocaine also brings with it more violence and other criminality than other drugs. In the first nine months of 2011, 12,903 people were killed in Mexico in drug-related violence predominantly related to the cocaine trade, which has brought the total of such deaths in Mexico since 2006 to 47,515 (HASC, 2012: 19). West Africa bears similar testimony to the corrosive effect of corruption and intimidation that accompanies cocaine trafficking with Guinea Bissau being labelled as a 'narco state' some years ago by UNODC (Vulliamy, 2008). Cocaine trafficking is firmly on the list of global national security issues. Effective money laundering and the ability of the traffickers to dislocate the act of supply geographically from the act of payment allow them to realize a lucrative criminal profit, which resources their resilience. Money laundering is increasingly assisted by the speed of automated payment and clearance systems as well as the existence of accessible and effective value transfer systems. Digital and e-currencies further assist efforts to launder proceeds via the cyber domain.

In summary, cocaine can be placed at the centre of a fairly extensive picture of harm and threat but the globalized scale of the problem and the resilience and flexibility of the traffickers poses a formidable challenge to efforts to reduce demand or supply. The lack of detailed knowledge in the UK about the nature of people in the clandestine community of users and lack of any useful audience segmentation also adds to the scale of this challenge.

A systems view

In thinking about cocaine as a wicked problem, the downside is the difficulty leaders will feel in meeting expectations of resolution and decisive, visionary, decision-making. On the upside is recognizing the likelihood that addressing cocaine as a problem that needs dynamic and ongoing interventions helps people deal with issues as they are and manage them over realistic timescales rather than place undue hope in short-term solutions. Understanding that for every action there may be desired and undesired, intentional and unintended consequences should lead planners to think explicitly about interventions in two ways: 1) connectedness and 2) risk. If there are connections that cause knock-on consequences, placing a risk-based analysis in a planning process is a necessary step. Risks involved should be explicitly stated so that accommodation might be obtained about how they might be mitigated or accepted. However, having some understanding about risk is problematic across large numbers of stakeholders (as exist in the cocaine context) as per wicked problem characteristic number 3 above. The issue of communicating complexity in unbounded problems is something that Checkland (1993) also addresses through his Soft Systems Methodology, which we turn to next.

Rich pictures in soft systems: The case of cocaine

Checkland (1993: 1) explains that 'the central concept "system" embodies the idea of a set of elements connected together which form a whole, this showing properties which are properties of the whole, rather than properties of its component parts'. From this definition, one introduces the notion of emergent properties through the interaction of entities in a system. In terms of cocaine, one cannot understand cocaine by examining users and suppliers in isolation from one another. In understanding their connectedness, one can start to examine patterns of life shaping how people live, work, use and purchase (e.g. see Pettiway, 1995, for more on what variables impact upon distances travelled by people to purchase and use crack). However, when one introduces many more variables, the ability to communicate and 'sanity check' one's understanding of the problem space (rather than the strict formulation of the problem), a narrative account soon becomes bogged down. Soft Systems Methodology was specifically developed to address open and seemingly unbounded problem spaces where problem definition was difficult. Consequently, Checkland as part of his Soft Systems Methodology (SSM) advocates the use of 'rich pictures' at an early stage in helping to explore the features of the problem situation. An example of a rich picture is shown in Figure 4.1 that tries to illustrate the many relationships. It allows a group through discussion to explore what they think are the key features and how they might relate and operate. Whilst here we only borrow one approach in the portfolio of SSM, Checkland goes on through several stages to develop system views and definitions before generating possible actions to improve the problem situation.

Perhaps when looking at the picture and the brief discussion of wicked problems, one might feel that a purposeful intervention with knowable outcomes is impossible. However, if one has decided to deal with the problem of drug use, then at least a more informed and risk-based view can be adopted. Exploring the relationship within the system can act as a prompt to identifying second-order consequences for an intervention at a particular point.

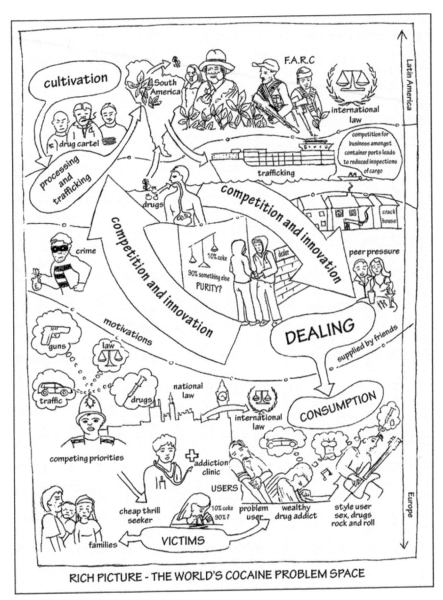

RICH PICTURE - THE WORLD'S COCAINE PROBLEM SPACE

FIGURE 4.1 Rich picture of the cocaine demarketing problem space

This leads to the next question: what should any particular intervention look like, and how should it be framed in the mind of the policy maker and planner? If the policy maker has, for example, already decided that a legal solution is the answer (now what's the question?) and made a public commitment on this, then of course the option space for resolutions has already been situated. One needs to recognize that we do not start with a blank slate. Rather, in any

context with a mixed set of interdependencies such as those explored in the rich picture, we can start to select which elements of the problem space might be addressed. This will be shaped by the planner's or policy maker's responsibilities and resources, but also crucially how they attribute cause and effect in the problem space.

Limits of responsibility and control

If we argue that the cocaine problem space includes everything from the production in South America, to its transit, wholesaling, retail and use (with processing at various stages along the way), there are clear limits to whether or not any one organization can deal with the whole problem space. For example, in the case of heroin, the United Kingdom, at the time of writing, has troops deployed in Afghanistan where their operations impact upon or coexist with poppy growing and production. The farming year can normally sustain two poppy crops, providing income for resource-stressed farmers, funding the insurgency and circulating money through the formal and informal economies (Goodhand, 2009). The UK also works in areas where heroin is trafficked, for example through the Balkans. Through its law-enforcement agencies, it targets traffickers and dealers. The UK also runs campaigns directed towards shaping user behaviour. At each stage, a variety of jurisdictions, public sector and third-sector agencies play a role, necessitating efforts to coordinate up, down and across entities over which no one individual or group has directive or resource control. Indeed, the UK Government, despite its physical presence in both the production and consumer domains of the heroin trade, faces dilemmas in coordinating policy with activities and reconciling competing imperatives (Caulkins *et al.*, 2011). For example, the issue of replacing income gained from poppy for poor farmers with alternative sources of income (say from high-yield wheat) has been problematic, given transportation issues, access to wheat markets and intimidation, highlighting a key characteristic of wicked problems, namely that, when one intervenes in a problem, the solution creates a further and different problem.

In addressing the cocaine problem space as a business function entailing products, services, supply and demand, one runs into the same problem of who does what and how coordination might be best achieved. Hirschman (1992b) discusses cocaine in the context of product innovation. Writing in 1995, she charts the development and diffusion of cocaine in its various product forms and describes crack users as displaying 'the ultimate product loyalty'. She positions the innovation of drug producers in offering new products such that the pattern of use cannot be separated from the producer–consumer, supply–demand relationship:

> Supply – in the face of decreased demand – is likely to continue to innovate novel product forms which will be demanded. Demand – in the face of lessened supply – will likely raise the potential profitability of cocaine production, drawing more dealers into the market ... the only viable solution

lies in deactivating both supply and demand sides of the cocaine market concurrently.

(Hirschman, 1992a: 137)

Hirschman can be forgiven for not having predicted specific innovation responses from suppliers in terms of the adulteration of cocaine with Active Pharmaceutical Ingredients such as benzocaine. APIs can extend or maintain the profitability of cocaine by allowing a small amount to go further and extend the market or, when cocaine supply is reduced, allow the maintenance of existing levels of use. Nevertheless, her argument to concurrently target supply and demand sides is well made, if problematic, given the coordination requirements already discussed. Fan and Holway (1994) disagree, arguing that drug policy is likely to be more effective when directed at demand than supply.

In terms of reducing demand and supply for cocaine, some initiatives have less obvious consequences. Wholesale legalization arguably does little to serve the interests of public health but one might see the attraction of this proposal from the perspective of countries whose personnel are getting killed or maimed trying to stem production. Relaxing enforcement at the user (or even minor social supply) end of the criminal justice spectrum might appear to serve the interests of treating the user as a victim rather than an offender but does it make treatment and rehabilitation any more likely where it is needed? Also from a law-enforcement perspective, what motivation would there be for a user to incriminate their supplier if demonstrating remorse and assistance to police was never going to be necessary to mitigate a court-imposed penalty? Would such a policy actually increase the demand for cocaine in the UK, thereby escalating the humanitarian cost and environmental harm in source and transit countries mentioned above?

As the international community works to enable coordination on supply and demand through, for example, the United Nations Commission on Narcotic Drugs,[1] the challenge of how to intervene still remains. Interest in specifically focusing on behavioural change has seen considerable growth in recent years as evidenced by the UK Government's Behavioural Insights Team or 'Nudge Unit' (see Thaler and Sunstein, 2009). There has been the exploration and adoption of frameworks such as MINDSPACE within government – a mnemonic that captures 'the most robust (non-coercive) influences on behaviour' and looks at the Messenger, Incentives, Norms, Defaults, Salience, Priming, Affect, Commitments and Ego (Dolan *et al.*, 2010). It seeks to make other approaches such as social marketing more effective. The theoretical underpinning of behavioural approaches is driven by the idea that attitudes (and a focus on attitudinal change) show a weak relationship with actual behaviour (Azjen, 1991; Darnton, 2008). An intervention focused on attitudinal change will underplay the structural factors at work in shaping the behaviour of illicit drug use. Of course, this creates tension when it comes to, for example, a legal system that focuses more on agency and personal choice whilst accepting some mitigating circumstances, or a narrative that constructs addiction and victimhood and downplays personal choice.

The planner and policy maker should therefore draw their own rich picture from their own organizational perspective and recognize that, whilst the rich picture earlier tries to encapsulate an international problem space, local systems will also be identifiable. Here the relationships at work will cross boundaries of responsibility and highlight areas needing collaboration. It might even challenge own assumptions about the way things work as one tries to discern a connected whole.

Social demarketing

The National Social Marketing Council (NSMC) use the French and Blair-Stevens (2007) behavioural change definition of social marketing as: 'The systematic application of marketing, alongside other concepts and techniques, to achieve specific behavioural goals, for a social good.' An intervention that is focused on behavioural goals keeps the idea of what people do at the centre of the process. It recognizes that there are many variables that impact upon people's behaviour that result from social structures as well as individual and group choices. In the cocaine problem space, the wide variety of impacting variables highlight this structure versus agency debate – addiction, disposable income, consumer preferences, deviance, the law, social context and so on. How one sees structure and agency shapes attribution for the cocaine problem and therefore the policy choices made. Social marketing techniques recognize that there are many reasons for why people behave as they do, and therefore many ways of resolving it.

In this section, we consider social marketing concepts and processes and illustrate some of the issues that social marketers working in the cocaine problem space have to negotiate as they plan interventions. Most planning processes take a cyclical approach starting with planning, implementing and reviewing. The NSMC advocate the following process for planning social marketing interventions: getting started; scope; develop; implement; evaluate and follow-up (NSMC, 2012). We discuss how cocaine might be demarketed using each of these stages next.

Getting started

NSMC identify three broad areas that are important to consider at this early stage as follows:

1. the issue or challenge you want to address;
2. the resources and assets you might be able to draw on along with any risks that you can identify;
3. initial plans and timescales.

As previously discussed, the identification of the challenge is limited by responsibilities and resources. Nevertheless, trying to frame the boundaries of the challenge is necessary to frame something achievable. For this illustration, let us assume the challenge is to reduce the use of cocaine and that a multi-agency approach at community level is possible. Planners should not feel constrained at this point that the challenge cannot be re-examined. Whilst any planning process is simplified to a number of steps, things learned later may have a bearing on initial assumptions. For example, the extent of multi-agency cooperation will become apparent as commitments and resource demands emerge. Recognition of the interconnected nature of the problem space is useful, perhaps drawing on the rich-picture technique discussed above. The requirement to start thinking about risks can also be informed by anticipating second-order consequences. In our context, resource risks may be obvious. Reputational risks might be more difficult to ascertain. However, a series of ethical issues must also be discussed, such as how to handle disclosure on drug use in a multi-agency context or how to deal with impact on neighbouring areas. It is useful to overlay alternative approaches to creative problem solving such as cycles of divergent and convergent thinking (Cropley, 2006). In starting with a divergent phase, one may aim to establish what the problem looks like and what is in and what is out. The convergent phase can then start to elicit and focus on its core elements. The next divergent cycle goes back out to see if one is still working on the same problem, or if the problem needs to be reframed. Diverging and converging cycles can help to maintain focus whilst avoiding the exploration of 'rabbit holes'.

Scope

On the question of scoping and devising the social marketing project, NSMC propose the following general guidelines:

- Bringing people together who might be important for the intervention.
- Forming a steering group; reviewing expectations and resources.
- Investigating what has already been done that can be learned from.
- Analysing factors that may affect the issue and what can be done.
- Carrying out secondary and primary research to provide the information needed to forge ahead.

From the demarketing cocaine perspective, of central importance is the degree to which we understand the audience for which behaviour change is planned and the behavioural goals for each audience. NSMC quite rightly suggest that goals should follow the standard SMART (strategic, measurable, actionable, realistic and timely) format. In our context, the key questions will be: whose cocaine use are we targeting for intervention and what do we mean by use? Problem use might already be driving the motivation for looking at the problem in the first place. Law-enforcement agencies may view it as a problem shaping anti-social behaviour and forms of acquisitive crime. Health agencies may see it differently to schools, parents, political representatives and neighbourhood watch schemes. Each stakeholder may attribute cause and effect in different ways.

Insights into the target audience

There is not a lot of precise knowledge about the nature of the cocaine user community in the UK. It has not previously been credibly segmented. Where cocaine users touch emergency, support and health services, insight is likely to flow into collection such as the annual British Crime Survey, now being conducted by the Office of National Statistics (ONS). Contact with the criminal justice system, including law enforcement, also provides knowledge on who is supplying and using cocaine. Studies and surveys by NGOs such as Drugscope add to the picture. Workplace substance abuse testing throws some light onto this knowledge gap but it is far from definitive. Further research in this area is critical if we are to effectively design credible interventions in reducing cocaine use. In its submission to the UK Parliamentary Home Affairs Select Committee Cocaine Trade Inquiry, the UK Drug Policy Commission (UKDPC) asked a seemingly intractable question – who actually uses cocaine? They concluded that:

> There is much diversity among cocaine uses and distinctions should of course be made between cocaine and crack use, different routes of administration (smoking injecting, snorting) and different patterns of use (recreational, problematic, dependent).
>
> *(UKDPC, 2009: 2)*

UKDPC (2009) note that cocaine is more common among those in their twenties, mostly males and those more likely to report higher usage of other drugs. Of those aged 16–25 years old, three-quarters report using it less than once a month. There is also a strong link between cocaine and heavy use of alcohol. From a personality perspective, Mendelson and Mello (1986) discuss two main drug personality types: the distressed sub-type, who uses to self-medicate to cope with depression and anxiety, and the sociopathic sub-type, who uses other drugs and alcohol impulsively to gratify their needs. A longitudinal study of first-time cocaine users in the USA (Khalsa et al., 1993) concluded that the mean age was 24 years old, that most people (76 per cent) were introduced to cocaine by a friend, that first-time use tended to be free (85 per cent), and that people consumed cocaine for the following reasons:

- To satisfy their curiosity (36 per cent);
- To facilitate socializing at parties (34 per cent);
- To have fun and celebrate (34 per cent);
- To relieve dysphoria (e.g. depression and anxiety) (15 per cent);
- To get 'high' (7 per cent);

- Because it was available (6 per cent);
- To enhance sexual pleasure or to procure sexual partners (3 per cent).

By contrast in the UK, one study finds that the age of first use of cocaine for a group of problem drug users was 16.6 years old and 16.7 years for crack cocaine (Parker, 2005), whilst another finds first use taking place for young users of cocaine at 18.4 years old and 19.4 years old for crack cocaine (Boys *et al.*, 2002). Unsurprisingly, this is the reason why many anti-drug use interventions have been targeted at first-time users. In an interesting counter-intuitive perspective, users may actually excessively consume drugs in an attempt to experience feelings of being able to control the uncontrollable in an otherwise meaningless world (McGovern and McGovern, 2011; Furst *et al.*, 1999) and young users feel it is better to consume cocaine than other drugs because if the drug is more expensive, it must be of better quality (Boys *et al.*, 2002). Hirschman (1992b) argues that, whilst cocaine was used as a 'tonic' when it was originally introduced into the USA at the end of the nineteenth century, by the end of the twentieth century, it was taken as a status symbol and to engender feelings of power and success. Ironically, despite the fact that many young people perceive the use of crack cocaine negatively (used by the 'scummy and the underclass'), many had inadvertently used crack cocaine without realizing it (Boys *et al.*, 2002).

When drugs do not satisfy users' motivations (i.e. they do not result in a pleasurable and satisfying outcome – the 'high'), suppliers are nevertheless often shown a degree of tolerance despite the fact that the product purchased is not what the user expects, often because finding another source of supply is difficult and risky (Fitchett and Smith, 2001). Many users therefore are trapped in specific buyer–dealer relationships.

This discussion on audiences points to one very important conclusion. Some of the references relate to a cocaine market around ten years ago. The trend in the mid- to late 2000s was for younger males to become increasingly more involved with cocaine, which is perhaps reflected by Parker's new-user ages in 2005 being younger than Boys *et al.* in 2002. This may also be influenced by what the UKDPC (2009) call the two-tier market hypothesis. This posits that many drug dealers now sell cheaper, less pure cocaine to a new market previously unable to afford cocaine. The market and its characteristics are not and have not been static, and it is important to note the point in time that an observation is made. Another point from this trending is that the trafficker and the user are not 'standing still' so designing interventions needs to take account of hitting 'moving targets'. This again reflects back to the nature of the wicked problem and the need for research to examine the local context.

The objectives of the intervention

A common theme in our discussion is the distinction between recreational users and heavy users. Another distinction is between the threshold of first use and development of a future cocaine career. In our discussion about who uses and how it is used, we need to develop behavioural goals around differing segments and whether we might, for example:

1. prevent first use of cocaine;
2. reduce the likelihood of an increased take-up of cocaine after first use;
3. reduce heavy use of crack;
4. decrease heavy alcohol use with the use of cocaine (an approach advocated by Boys *et al.*, 2002).

Each form of intervention requires its own form of design. For example, Sohler Everingham *et al.* (1995) argue that prevention programmes for first-time users must be supplemented by programmes encouraging heavy users to quit or reduce their consumption if cocaine use is to be reduced more generally. Importantly, for crack cocaine users, confidential counselling should be available without necessarily requiring them to attend a clinic (Brian *et al.*, 1998). Existing users undergoing treatment also require considerable support, comprising individual sessions, peer support, partner or family therapy treatment contracts and frequent monitoring of urine to test drug use levels and abstinence (Strang *et al.*, 1993). Others have argued that, in social marketing, it is important to concentrate not purely on the individuals from whom behaviour change is sought, but also on others in government who can effect behaviour change at the systemic level (Hastings *et al.*, 2000). This begs the question of who else should be targeted in any particular intervention at this higher, systemic level.

There is also some contention about whether or not the lower socio-economic class users should be emphasized in targeting rather than higher social class users because their health costs will have a greater impact on the NHS (NSMC, 2012). The EMCDDA comment above on the underestimation of health consequences points to the difficulty of assessing and attributing costs to health. In terms of identifying successful levers for discouraging cocaine use, the NSMC muse over whether or not it is possible to reduce cocaine consumption by pointing out the negative environmental impacts that cocaine manufacture causes in host countries (NSMC, 2012). Our view is that this is not likely to be possible given that people using cocaine are unlikely to consider such moral perspectives. Hirschman (1992b), for example, has previously argued that users do not make decisions about drug consumption on moral grounds.

Development

The NSMC propose that the development stage is when a specific programme, campaign or intervention is developed based on the scoping stage. Pre-testing ideas with the audience is essential but one should also be careful to minimize the impact of the intervention on other audiences who may be unintended but affected nevertheless. For example, Furst *et al.* (1999) examine how the stigmatized image of the 'crack head' may have had an impact on the decline of use of crack in New York. They note that some 'misguided drug experimenters' may have been directed towards heroin, thinking it to be less destructive (Furst *et al.*, 1999). Lavack (2007) discusses using social marketing to 'de-stigmatize addiction' and argues that addicts do not seek help because of that stigma. She points out that, were social marketing to be successful, there may be an increased take-up of treatment services, which would also need to be planned for. In our context, perhaps it is conceivable that stigmatization used to prevent initial take-up of cocaine among young people may also have the effect of stigmatizing addicts and deterring heavy users from seeking help. These knock-on effects impact on services and behaviours and reinforce the need for thinking through actions and consequences.

At this stage of the intervention, it is necessary to consider the social marketing mix, in terms of the 4Ps as follows:

- Product: Shiu *et al.* (2009) frame the 'product' in a discussion of the demarketing of tobacco as product replacement and displacement. In terms of cocaine, we may attempt to think about ways of generating negative views of cocaine products, cocaine use and cocaine dealers. Additionally, one might consider the availability of services to support potential users who are wrestling with contradictory information received from friends, the press and others.
- Price: Lefebvre (2011) argues that price in social marketing stretches beyond monetary value to include other rewards and punishments for everyday behaviour, including psychological, social and geographic considerations. For example, peer pressure plays a very strong role in affecting use of drugs. This might be seen as an exchange relationship where use of the drug is exchanged for belonging.
- Place: A number of studies highlight the role of the peer group in shaping usage. For example, Smith and Fitchett (2002), in their study on youth illicit drug consumption, find that the notion of a predatory dealer coercing young people into first use is given little credence by users. Rather, if drug use is observed around the group, there is a greater propensity to think of it as common and everyday. Peer judgement becomes an important influence and qualifier in this context. This has a bearing on where and how young people access services, and where they hear positive and negative messages about competing services is a key consideration. Running information campaigns aimed at young target audiences in schools and vocational centres regarding the negative consequences of drug use appear to reduce the percentage of adolescent users (Block *et al.*, 2002; Duarte *et al.*, 2005), although Smith and Fitchett (2002) in contrast argue that this is hampered by a credibility gap, in that authority sources are not perceived to know what they are talking about, and Block *et al.* (2002) qualify their finding by arguing that anti-drug campaigns do not appear to impact on those adolescents

already using. Notably, in relation to anti-drug advertising concerning cocaine, the evidence for its effectiveness is weak (UKDPC, 2009).

• Promotion: Old-style one-way communication models need to be replaced with approaches that surround the audience with 'programs and messages and provide them with multiple opportunities to be exposed to behaviors, products, services and communications in order to lead to the behavior change' (Lefebvre, 2011: 64). Interestingly, the press has an important role to play in this regard and can be useful in conveying anti-drug messages if it reports events the public find interesting (Fan and Holway, 1994). Of course, this speaks to the need for coordinated approaches undertaken over the long term.

Implement, evaluate and follow-up

Previous anti-cocaine campaigns have not necessarily been effective. For example, the Scottish Government's 'Know the Score' campaign in 2005/6 aimed to focus on the link between cocaine use and heart attacks but failed to alter young people's usage behaviour (UKDPC, 2009). In contrast, in 2009/10, the UK Government ran an anti-cocaine use campaign called 'Frank', which, according to Home Office research, achieved clear cut-through with its audience: 67 per cent of those surveyed agreed the advertisement had made them realize how risky it was to take cocaine and 63 per cent said they would be less likely to take it as a result (UKDPC, 2009). Exactly what ingredients are necessary for a successful anti-cocaine campaign are, however, unknown at this point.

The implementation and evaluation stages of the intervention should be continuously monitored. This is itself part of the approach to risk – it allows for early warning and the ability to change course, as necessary. Naturally, a formal evaluation of the intervention facilitates discussion about what has been learned for future interventions. Assessment of success is easier when a behavioural change approach is adopted as it is normally easier to benchmark and observe than attitudinal changes. However, measures that seek to track the purity of drugs on the street will require close cooperation with law-enforcement agencies or specific permission to undertake such research (Johnson and Golub, 2007). According to Lavack (2007), successful social marketing programmes should include: clear goals and objectives; multiple target audiences and messages customized for each target audience; the use of public relations and paid media; advocacy campaigns and media monitoring; handbooks and guides to aid community involvement; mass media campaigns, telephone help lines and an evaluation framework.

Emerging principles

The discussion so far has attempted to illustrate some of the issues involved in moving from a picture of a complex problem space to the planning of tangible social demarketing interventions, with specific relevance to the demarketing of cocaine. The characteristics of a wicked problem apply and suggest that framing the problem as a continuous management process, rather than its ultimate resolution is a more realistic perspective. If this is the case, and we believe it is, then the following principles might be adopted for dealing with the demarketing of cocaine.

1. Think soft systems – to explore the problem space, its interconnectedness and to anticipate second-order effects.
2. Coordinate across multiple strands – a coordinated approach is required to marry persuasive messaging with the social structures that shape behaviour.
3. Integrate policy and behaviour change initiatives. Behaviour change initiatives do not start in the absence of policy. Policy can open up and close down the solutions that might be adopted. Having an understanding of behavioural outcomes stemming from policy and change programmes will at least help to identify where there is conflict but also potential synergy.
4. Focus on behaviours of specific segments. Thinking behaviourally keeps plans and resources focused on tangible outcomes. It also helps with assessing the effectiveness of any intervention. The heterogeneity of individuals and groups means that specific audiences need specific treatment.
5. Harness the power of friends. Peer groups have a huge impact on the take-up of drugs and their subsequent patterns of use. Peers will help reduce drug use.
6. Beware message fratricide. Message for one audience can have unintended consequences with another audience. Ensure messages are consistent and reinforcing.
7. Dynamically evaluate and adapt – not just to measure success but to change course and grab opportunities.
8. Sustain – long-term behavioural change needs to be embedded through persistent management of the problem.

Conclusion

In this chapter, we have attempted to chart an analytical pathway for the planner and policy maker that can take them from the strategic picture to the local. We have not produced a set of specific interventions that will work everywhere. Rather, we believe a more useful outcome from our discussion is the realization that there is no one solution that can be used everywhere. There is utility in examining the cocaine problem space through the lens of wicked problems and that soft systems method provides a way by which understanding can be checked and potential second-order effects identified. Only then can one start to think about interventions at the local level through a social demarketing approach. That is when the planner has to 'add local'. What we also hope to have shown is that the problem space can be considered from numerous perspectives, and what perspective we adopt impacts on what we regard as the solution. We have highlighted both the demand and supply side of the 'wicked' problem, in that the task is highly complex, not least because it involves so many potential target audiences and so many stakeholders in the process of distributing, supplying and consuming cocaine. Moreover, social marketing interventions in Western Europe will look very different from social marketing in developing economies – a problem for planners working in Whitehall or Brussels and wanting to intervene across the problem. So interventions need to be clearly thought through, not only because they will need to be tailored to different communities, but also because interventions on one audience can impact on another and exacerbate the problem. Further research is needed to understand the moving target of users' motivations for taking cocaine and to segment users locally in a sophisticated way so as to enable the design of specific, targeted messages for each segment. Demarketing interventions could be aimed at cultivators, traffickers, first-time users, early users, heavy users, crack users and cocaine/alcohol users but each intervention would need to be designed differently to take account of the different users and the contexts in which they use. In these circumstances, we hope that the broad, principled approach, funnelling from big picture to local intervention, can help policy makers and planners avoid analysis paralysis, and find ways for dealing with (managing) this wicked problem.

Note

1 See http://www.undrugcontrol.info/en/un-drug-control/cnd accessed on 15 December 2012.

References

Ajzen, I. (1991), 'The theory of planned behavior', *Organizational Behavior and Human Decision Processes*, 50, 179–211.

Block, L.G., Morwitz, V.G., Putsis, W.P. and Sen, S.K. (2002), 'Assessing the impact of antidrug advertising on adolescent drug consumption: Result from a behavioural economic model', *American Journal of Public Health*, 92, 8, 1346–51.

Boys, A., Dobson, J., Marsden, J. and Strang, J. (2002), '"Rich Man's Speed": A qualitative study of young cocaine users', *Drugs: Education, Prevention and Policy*, 9, 2, 195–210.

Brian, K., Parker, H. and Bottomley, T. (1998), *Evolving crack cocaine careers: New users, quitters and long term combination drug users in N.W. England*, Manchester: University of Manchester. Retrieved from: http://library.npia.police.uk/docs/homisc/occ-evolving.pdf, accessed 21 December 2012.

Caulkins, J.P., Kulick, J.D. and Kleiman, M.A.R. (2011), 'Think again: The Afghan drug trade', Foreign Policy April, retrieved from: http://www.foreignpolicy.com/articles/2011/04/01/think_again_the_afghan_drug_trade?page=full, accessed 15 December 2012.

Checkland, P. (1993), *Systems Thinking, Systems Practice*, Chichester: John Wiley & Sons.

Cropley, A. (2006), 'In praise of convergent thinking', *Creativity Research Journal*, 18, 3, 391–404.

Darnton, A. (2008), *Practical Guide: An Overview of Behavior Change Models and their Uses*, London: Government Social Research Unit.

Dolan, P., Hallsworth, H., Halpern, D., King, K. and Vlaev, I. (2010), *Mindspace: Influencing Behaviour Through Public Policy*, HMG Cabinet Office/Institute for Government, March, retrieved from: http://www.instituteforgovernment.org.uk/publications/mindspace, accessed 15 December 2012.

Duarte, R., Escario, J.J. and Molina, J. A. (2005), 'Participation and consumption of illegal drugs among adolescents', *International Advances in Economic Research*, 11, 399–415.

European Monitoring Centre for Drugs and Drug Addiction (2012), *Annual Report 2012 – The state of the drugs problem in Europe*, Lisbon: EMCDDA.

Fan, D.P. and Holway, W.B. (1994), 'Media coverage of cocaine and its impact on usage patterns', *International Journal of Public Opinion Research*, 6, 2, 139–62.

Fitchett, J.A. and Smith, A. (2001), 'Consumer behaviour in an unregulated market: The satisfactions and dissatisfactions of illicit drug consumption', *Journal of Consumer Behaviour*, 1, 4, 355–68.

French, J. and Blair-Stevens, C. (2007), *Big Pocket Guide – Social marketing* (2nd edition), London: National Consumer Council/Department of Health.

Furst, R.T., Johnson, B.D., Dunlap, E. and Curtis, R. (1999). 'The stigmatized image of the "crack head": A sociocultural explorations of a barrier to cocaine smoking among a cohort of youth in New York City', *Deviant Behavior*, 20, 2, 153–81.

Goodhand, J. (2009), *Bandits, Borderlands and Opium Wars: Afghan State-building viewed from the margins*, DIIS Working Paper 26, Copenhagen: Danish Institute for international Studies.

Gossop, M., Manning, V. and Ridge, G. (2006), 'Concurrent use of alcohol and cocaine: Differences in patterns of use and problems among users of crack cocaine and cocaine powder', *Alcohol and Alcoholism*, 41, 2, 121–25.

Green A., Pickering, R., Foster, R. and Stimson, G.V. (1994), 'Who uses cocaine? Social profiles of cocaine users', *Addiction Research*, 2, 2, 141–54.

Hammersley, R. and Ditton, J. (1994), 'Cocaine careers in a sample of Scottish users', *Addiction Research*, 2, 1, 51–69.

HASC (2012) *Drugs: Breaking the cycle* 2012, House of Commons Home Affairs Select Committee, London: The Stationery Office.

Hastings, G., MacFadyen, L. and Anderson, S. (2000), 'Whose behaviour is it anyway? The border potential of social marketing', *Social Marketing Quarterly*, 6, 2, 46–58.

Hirschman, E.C. (1992b), 'Cocaine as innovation: A social-symbolic account', *Advances in Consumer Research*, 19, 129–39.

Hirschman, E. (1992b), 'The consciousness of addiction: Toward a general theory of compulsive consumption', *Journal of Consumer Research*, 19, 155–79.

Johnson, B.D. and Golub, A. (2007), 'The potential of accurately measuring behavioural and economic dimensions of consumption, prices and market for illegal drugs', *Drug and Alcohol Dependence*, 90, S1, S16–S26.

Khalsa, M.E., Paredes, A. and Anglin, D.M. (1993), 'Cocaine dependence: Behavioural dimensions and patterns of progression', *Clinical Update*, 2, 4, 330–45.

Lavack, A. (2007), 'Using social marketing to de-stigmatize addictions: A review', *Addiction Research and Theory*, 15, 5, 479–92.

Lefebvre, R.C. (2011), 'An integrative model of social marketing', *Journal of Social Marketing*, 1, 1, 54–72.

Mendelson, J. and Mello, N. (1986), *The Addictive Personality*, New York: Chelsea House.

McGovern, R. and McGovern, W. (2011), 'Voluntary risk-taking and heavy-end crack cocaine use: An edgework perspective', *Health, Risk and Society*, 13, 5, 487–500.

NSMC (2012), *Reducing Cocaine Usage in the UK: Shared responsibility*, London: National Social Marketing Centre.

Parker, H. (2005), 'Normalization as a barometer: Recreational drug use and the consumption of leisure by young Britons', *Addiction Research and Theory*, 13, 3, 205–15.

Pettiway, L.E. (1995), 'Copping crack: The travel behaviour of crack users', *Justice Quarterly*, 12, 3, 499–524.

Power, R., Green, A., Foster, R. and Stimson, G. (1995), 'A qualitative study of the purchasing and distribution patterns of cocaine and crack users in England and Wales', *Addiction Research*, 2, 4, 363–79.

Rittel, H.W.J. and Webber, M.M. (1973), 'Dilemmas in a General Theory of Planning', *Policy Sciences*, 4, 155–69.

Smith, A. and Fitchett, J.A. (2002), '"The first time I took acid I was in heaven": A Consumer research inquiry into youth illicit drug consumption', *Management Decision*, 40, 4, 372–82.

Shiu, E., Hassan, L.M. and Walsh, G. (2009), 'Demarketing tobacco through governmental polices – The 4Ps revisited', *Journal of Business Research*, 69, 269–78.

Sohler Everingham, S.M., Rydell, P.C. and Caulkins, J.P. (1995), 'Cocaine consumption in the United States: Estimating past trends and future scenarios', *Socio-Economic Planning Sciences*, 29, 4, 305–14.

Stockley, D. (1992), *Drug Warning*, London: Optima Books.

Strang, J., Johns, A. and Caan, W. (1993), 'Cocaine in the UK – 1991', *British Journal of Psychiatry*, 162, 1–13.

Thaler, R.H. and Sunstein, C.R. (2009), *Nudge: Improving decisions about health, wealth and happiness*, London: Penguin.

UKDPC (2009), *Submission to the Home Affairs Select Committee Cocaine Trade Inquiry*, UK Drug Policy Commission, London: HMSO. Retrieved from: *http://www.ukdpc.org.uk/wp-content/uploads/Briefing%20-%20Submission%20to%20the%20Home%20Affairs%20Committee%20cocaine%20trade%20inquiry.pdf*, accessed 21 December 2012.

UK Focal Point on Drugs (2010), *United Kingdom Drug Situation: Annual report to the European Monitoring Centre for Drugs and Drug Addiction (EMCDDA)*, London: Department of Health.

——(2011), *National Report (2010 data) for EMCDDA*, October, London: Department of Health.

——(2012), *National Report (2011 data) for EMCDDA*, October, London: Department of Health.

UNODC (2012), *World Drugs Report 2012*, UN Organized Drugs and Crime: Vienna.

Vulliamy, E. (2008), 'How a tiny West African country became the world's first narco state', *The Observer*, 9 March.

Websites

http://www.cabinetoffice.gov.uk/behavioural-insights-team
http://www.thensmc.com/
http://socialmarketing-toolbox.com/
http://www.ukdpc.org.uk/
http://www.undrugcontrol.info/en/un-drug-control/cnd

5

COUNTER-MARKETING CASE STUDIES

Clive Boddy

The aim of this chapter is to provide some examples of counter-marketing initiatives in order to help describe what counter-marketing is and how it can be used. Counter-marketing involves the active demarketing of something or the use of marketing activities to counter the effects of other marketing activities. Demarketing is when those involved in the marketing of a product or service attempt to reduce the demand for it. This can be done via merely ceasing marketing activities such as promotions, advertising and supply or via more active counter-marketing activities such as raising the price. Counter-marketing is when attempts are made to reduce the demand for a product or service via the use of proactive marketing measures such as promoting reasons why a product or service should not be used because of, for example, side effects or other effects deemed to be undesirable.

Counter-marketing is thus where there is a marketing campaign by an organization aiming to slow down or to stop a consumption or behavioural activity that is being or has been marketed or otherwise promoted by that organization or by another organization. Counter-marketing is usually carried out where the product or service in question is deemed to be detrimental to individual or societal wellbeing. Counter-marketing can be undertaken by either the originating corporation or by those who are opposed, for whatever reason, to the further marketing of the product or service. Counter-marketing is thus concerned with managing social change and with shaping demand to conform to long-term objectives such as having a healthy and sustainable society (Cullwick 1975).

Examples of externally driven counter-marketing include the anti-smoking, anti-drinking and anti-illegal-drug use campaigns run by various governments throughout the world to counter the efforts of tobacco and alcohol companies and drug dealers. Governments are concerned with the costs to society of ill-health directly due to illegal (and legal) drug and alcohol usage, such as reduced immune system function, mental health deterioration and increased liver damage to individuals. Governments are also concerned with the costs incurred indirectly from such concomitant issues as increased rates of crime and of accidents due to drug- and alcohol-related cognitive impairment. Illegal drug dependency can also lead to wasted economic resources in terms of personal productivity, misallocation of financial resources and crime related to individuals seeking to acquire from others the financial resources that they crave in order to purchase more illegal drugs. Counter-marketing in response to this can take the form of promoting the awareness of the ill-effects of long-term drug use as well as of providing safer alternatives to illegal drugs for users to take instead. This provision of substitutes is an attempt to persuade illegal drug users that there are other products that will satisfy their expectations and this aim of managing social change is an accepted form of demarketing or counter-marketing (Cullwick 1975). Trade bodies and corporations may also initiate and run these counter-marketing campaigns and, for example, McDonald's has run anti-litter-dropping campaigns, alcoholic beverage manufacturers have run anti-drinking and driving campaigns and sections of the gambling industry have run segmented counter-gambling campaigns. Some examples of these are discussed below.

Internally originated counter-marketing is where the originating organization not only organizes the demarketing of a product or service but also actively markets against its further use. Examples of this would include where a product is found to be dangerously faulty, in which case an organization may issue a statement of product recall asking for customers to return the product so that it can be either repaired or replaced. The recall and repair of some Toyota cars by the manufacturer a few years ago would be an example of an internal counter-marketing effort. Here Toyota issued marketing communications materials recalling thousands of cars around the world because of a fault. Toyota did not seek to demarket its cars but to reassure customers that it would always repair them if faulty. In contrast, Ford, when its Pinto model was found to be in danger of bursting into flames after rear collisions, decided, for mainly financial reasons, not to undertake any counter-marketing and did not recall the model for repairs (Judkins 1989). Counter-marketing initiatives towards the Ford Pinto then took place by external organizations and consumer groups as reports of Pinto drivers and passengers burning to death continued to be reported in the press in the USA in the 1970s (Bonamici 2005). The differences between the approach to counter-marketing of these two car giants is illuminating. By managing its own counter-marketing, Toyota largely remained in control of its corporate image and reputation and arguably only its reputation for reliability was damaged (and only probably in the short term), whereas its reputation for trustworthiness and doing the right thing in taking ethical action was enhanced. Such management of corporate reputation and image is important for companies to maintain (Boddy 2012). On the other hand, Ford took an unethical decision not to counter-market the Pinto and people are still writing about this in disgust 40 years later.

Another example of internally originated counter-marketing comes from the hydro-electric power generation sector in the USA. Here a drought meant that hydro power turbines had reduced water flow to drive them and the electric power supplier could not produce as much electricity as was usually needed for the population served. The electric power company therefore actively demarketed, i.e. it counter-marketed demand, by explaining the situation to customers in marketing communications materials and making suggestions as to how they could reduce their demand for electricity until normal supply was resumed (AMA 1974).

Counter alcoholic beverages marketing campaigns

A range of alcoholic beverages was introduced into the UK market in 1994 that became popularly called 'alcopops' because of their sweet, fruity taste, bright colours, bright packaging, differently shaped bottles and common appeal to underage teenage drinkers (Barnard and Forsyth 1998). Their popularity among this age group caused much concern among adults and the drinks became subject to various counter-marketing efforts. For example, one UK cooperative group of shops even decided to de-list (no longer stock or sell) the drinks because of their concern over the damaging effects of underage drinking (Barnard and Forsyth 1998). Also in the UK, another supermarket was forced to clear its shelves of an own-label 'alcopop' after a consumer complaint to a drinks marketing body (Jardine 1999).

In the UK, these counter-marketing efforts eventually led to the withdrawal of one of the more controversial brands, 'Hooch', and it is no longer sold in the UK (Anonymous 1997a). Similarly, in Australia, the marketing of these 'alcopop' drinks was restricted in terms of the packaging the manufacturers could use in order to try to reduce the products' appeal to the young. Stories about 'alcopops' in the popular press proliferated and they were pejoratively described as being 'aimed at kids' (children) (Leonhardt and Dawley 1996).

Counter-marketing initiatives against such products that are perceived to be harmful continue to be started by consumer groups and recently in America some local community groups attempted to disrupt the sale of 'alcopops' in their local areas to prevent their sale to children. In Marin county, these groups attempted to persuade a convenience store to de-select such products (Newswire 2012), whereas in New York attempts were made to ban their advertising near schools (Melillo 2002). Reports that beverages containing alcohol are being marketed to underage drinkers in the United States are reported on in the press, reflecting society's continuing concern with this issue, and the perceived marketing of such products is attacked in attempts at counter-marketing such products (Melillo 2001). These examples concerning 'alcopops' demonstrate the power that counter-marketing efforts can have. Perhaps recognizing this, Starbucks (a coffee drink retail chain) recently responded to public pressure over the revelation that it had not paid UK corporation tax by voluntarily agreeing to pay 20 million pounds in corporation tax amid fears of a growing consumer boycott (Campbell 2012).

Counter gambling marketing campaigns

For the majority of gamblers most of the time, gambling is an unproblematic activity that involves small amounts of money spent irregularly for the thrill of betting on uncertain outcomes and the possibility, however unlikely, of winning an amount of money. However, for a minority of gamblers, betting is compulsive to the point of addiction and the amounts spent are problematic for the gamblers and their families and for the societies in which the gamblers live. Casinos in some Western countries such as Canada, have a responsibility to their customers and this includes a duty of care, meaning that, officially at least, counter-marketing activities take place towards problem gamblers to dissuade them from over-spending.

These counter-marketing activities include the promotion of publicized codes of conduct, such as those promoting responsible gambling that is affordable and non-harmful. Some casinos have a scheme whereby problem gamblers can volunteer to be barred from the casino so that their gambling is subject to this level of imposed control. Counter-marketing could also be managed through the relationship marketing techniques and tools that casinos and other gambling providers use such as loyalty card schemes, which would enable the identification of problem gamblers towards whom counter-marketing initiatives could be aimed. Other research-based suggestions to reduce problem levels of gambling include restricting access to sources of money such as ATM machines within casinos, restricting access to the young and restricting the venue opening hours and access to the provision of alcoholic beverages (Williams, West and Simpson 2007).

In another article about gambling, Beeton and Pinge (2003) argue that Australians are not taking their full annual holidays, which could lead to individual well-being and community health issues and (as a competitor for financial resources) impact the viability of the domestic tourism industry. They argue that competition for discretionary income from other sources of recreational activities such as gambling will continue to impact on the tourism sector, requiring demarketing activities as a means to limit gambling expenditure and increase tourism (Beeton and Pinge 2003). This is another example of arguments for counter-marketing being put forward to help shape what is argued to be a socially desirable outcome. Other examples of counter-marketing in the tourism sector are discussed below.

Counter tourism marketing campaigns

Tourism has been identified as one of the main areas of business where demarketing is practised for various reasons but with the overall aim of deterring or deflecting visitors (Medway, Warnaby and Dharni 2011; Beeton and Pinge 2003). Such downward management of demand may be to preserve an environment or site of historical interest, to cope with crisis situations, such as the outbreak of diseases or civil unrest, or to stimulate some kinds of demand rather than others.

As an example of this, Clements (1989) discusses the implementation of a segmented and selective counter tourism marketing campaign in Cyprus in the 1980s. This was designed to dissuade rowdy hooligan tourist elements from visiting Cyprus as this had the potential to generate adverse publicity and give a poor image to Cyprus (as a holiday brand destination) to mainstream tourists. Cyprus had positioned itself as a more prestigious destination than certain other Mediterranean countries and aimed at a post-thirty-year-old and middle- to high-income group (Clements 1989). Cyprus achieved this through adopting a strategic approach to tourism development at the governmental level through the use of the usual marketing tools, including attempts to control the product offering, i.e. to develop more up-market hotels rather than self-catering accommodation; through premium pricing; and through promotional and advertising activities that targeted the preferred, older, richer tourist and their families. The Cyprus Tourism Organization monitored tourist arrivals by demographic information to make sure that the policy was working, and in the 1980s market research showed that it was. This sort of marketing activity has been described as passive place demarketing as it entails the emphasis of some attributes (e.g. premium quality) and this may automatically mean that the alternative attributes (e.g. low cost) are de-emphasized (Medway, Warnaby and Dharni 2011).

As another example of tourism counter-marketing, a little discussed element of the 2012 London Olympics was the campaign to dissuade local domestic tourism during the time of the Olympic Games in order to prevent the over-crowding and traffic delays that may otherwise have resulted in internationally poor publicity for the Games. This counter place marketing took several forms. Dedicated traffic lanes through busy areas of London were established for the sole use of Games-relevant traffic.

Anecdotally, this had mixed results as Londoners were unsure whether and when they could use the traffic lanes concerned, while foreign visitors to the Games were unaware of the dedicated traffic lanes and equally confused by them. Perhaps to address this confusion, towards the end of the Games, notices went up that the traffic lanes were open to everyone. Local people were also informed that the period of the Games was a good time to leave London and visit elsewhere, and British Airways ran advertisements that promoted overseas travel during this time. Again anecdotally, some local shopkeepers complained about this because they did not experience the footfall (number of customer visits) and level of customer spending that they anticipated. Within a counter-marketing effort like this, different stakeholders may have conflicting agendas, and so, while it was deemed to be important for the Games organizers to appear well organized and to get competitors and customers to the Games on time, this may have conflicted with other London transport users who may have suffered from increased traffic congestion and with shopkeepers who may have had lower numbers of domestic customers than they expected. It appears then that the counter local tourism campaign staged at the London Olympics may have been a failure in that it was a bit too successful in persuading too many local people to stay away from central and east London during the course of the Games. This is a consistent danger of counter place marketing activities and this was also reported to have happened when authorities counter-marketed the

British countryside during the Foot and Mouth (a disease affecting cattle in particular) crisis of 2001 (Medway and Warnaby 2008). After the crisis was over, rural economies continued to suffer from a lack of tourists at the very time that economic support was needed to supplement the losses to the rural economy from the ravages of the disease.

Other types of tourist destination may have built up a particular image and association in customer minds resulting in seasonal demand at some times of the year. For example, in Australia, the ski resort at Mount Kosciuszko (Australia's highest mountain, located in the Snowy Mountains near Canberra) was often full in winter but with extensive underused facilities, including hotels, restaurants and lifts, in summer. A campaign to counter the image of the area as just a winter destination was therefore undertaken with the aim of marketing the area as a place of natural beauty suitable for hikers, walkers and admirers of mountain scenery in summer. Such efforts are also to be found at other ski resorts around the world and this can be envisaged as counter-marketing the dominant image of being snow-sports destinations that these resorts have built up over many years.

Further types of tourist destinations such as National Parks may also be in need of demarketing and counter-marketing activities in order to manage excessive demand at certain time of the year. Groff discusses this in relation to National Parks in the USA where park managers are faced with the task of reducing demand without alienating customers (Groff 1998). It is recognized that in this type of environment excessive demand can reduce the quality of the visitor experience, as well as damaging the physical resource itself through overuse. Groff calls for the use of all the standard marketing tools in approaching the task of reducing demand.

This can include demarketing activities, for example stopping all advertising and promotional activity at certain times of the year, and counter-marketing, for example putting out press releases that the park is suffering from over-crowding to discourage further visitors (Groff 1998). Demarketing could also include closing the park to further visitors once it is full, increasing the entry price at peak seasons and issuing licences to take part in certain activities. For example, river rafting on the Colorado river is reported by Groff to be subject to such high levels of demand that the experience would be demeaned if all demand was met because the river would become overcrowded with boats. Therefore, demand is managed through a licensing system, which limits the number of boats on the river.

Similarly, the demand for off-road car travel is so great in some US National Parks that it would damage the physical environment if left unmanaged and the park management has to consider the dual aims of providing a quality visitor experience with that of protecting the resource of the park for long-term sustain-ability. Counter-marketing activities could include the marketing of alternative venues or areas of natural beauty if there are any substitutes available. This could include advertising and promoting those alternatives, as well as offering discounts to those alternative place offerings.

Counter-marketing food marketing

The health problems related to a processed food diet and an unhealthy, sedentary lifestyle have been compared to those that are related to tobacco smoking with similar financial costs to the health services of the countries concerned (Kavas and Kavas 2011). In particular, obesity is related to increased likelihood of diabetes, heart problems and cancer (Thomas 2009) and these present the individual with personal problems and health costs. To counter the increasing consumption of fat-, salt- and sugar-laden pre-processed foods and thereby promote a healthier, less diseased and less obese population, the US Department of Agriculture ran a 'five-a-day' campaign to try to increase the consumption of fresh vegetables and fruit (Andreasen 2002). More recently, this campaign has also been replicated in the United Kingdom and can be envisaged as governmental counter-marketing to the extensive fast food marketing from profit-oriented food corporations.

Kavas and Kavas (2011) suggest that subsidizing fresh food for children and increasing the price of high-calorie foods may provide a price method of counter-marketing fast food marketing and that curtailment of some fast food advertising directed at children may also be useful because food habits established in childhood tend to remain throughout adulthood. Similarly in the USA, a campaign to reduce the proportion of obese and overweight adults and promote the consumption of fruits and vegetables within a Hispanic community was launched in one specific area of the country (Rivera *et al.* 2010). This can again be envisaged as counter-marketing against processed food companies to promote healthy, fresh food consumption choices.

Counter-marketing campaigns directed against particular food companies have included separate campaigns in various countries against McDonald's (Botterill and Kline 2007). In response to consumer complaints and counter-marketing efforts concerning the environment, McDonald's removed its Styrofoam packaging and replaced it with cardboard boxes, and in response to counter-marketing based on health concerns it has added fruit, vegetables and fruit juice to its menu (Botterill and Kline 2007).

At other times, McDonald's has taken a more proactive approach, for example, by sending its representative to public meetings concerning new restaurant openings; these people then counter local opposition by extolling the virtues of having a local restaurant in terms of job creation and stimulating the local economy and by promising to be a good citizen and to pick up any litter dropped by customers. However, in other cases, McDonald's has countered counter-marketing activities by taking legal action. One well-known example of this from the UK became known as the McLibel case. This stemmed from action in the 1980s when a group of Greenpeace activists engaged in counter-marketing against McDonald's by distributing a leaflet outlining the costs to society of McDonald's global quest for profit. To counter the consumer-based counter-marketing, McDonald's sued the authors of the leaflet. The ensuing trial lasted ten years as McDonald's spent a reported £10m on lawyers to sue the authors of the leaflet for libel. This helped galvanize sections of public opinion against McDonald's in the UK and has been described as the world's biggest corporate public relations disaster. A 1997 judgment eventually ruled in McDonald's favour on some points and fined the plaintiffs £96,000; however, claims that McDonald's suppressed labour markets, made deceptive claims about its food and provided a diet that was unhealthy to long-term consumers and exploited children's credulity with its promotions were ruled by the judge to not be libellous (Botterill and Kline 2007).

In France, a social marketing programme to counter childhood obesity reportedly used a variety of counter-marketing techniques in order to achieve its objectives (Henley, Raffin and Caemmerer 2011). The campaign engaged opinion leaders in the form of town mayors who would also have the authority and budgets to achieve objectives such as providing cycle paths and parks for children to exercise in. The social marketing counter-marketing campaign focused on the benefits of healthy eating and exercise, such as the fun involved in physical and sporting activity rather than on the negative consequences of becoming unhealthy and obese, and it communicated these benefits in a way designed to attract awareness and interest (Henley, Raffin and Caemmerer 2011). The French campaign also encouraged supermarkets and school cafeterias to display fresh fruit where children would see it and could pick it up themselves and easily purchase it. The campaign measured its success in terms of reducing the body mass index of children in the areas where the counter-marketing campaign ran and in terms of other behavioural measures such as the weekly consumption of French fries. Both of these measures improved from 2005 to 2009 during the course of the campaign.

The marketing of milk powder for babies has come under continued fired from health professionals as it has given the impression that such milk may be better than mother's natural breast-milk.

Breastfeeding is better because it promotes the baby's health in terms of lower rates of infections and the World Health Organization recommends exclusive breastfeeding for the first sixth months of a baby's life (Lowry *et al.* 2009). Consumer groups concerned about the issue have engaged in a series of counter-marketing initiatives over many years aimed at promoting breast-milk instead of milk power and including marketing communications materials from groups such as 'Baby Milk Action' to the effect that milk powder manufacturers should desist from making misleading claims about the relative nutritional value of milk powder compared to natural breast-milk (Anonymous 2007a).

Other counter-marketing efforts included the promotion of the 'International Code of Marketing of Breast-milk Substitutes' and asking doctors to help in raising the awareness of the benefits of breastfeeding (Cheetham and Lee 1994). In partial response to consumer concerns, 'The International Code of Marketing of Breast-milk Substitutes' was written by the World Health Organization with input from the United Nations International Children's Emergency Fund (UNICEF), and agreed by the World Health Assembly in 1981 (Greer 1984). In the USA, leaflets ('Breast-milk or Formula: Making the Right Choice for your Baby') concerning breast-milk were issued by governmental health organizations to promote breastfeeding (Anonymous 1997b). Companies such as Nestlé, seen as marketing powdered milk too aggressively, especially in third world countries, were attacked by consumer groups and counter-marketing calls to boycott their products were made (Brady 2011; Morris 1979). The Nestlé boycott was reported as being the most visible and precedent-setting manifestation of the controversy over the marketing of infant milk formula (Post 1985) and this must attest to the power and influence of well-directed consumer-based counter-marketing efforts. Other counter-marketing initiatives in the form of boycotts are discussed below.

Consumer boycotts as counter-marketing

Boycotts can be called for because of a variety of reasons, including political reasons, and, for example, in the USA, the French opposition to the war in Iraq in early 2003 prompted calls for a boycott of French wine (Chavis and Leslie 2009). This boycott resulted in some decline in French wine sales in the USA.

Consumer counter-marketing in the form of calls for boycotts on goods and services can also be called for reasons of environmental concern (Anonymous 2007b; Gueterbock 2004) and, for example, in Canada, Greenpeace urged Canadian consumers to boycott the products of Kellogg's because of their use of genetically modified foodstuffs (Anonymous 2000).

Counter-marketing energy and resource marketing

An advertising campaign on television and in newspapers was the counter-marketing vehicle for demarketing electric power consumption in Israel. This counter-marketing campaign was aimed at all consumers and coincided with a separate TV consumerism show on the similar theme of electricity over-use and how to restrict it (Deutsch and Lieberman 1985). Research indicated a 6 per cent downward shift in demand for electric power during the course of the counter-marketing campaign.

Peattie and Peattie (2009) point out that counter-marketing could be used to help move world patterns of consumption and development towards a more sustainable level for economies and societies. The promotion by marketing of responsible consumption and simpler, more sustainable styles of living could, for example, decrease total energy demand and help lower CO_2 emissions (Peattie and Peattie, 2009). This is an example of social marketing, which is the use of marketing to modify consumer behaviour in order to benefit the consumer and wider groups in society. Social marketing has a deep experience of counter-marketing initiatives gained from a relatively long history of involvement in such areas as the counter-marketing of drug, alcohol and tobacco consumption. Peattie and Peattie (2009) suggest that the widespread social movement towards downsizing, which is the deliberate trading off of a high-income, high-stress life for a lower-income, more satisfying and lower-stress life, could be utilized by counter consumption marketing to increase the appeal of a lower consumption lifestyle. They note that such counter consumption marketing is otherwise difficult to communicate and propagate because of the dominant social paradigm towards a high and increasing level of consumption.

As another example of counter-marketing energy usage, in the UK in December 2012, the large increases in retail electricity and gas prices have been in the news and the subject of debate in the House of Commons because the rises in price from the power companies involved are much bigger than inflation and (falling) real incomes. To counter demand for power, TV news programmes have demonstrated how households can cut their usage by such actions as turning electric plugs for appliances off when they are not in use and increasing the levels of insulation in house lofts and wall cavities.

Forced counter-marketing

Rarely, a corporation may have to engage in counter-marketing its own products in response to legal or other external developments. For example, Eastman Kodak had to withdraw from the instant photography market in 1986 when, as the result of a court case, it was effectively barred from the further making or selling of instant cameras and films. The injunction stemmed from a legal issue over patents that Kodak lost to the Polaroid corporation. Kodak attempted to leave customers satisfied by instigating a demarketing strategy whereby it started a cost-free telephone helpline for customers and offered to exchange customers' existing Kodak instant cameras for other products or for shares in the company despite this move potentially costing up to US$80m at the time (Higgins 1986). This was seen as a positive way for Kodak to manage the product demarketing that was forced on the company. In this way, Kodak managed its reputation and thus ensured that any damage to its reputation was minimized.

Consumer-driven counter-marketing

This is counter-marketing starting at the consumer level rather than that originating from companies, and with the increasing use of social media it is becoming easier and faster for such consumer-driven counter-marketing to take place.

Often, such counter-marketing is fuelled by anti-consumption movements, which may be permanent or in response to specific events (Lee and Fernandez 2009), such as the issues around baby milk powder marketing and fast food marketing discussed above. For example, in the UK, the recent news regarding the avoidance, through legal accounting policies, of paying large amounts of corporate tax by major multinationals like Starbucks and Google, despite their earning very large revenues in the UK, has become the subject of popular debate in the media and on social media networks. Campaigns based around social media and aimed at stopping consumption of the products concerned for moral reasons have been started. Such retaliatory counter-marketing campaigns can be expected to grow in importance in the future as consumers take steps to avoid brands that are seen as betraying the moral norms and practices of society.

Counter-marketing to diplomatically shed clients/customers

Gordon (2006), in a conceptual article on the management of marketing relationships with wasteful or worthless customers, makes a number of insightful comments that this author can agree with from practical experience of running a business. Gordon's article discusses how businesses have to concentrate on profitable, satisfied customers rather than unprofitable, dissatisfied customers to achieve success (Gordon 2006). To add qualitatively to Gordon's article, his main points will be illustrated with an example from this author's experience of turning around a marketing research business in the late 1980s.

Gordon says that dropping (demarketing) customers/clients should be built into a company's practices, and from my experience that is certainly true to an extent that is hard to imagine for someone who has not had business experience. In 1987, I took over the management of a market research company when the Managing Director left to form a competitive research company, taking the Data Processing Manager, the Deputy Fieldwork Manager and the Company Accountant with him. An initial examination of the accounts of the market research company that I took over revealed that our single major client, representing almost half of all business, had been given an ongoing (yearly) and huge discount (of around 50 per cent) to attract and keep them as clients.

However, they were dissatisfied, nit-picking and focused on minute detail rather than on making strategic decisions based on our research findings and recommendations. This meant that they tied up around 75 per cent of all research, fieldwork and data processing staff most of the time, leaving us with little time for other clients and no time for pitching to new clients. Additionally, after the direct costs of servicing their business, the remaining revenue (gross profit) from them made little contribution towards overheads and, to make matters worse, the contract we had with them included an exclusivity element, meaning that we could not deal with any competitive companies. Gordon reports that customers who are not profitable and are not likely to be profitable must be regarded as the company's past rather than their future and should be shed (Gordon 2006). In the research business I was running at the time, I quickly realized that we had to get rid of the client as soon as possible or remain stuck in an unprofitable and mutually dissatisfied situation.

However, there were political forces involved, as the client contact was the regional (Asia-Pacific) Managing Director who was a drinking buddy with my boss, i.e. my regional Managing Director. Gordon mentions that there are significant risks to getting rid of unwanted customers and that a scorned customer may go on to damage a company's reputation (Gordon 2006). Some counter-marketing was therefore called for to limit the possible political damage to the company's reputation (and my career) when the client complained to my boss about my counter-marketing towards them. I realized that it would be better for the company's reputation if the client left of their own accord rather than if I asked them to leave, because a spurned client may be vindictive, whereas an indignant client may be of the opinion that the withdrawal of their business is sufficient 'punishment'. Luckily, the annual contract with the client was up for review just after I took over the management of the research company concerned.

I pre-warned my boss that the client had been given both exclusivity and an unsustainable discount, neither of which could be maintained if the market research company I was now running was to be turned around and made profitable according to plan. I also warned him that I planned to increase our quote to this client in line with market rates and that we may well lose them (our biggest client) because of this. After receiving the new quote for annual research, excluding exclusivity, the client decided to take their business to another research company. Although recognizing that there are many reasons for the success or failure of market research companies (Boddy 2001) in line with Gordon's arguments concerning the counter-marketing of clients, I regard this demarketing of an unprofitable client as the single biggest contribution to the success, at that pivotal time, for the market research company concerned.

With the resources of staff at all levels that were freed up by the client's departure, we could concentrate on properly servicing other existing clients and on gaining new clients and our annual sales went up by about 62 per cent for the rest of that year with further dramatic growth the year after, which set the company on a course of continued success. The market research company concerned, which was in Taiwan, became one of the world's fastest-growing market research offices at that time. As Gordon suggests in his article, the costs of servicing and communicating with a customer who has discounts applied to them and is still not satisfied may be too great for a mutually beneficial relationship to continue and the overall profitability of a company would be greater if no such bad customers existed, which means that some customers need to be shed, in which case counter-marketing may have to take place to sensitively and diplomatically demarket such customers (Gordon 2006).

Counter-marketing to make it difficult or impossible for some customers to purchase certain goods may also be practised by some sections of industry and one example of this is the firearm (handgun) industry in the USA where manu-facturers take steps to limit the diversion of guns to customers such as convicted criminals who are not legally allowed to own them (Gundlach, Bradford and Wilkie 2010). Appeals to such customers via advertising and other marketing communications materials aimed at their conscience would probably not be effective because some criminals choose to ignore their conscience, while others, such as psychopaths, have no conscience to begin with (Hare 1999; Boddy 2006).

Therefore, counter-marketing efforts are aimed at the distribution channel rather than at the target audience of concern. Gundlach, Bradford and Wilkie's innovative study showed that counter-marketing initiatives aimed at the dis-tribution chain and, for example, at limiting the distribution of handguns to established retailers with physical retail stores did reduce the diversion of guns into the hand of criminals and the number of resulting crimes that were committed. However, Gundlach, Bradford and Wilkie's study (2010) also showed that gun industry manufacturers varied widely in their use of the counter-marketing tools that were available to them and on average used only one method of counter-marketing with the result that a significant amount of diversion of guns into illegal hands still occurred.

Handgun counter-marketing efforts also included governmental departments working with trade organizations to help prevent guns falling into undesirable hands. For example, a joint programme from the US department of Alcohol, Firearms and Tobacco together with a trade body, the National Shooting Sports Foundation, was aimed at persuading people not to buy handguns for other people who couldn't legally buy handguns themselves (Gundlach, Bradford and Wilkie 2010).

The programme was called 'Don't lie for the other guy' and it had similar aims as other organizations such as 'Mayors Against Illegal Guns' in trying to prevent handguns getting to criminals. Despite these various counter-marketing efforts, Gundlach, Bradford and Wilkie's research showed that 10.1 per cent (135,000 handguns) of all handguns distributed in 1996 in the USA had been used in a violent crime by 2000. Further, it was evident that some manufacturers were much more successful at counter-marketing than others because, while one manufacturer had only 1 per cent of their handguns used in violent crime in the proceeding four years, this was up to 55 per cent for another manufacturer, with the other manufacturers falling in between these figures (Gundlach, Bradford and Wilkie 2010).

Market research in counter-marketing

In order to design and implement counter-marketing campaigns that have a real chance of changing people's behaviour in desirable directions, market research is absolutely essential. In designing campaigns, it must be recognized that what drives and motivates the initiators of the counter-marketing campaign will not necessarily drive and motivate the target audience. For example, communications based on rational models of decision making such as 'don't smoke because it is bad for you' run the risk of increasing smoking rather than reducing it as the target audience emotionally reacts against the transparent manipulativeness of the message. On the other hand, US counter-marketers have found that, with adolescents, pointing out to them how the tobacco industry works and tries to manipulate them into smoking has a more positive effect on non-smoking as the adolescents react against the tobacco industry rather than their opponents (Johnson *et al.* 2008; Zucker *et al.* 2000). Market research into what counter-marketing efforts are attempting to communicate can help counter-marketers to craft messages that will be effective rather than counter-productive.

An understanding of the possible benefits of behaviour change from the point of view of the target audience is necessary in order to craft appeals that will have any chance of working effectively. For example, Henley, Raffin and Caemmerer (2011), in the French anti-childhood obesity campaign discussed above, describe how focus groups and in-depth interviews were conducted in order to help develop messages that would appeal to and motivate children and their carers. Counter-marketing campaigns focused on the positive benefits of an active, healthy lifestyle rather than the negative consequences of a bad diet, and were more effective because of this.

Similarly, Lowry and colleagues describe how social advertising materials aimed at increasing breastfeeding were tested via market research for use in a specific area of the UK and were adapted for that area based on research findings (Lowry *et al.* 2009). Such market research can ensure that the words used in such advertising and other marketing communications materials are understood by, relevant to and motivational towards the target audience to maximize their chance of communicating effectively. Similarly, in a campaign run in Liverpool, research established that it was the motivation that the target audience lacked rather than knowledge of the rational reasons why becoming healthier was desirable (Thomas 2009). Basing the counter-marketing campaign around these motivational elements allowed it to be successful in reducing obesity.

Groff reports that, in designing demarketing or counter-marketing to help reduce demand-related problems in National Park usage, the needs of customers (visitors) have to be researched so that these can be understood (Groff 1998). This could, for example, help to determine at what levels of visitor numbers it is considered that overcrowding is taking place so that demand can be managed down to those levels.

Similarly, market research could help determine whether certain visitor segments (e.g. off-road car users, speed boat users) were perceived by other visitors to be undesirable or not. For example, in the Lake District National Park in England, the speed limit on Lake Windermere was reduced to 10mph in 1991 (Collins 2011) to limit speed boat users who were perceived to be a minority of users who were making the lake polluted and dangerous to use for other visitors, especially those in small canoes, sail boats and yachts. This also reduced noise and fuel pollution from the motors of the speed boats and added to the visual serenity of the lake.

Counter-marketing activities by consumer groups can be seen as a useful source of market research information concerning what some consumers perceive to be wrong with a service or product. A company can then assess the extent of these concerns via more structured research and, if necessary, it can then address these concerns through changing the packaging or adding to the product offering just as McDonald's has sometimes done as discussed above. Gundlach, Bradford and Wilkie's (2010) forensic market research into handgun counter-marketing illustrates how research can help to understand the range of counter-marketing initiatives that are possible in specific markets. This understanding can allow corporations to undertake counter-marketing efforts that they otherwise would not have thought of themselves as well as giving regulatory bodies a broader understanding of the issues involved.

Conclusions

Counter-marketing can be initiated by the company that originally marketed a product or service but more often it is externally driven. Such external counter-marketing campaigns are often started by consumer groups who are concerned at what they deem to be inappropriate marketing. These campaigns include counter-marketing against the promotion of alcoholic drinks, the design, taste, packaging and advertising of which appeal to teenage drinkers. Also they include counter-marketing against the promotion of tobacco products.

Counter-marketing can also be initiated by trade bodies as part of self-regulatory activities in a particular industry or business sector. Governmental or quasi-governmental organizations can also engage in counter-marketing activities that are deemed to be in the public interest.

Counter-marketing campaigns can include calls for boycotts of products or classes of products or even of all products from certain companies or countries. Companies may also instigate their own demarketing and counter-marketing if, for example, products are found to be faulty and in need of repair or if they are finding their way into the hands of those not entitled to use them because of age restrictions or other legal restrictions. This counter-marketing allows those companies to manage their own corporate reputation rather than leaving this up to chance.

Case study questions

1. Why might counter-marketing campaigns aimed at reducing cigarette smoking have the opposite effect?
2. How might a company demarket to undesirable market segments?
3. What has been the effect of counter-marketing by pressure groups?
4. Why might an energy supplier counter-market its own product?
5. What is forced counter-marketing, and how does it come about?

References

AMA 1974, 'Utilities share Marketing Firm of the Year Award for demarketing.' *Marketing News*, vol. 8, no. 2, p. 7.

Andreasen, A. R. 2002, 'Marketing social marketing in the social change marketplace.' *Journal of Public Policy and Marketing*, vol. 21, no. 1, pp. 3–13.

Anonymous 1997a, 'Bass hikes its Hooch brand.' *Marketing Event*, p. 7.

——1997b, 'Free publications give advice about young children's health.' *FDA Consumer*, vol. 31, no. 3, p. 6.

——2000, 'Greenpeace asks Canadians to boycott Kellogg food items.' *Marketing News*, vol. 34, no. 9, p. 52.

——2007a, 'Breast Is Best "Victory".' *Ecologist*, vol. 37, no. 4, p. 9.

——2007b, 'Consumers back boycott of brands that fail eco test.' *Marketing Week*, vol. 30, no. 22, p. 10.

Barnard, M. and Forsyth, A. J. M. 1998, 'Alcopops and under-age drinking: Changing trends in drink preference', *Health Education*, vol. 6, no. November, pp. 208–212.

Beeton, S. and Pinge, I. 2003, 'Casting the holiday dice: Demarketing gambling to encourage local tourism.' *Current Issues in Tourism*, vol. 6, no. 4, pp. 309–322.

Boddy, C. R. 2001, 'Perceived Reasons for the Success of the UK Market Research Industry.' *International Journal of Market Research*, vol. 43, no. 1, pp. 29–41.

——2006, 'The dark side of management decisions: Organisational psychopaths.' *Management Decision*, vol. 44, no. 9/10, pp. 1461–1475.

——2012, 'The impact of corporate psychopaths on corporate reputation and marketing.' *The Marketing Review*, vol. 12, no. 1, pp. 79–89.

Bonamici, K. 2005, '1972: Ford decides to let the Pinto explode. (cover story)' *Fortune International* (Europe), vol. 151, no. 11, pp. 43–44.

Botterill, J. and Kline, S. 2007, 'From McLibel to McLettuce: childhood, spin and re-branding.' *Society and Business Review*, vol. 2, no. 1, pp. 74–97.

Brady, M. 2011, 'Why boycott Nestle?' *New Internationalist*, pp. 6–7.

Campbell, P. 2012, 'Starbucks to hand £20m to taxman amid fears of consumer boycott.' *Daily Mail*, p. 2.

Chavis, L. and Leslie, P. 2009, 'Consumer boycotts: The impact of the Iraq war on French wine sales in the U.S.' *Quantitative Marketing and Economics*, vol. 7, no. 1, pp. 37–67.

Cheetham, N. and Lee, V. 1994, 'Doctors asked to pledge support for breastfeeding.' *Nation's Health*, vol. 24, no. 7, p. 12.

Clements, M. A. 1989, 'Selecting tourist traffic by demarketing.' *Tourism Management*, June, pp. 89–94.

Collins, M. 2011, 'The politics of the environment, and noisy sports: two totally different outcomes in the Lake District National Park for powerboating and off-road motoring.' *Leisure Studies*, vol. 30, no. 4, pp. 423–452.

Cullwick, D. 1975, 'Positioning demarketing strategy.' *Journal of Marketing*, vol. 39, no. 2, pp. 51–57.

Deutsch, J. and Lieberman, Y. 1985, 'Effects of a public advertising campaign on consumer behavior in a demarketing situation.' *International Journal of Research in Marketing*, vol. 2, pp. 287–296.

Gordon, I. 2006, 'Relationship demarketing: Managing wasteful or worthless customer relationships.' *Ivey Business Journal*, vol. 70, no. 4, pp. 1–4.

Greer, T. V. 1984, 'The future of the international code of marketing of breastmilk sub-stitutes: The Socio-legal context.' *International Marketing Review*, vol. 1, no. 3, p. 33.

Groff, C. 1998, 'Demarketing in park and recreation management.' *Managing Leisure*, vol. 3, no. 3, pp. 128–135.

Gueterbock, R. 2004, 'Greenpeace campaign case study – StopEsso.' *Journal of Consumer Behaviour*, vol. 3, no. 3, pp. 265–271.

Gundlach, G. T., Bradford, K. D. and Wilkie, W. L. 2010, 'Countermarketing and demar-keting against product diversion: Forensic research in the firearms industry.' *Journal of Public Policy and Marketing*, vol. 29, no. 1, pp. 103–122.

Hare, R. 1999, *Without Conscience: The disturbing word of the psychopaths among us*, Guildford Press, New York.

Henley, N., Raffin, S. and Caemmerer, B. 2011, 'The application of marketing principles to a social marketing campaign.' *Marketing Intelligence and Planning*, vol. 29, no. 7, pp. 697–706.

Higgins, K. T. 1986, 'Kodak "stands tall" with consumers while demarketing instant photo line.' *Marketing News*, vol. 20, no. 3, pp. 1–16.

Jardine, A. 1999, 'Portman forces Asda to ditch alcopop.' *Marketing*, p. 2.

Johnson, D. M., Wine, L. A., Zack, S., Zimmer, E., Wang, J. H., Weitzel-O'Neill, P. A., Claflin, V. and Tercyak, K. P. 2008, 'Designing a tobacco counter-marketing campaign for African American youth.' *Tobacco Induced Diseases*, vol. 4, no. 1, p. 7.

Judkins, B. M. 1989, 'Corporate crime under attack: The Ford Pinto case and beyond (book).' *Social Forces*, vol. 67, no. 3, pp. 818–819.

Kavas, A. and Kavas, A. 2011, 'Are demarketing tools used in reducing smoking applicable to the global obesity challenge?' *International Journal of Business Research*, vol. 11, no. 2, pp. 201–207.

Lee, M. S. W. and Fernandez, K. V. 2009, 'Anti-consumption: An overview and research agenda.' *Journal of Business Research*, vol. 62, pp. 145–147.

Leonhardt, D. and Dawley, H. 1996, 'A Little Booze For The Kiddies?' *Business Week*, no. 3494, p. 158.

Lowry, R. J., Billett, A., Buchanan, C. and Whiston, S. 2009, 'Increasing breastfeeding and reducing smoking in pregnancy: a social marketing success improving life chances for children.' *Perspectives in Public Health*, vol. 129, no. 6, pp. 277–280.

Medway, D. and Warnaby, G. (2008) 'Alternative Perspectives on Marketing and the Place Brand.' *European Journal of Marketing*, vol. 42, no. 5 and 6, pp. 641–653.

Medway, D., Warnaby, G. and Dharni, S. 2011, 'Demarketing places: Rationales and strategies.' *Journal of Marketing Management*, vol. 27, no. 1/2, pp. 124–142.

Melillo, W. 2001, 'Ads for "alcopops" are under fire.' *Adweek* New England Edition, vol. 38, no. 19, p. 61.

——2002, 'New York assembly takes aim at "alcopops" ads.' *Adweek* Eastern Edition, vol. 43, no. 43, p. 2.

Morris, D. 1979, 'Boycott of Nestle hurts but it doesn't cut sales.' *Marketing News*, vol. 12, no. 19, pp. 1–3.

Newswire 2012, 'Alcopop-free zones: Marin advances as San Rafael city council to vote on resolution of support youth rally to ask Albert Park 7-Eleven to stop selling alcopops.' In *PR Newswire US*.

Peattie, K. and Peattie, S. (2009) 'Social marketing: A pathway to consumption reduction?' *Journal of Business Research*, vol. 62 (2), pp. 260–268.

Post, J. E. 1985, 'Assessing the Nestle boycott: Corporate accountability and human rights.' *California Management Review*, vol. 27, no. 2, pp. 113–131.

Rivera, F. I., Lieberman, L. S., Rivadeneyra, G. M. and Sallas, A. M. 2010, 'Using a social marketing framework to transform an education program: Lessons from the Hispanic Obesity Prevention and Education (PESO) Program.' *Social Marketing Quarterly*, vol. 16, no. 2, pp. 2–17.

Thomas, J. 2009, 'Addressing obesity through social marketing: "Liverpool's Challenge".' *Perspectives in Public Health*, vol. 129, no. 6, p. 254.

Williams, R. J., West, B. L. and Simpson, R. I. 2007, *Prevention of problem gambling: A comprehensive review of the evidence*. Report prepared for the Ontario Problem Gambling Research Centre, Guelph, Ontario, CANADA., Ontario Problem Gambling Research Centre, Ontario.

Zucker, D., Hopkins, R. S., Sly, D. F., Urich, J., Kershaw, J. M. and Solari, S. 2000, 'Florida's "truth" campaign: a counter-marketing, anti-tobacco media campaign.' *Journal of Public Health Management and Practice*, vol. 6, no. 3, pp. 1–6.

6
GENERAL DEMARKETING
Heather Skinner

Introduction

According to Kotler and Levy (1971: 75), general demarketing 'is required when a company wants to shrink the level of total demand', and 'acts by discouraging customers in general or a certain class of customers in particular on either a temporary or permanent basis'. It may be surprising to realize that there would be times that a company would actively seek to decrease demand for its goods and services, especially as Kotler and Levy point out that 'the popular conception of marketing is that it deals with the problem of furthering or expanding demand' (1971: 74). Indeed, when the term 'marketing' is used by critics, 'it is meant to cover all the ways used by marketing to tempt the consumer into buying' (O'Shaughnessy and O'Shaughnessy, 2002: 525).

To understand why and how a company may be forced to, or choose to, engage in demarketing activities it is therefore interesting to see how such a demand-generation view of marketing has developed.

Do marketers generate demand or meet it?

Historically, marketing had been viewed mainly from a social and economic perspective. According to Webster (1992: 2), this perspective changed only in 1948 when marketing was defined as 'the performance of business activities directed toward, and incident to, the flow of goods and services from producer to consumer or user' (American Marketing Association, 1948: 210), a perspective that further developed in the 1950s and 1960s when a managerial focus emerged to the study of marketing. Webster also found that, as marketing became a more decentralized function, particularly in larger organizations, 'the task of the marketing function was first to develop a thorough understanding of the marketplace to ensure that the firm was producing goods and services required and desired by the consumer', employing an effective approach to managing elements of the marketing mix in order to generate customer demand (Webster, 1992: 4). This perspective begins to point to some of the practical managerial issues involved in responding to a 'thorough understanding of the marketplace', where the marketer's challenge is to ensure not only that the supply of goods and services deemed to be desired by the marketplace is delivered by the producer to the consumer, but also that this supply, in an ideal world, would meet the demand that the marketer has been involved in generating through the firm's mix management activities. It is also worth acknowledging that a more production-oriented rather than marketing-oriented firm may respond to marketplace conditions of limited competition and excess demand by focusing more on profit maximization through increased production (Kaur and Sharma, 2009). Such different organizational orientations and focus on different organizational functions and activities help illustrate the tensions involved in delivering on the marketing concept: if firms are undertaking activities to meet customer demand, then there should be no need for demarketing; if marketing is instead about generating demand, it would seem logical to assume that marketing activities could affect demand either by increasing or decreasing it.

However, it is also recognized that affecting supply and demand can be out of the control of the marketer. For example, Patsiaouras and Fitchett (2012: 161) discuss the economic depression of the 1930s and the European wartime and post-war economy where demand for consumer products decreased through macro-environmental factors, and when even 'everyday commodities such as butter and eggs, and consumer electronics and technologies, took on luxury signification'. Nowadays in developed economies, it is more usual for consumption, at least in consumer markets, to be viewed as feeding the needs of an ever-demanding, hedonistic consumer who can discover 'the meaning of life ... through acquisition; [and] that the hedonistic experience of material accumulation is the core object of existence on earth' (O'Shaughnessy and O'Shaughnessy, 2002: 524).

Many authors note that the marketer's challenges have become much more complex as the marketplace, and therefore competition for market share, has become globalized. However, while overall demand for certain goods and services may indeed be globalized, demand may not be at equal levels in all of a firm's global markets. Thus, globalization can cause problems for firms who may face wider geographical spread of excess demand, or pockets of excess demand in different countries, which means their marketing efforts may be required to focus on stimulating demand in some markets, while demarketing in others.

Contexts for general demarketing

General scarcity economies

The above example of Europe between the 1930s and 1950s, where the economies of entire nations were 'plunged into a state of widespread product shortages' (Kotler and Levy, 1971: 74) illustrates that 'at times excess demand can characterize a whole economy, and at other times, only a limited number of firms. Even in the absence of a general scarcity economy, there are always individual sellers who are facing excess demand for one or more of their products' (ibid p. 75). In times of general scarcity, the role of marketing is not decided at the level of the organization, as macro-environmental factors may come into play that are out of the control of the marketer and the firm. In such contexts, marketing may be perceived as having less relevance and importance than in times of excess supply, where the role of marketing in affecting the flow of goods and services between producer and consumer is more clearly evident.

Sectoral general demarketing

It is interesting to note that the criticisms of marketing identified at the outset of this chapter are usually levied against private sector consumer marketing activities 'with next to nothing to say on business-to-business marketing. Not-for-profit marketing is similarly ignored' (O'Shaughnessy and O'Shaughnessy, 2002: 526). However, general demarketing can be evidenced in both of these sectors.

One good example comes from the industrial business-to-business sector. Three strategic economic options have been identified as being appropriate for oil-exporters facing a future of increased demand for energy while the world's finite natural resources are diminishing:

> (a) to increase exports to meet increasing demand; (b) to freeze exports at their current levels; or (c) to reduce exports. The last two choices are in the order of demarketing. The first might also involve demarketing if the rates of increase were kept deliberately lower than what rates of growth in demand warrant and what the production capacities make possible.
>
> *(Saddik, 1977: 281)*

Against this background, Saddik (1977) explored the demarketing mix for the oil industry.

> Place: Reduce the distribution of oil-exports, thus minimizing supply to oil-importing countries.
> Price: Oil-exporting countries could simply raise oil prices with the assumption that demand would then decrease.

In practice, both of these demarketing mix elements work in conjunction with each other, because, as supply is reduced, price often rises to a higher equilibrium level. 'Assuming that an equilibrium situation existed in the first place, the two courses of action lead to the same result. The oil-exporting countries have, in practice, followed both courses, producing a reinforcement effect between the two demarketing mix elements' (Saddik, 1977: 282).

Product and promotion activities can be similarly reinforcing of each other.

> Product: In this context, demarketing also involves seeking alternative substitute products to oil and gas that can meet consumers' long-term future energy needs.
> Promotion: When promoting as part of a demarketing mix, it is recognized that the main objective of marketing communications changes. In the case of

oil-exporting countries, their communication imperatives were: To convince their customer nations that their demarketing strategies were appropriate and were not simply designed to hold their customer nations to ransom over prices and export levels; to encourage customers to switch to alternative energy products; and also to attract innovative responses through technology and knowledge to develop alternative energy solutions.

Saddik also noted that other demarketing activities such as 'stricter credit terms, a decreasing level of customer services and abolition of discount policies are not uncommon in the oil market of today' (1977: 283).

When demarketing occurs, it is therefore evident that traditional marketing activities are used, 'but in reverse: for example, the marketing mix variables are adjusted to "cool" demand' (Sodhi, 2011: 181).

Demarketing is also used in the not-for-profit and public sectors, 'to curb consumption or injurious consumption and the task of the marketer is to promote deconsumption of a product/behavior' (Sodhi, 2011: 181), particularly 'where environmental impacts are most severe' (Wall, 2007: 123). O'Shaughnessy and O'Shaughnessy (2002: 544) identify the existence of organizations committed to reducing consumer demand through demarketing activities, for example, 'in the USA, the organization called "Buy Nothing Day" (BND) argues that over-consumption is wrecking the environment and dragging down the quality of life'. However, when marketing is employed in the public and not-for-profit sectors, whether or not the objective is to influence behaviour that involves, decreasing demand, for example curbing the consumption of alcohol or cigarettes, or increasing demand, for example by encouraging increased participation in physical activity, such marketing activities are more usually all defined as 'social marketing'. No distinction tends to be made for those marketing activities designed to curb consumption that would, otherwise, be defined as 'demarketing'. This is evident in the following definition of social marketing as 'the adaption of commercial marketing techniques to programmes designed to influence the voluntary behaviour of target audiences to improve their personal welfare and that of society of which they are part' (Andreasen, 1994: 110), a definition that focuses only on the voluntary behaviour change, and not on whether that change involves increasing or decreasing attendant consumption.

The term 'counter-marketing' can also be applied when the aim of the demarketing activities is not just to shrink the level of total demand, as indicated by Kotler and Levy, but to stop consumption completely of, for example, tobacco-related products (Farrelly et al., 2002). However, more recently, Kotler has called for a more proactive approach to all marketing activities for sustainability, in order to 'demarket/countermarket certain products, technologies, and marginal consumer segments (e.g., consumers who cannot afford expensive homes)' (Achrol and Kotler, 2012: 45), concluding that a 'new consumption philosophy of customer care' can mean 'demarketing and countermarketing as often as it means marketing' (ibid p50). In this article, the authors do not articulate any distinction between 'demarketing' and 'counter-marketing'. Moreover, the example they give of demarketing or counter-marketing to marginal consumer segments could seem to be more related to selective demarketing, the objective of which, according to Kotler and Levy's earlier paper, is to 'discourage the demand coming from certain customer classes' (1971: 75), rather than general demarketing, which aims to reduce total overall demand.

Organizational demarketing for temporary shortages

Webster (1992: 15) proposed that marketing, which should remain 'focused on the ever-changing customer in the global marketplace', has three different strategic roles within organizations, affecting: the corporation as a whole; one of the corporation's businesses; or its Strategic Business Units (SBU). It is more difficult to perceive of an occasion where an entire corporation would actively choose to decrease total demand through general demarketing than viewing demarketing as a strategic approach to be pursued at the level of a corporation's individual business or SBU.

Kotler and Levy's (1971) article identified the following cases where general demarketing could be seen to be at the level of the corporation when facing temporary shortages in supply that was unable to keep up with customer demand at the early growth stage of the product lifecycle when new products were introduced into the market in the 1960s. These included Eastman Kodak when it introduced its new Instamatic camera; Wilkinson Sword's new stainless steel blade; and Anheuser-Busch's Budweiser beer. However, in each of these cases, demand reduction was only sought for a particular product, and not for the corporation's overall output.

The other example provided by Kotler and Levy is that of savings and loan associations that 'faced an oversupply of savings relative to their ability to invest the funds and sought means to discourage the savings customers. They were willing to encourage small accounts, but refused large depositors' (1971: 75). However, while classified as general demarketing in that article, it could be seen that this provides a better example of selective demarketing, as the activities were aimed at a particular segment of customers – large-deposit savers.

One example in the extant literature of general demarketing to deal with a temporary shortage at the corporate level has been provided by Arlbjørn and Lüthje (2012) who explore the case of a global manufacturing organization headquartered in one country where product development also takes place, with its manufacturing taking place in 4 countries on 2 continents, and customers based in more than 130 countries around the world. In this case, general demarketing at a corporate level was required due to problems in the corporation's supply chain:

> inadequate inventory management went beyond the deliveries to the customers because the company could not keep up with the demand for some of its products. For other products, the company had too many on inventory that became obsolete.
>
> *(ibid p1058)*

Kotler and Levy (1971: 76–77) identify a wide range of demarketing activities that can be appropriately employed by a company facing temporary shortages in supply in order to encourage deconsuming through demand reduction. These can also be mapped against the different elements of the demarketing mix:

Product: 'Reduce product quality or content, either to encourage deconsuming or to make more of the product available and thus demarket at a slower rate'.

Place: 'Curtail the number of distribution outlets, using the product shortage as an opportunity to eliminate undesirable dealers and/or customers'. Kotler and Levy also suggest a range of distribution strategies that allocate products either on the basis of:

- First-come, first-served, which is usually deemed by existing customers to be a fair method of allocating supplies, but which can be deemed unfair by new customers.
- Proportional demand, which means allocating a decided proportion of each customer's overall order. While this can also be seen as a fair and equitable solution, it will leave some customers without enough supply to meet their needs. This may lead to the customer organization being unable to meet its own consumers' demand, requiring similar demarketing activities to be undertaken throughout the entire supply chain, or to some customers seeking alternative suppliers, to which they may then become loyal at the expense of their original supplier.
- Favoured customers, where the customers deemed by the supplying company to be more valuable will get their orders filled, but, due to demand exceeding supply, other customers will end up with either no or a limited supply of its required products.
- Highest bid, where 'the supply goes to those customers who offer the highest premium for early delivery. While many people consider this an exploitative strategy, economists typically argue that it makes the most sense since the product flows to those who presumably need it most'.

However, Kotler and Levy noted that each one of these approaches will lead to some customers being disappointed. When utilizing such allocation strategies to deal with temporary shortages, they warn that 'if the company seeks to maximize its long-run, rather than short-run profits, it should choose solutions that minimize the total disappointment of customers during the period in question'.

Price: When attempting to discourage demand through pricing mechanisms when demarketing, it is most usual to see product costs rising, although other costs can be raised, including the psychological costs of 'the time and expense necessary for the buyer to procure the product or service'.

Promotion: Kotler and Levy identify a range of promotional demarketing mix activities that can be employed to curtail demand, including: reducing advertising expenditure; modifying the message content; reducing other promotional activities including all forms of sales promotions; and to 'cut back salesmen's selling time on the product and their entertainment budgets, asking them to concentrate on other products, spend more time in service and intelligence work and learn to say no in a way that customers find acceptable'.

Kotler and Levy do, however, warn that such activities must not be undertaken in isolation, but, rather, it must be seen that all demarketing mix activities should work together, reinforcing each other, with an attendant marketing eye being kept on 'the elasticity and cross-elasticities of the different instruments, i.e., their impact on demand when employed with varying intensity, both individually and in combination. Otherwise, the demarketing programme may over-inhibit demand, and the company may find itself facing a shortage of customers' (1971: 76). However, while Kotler and Levy identify these strategies as being appropriate to deal with times of temporary shortages, it can be seen that many of these demarketing activities could also be employed to deal with more general chronic overpopularity of products and services.

Organizational demarketing for chronic overpopularity

With regard to general demarketing being required to deal not with temporary shortages, but to deal instead with what Kotler and Levy refer to as 'chronic overpopularity' (1971: 77), the examples they give are all from the service sector. The first is a tourism marketing issue. It is interesting to compare this example of general demarketing with other issues relating to reducing demand relating to the consumption of places in the chapter in this book on synchro-marketing. Kotler and Levy identify two cases where general demarketing of places has been undertaken due to overpopularity.

BALI

> The island of Bali in the South Pacific has long been a tourist's dream. In recent years, it has attracted a larger number of tourists than can be handled comfortably with its facilities. The island is in danger of becoming overcrowded and spoiled.

OREGON

> Because of fear that the area's natural beauty will be spoiled by congestion, officials in the state of Oregon are demarketing to prospective settlers.

The third example offered by Kotler and Levy concerns a popular London restaurant. Although the restaurant is fully booked for months in advance, 'tourists without reservations crowd around in the hope of cancellations. They add noise and detract from the intended atmosphere of leisurely dining'.

Bali's demarketing strategy 'is to reduce the island's attractiveness to middle-income tourists while maintaining or increasing its appeal to high-income tourists'. Oregon 'does promote tourist trade; the governor encourages people to visit so long as they do not stay'. However, given that each of these cases describes places where only certain segments of consumers are actively not wanted, it could be seen that these places are practising selective rather than general demarketing. The London restaurant can be seen to have practised general demarketing to reduce overall total demand. 'They added a doorman who discouraged people from waiting for cancellations and from phoning about the availability of reservations. They also raised the prices.'

Heritage tourism demarketing

Examples of general demarketing through raising prices, and/or limiting access, can often be seen in tourism marketing (Medway *et al.*, 2011), particularly when considering the preservation of heritage in a tourism context. Globalization has already been mentioned as one of the challenges facing marketers that can lead to a focus on demarketing activities, due to either unequal demand being spread across a corporation's global markets, requiring some form of overall general demarketing, or where a company's global operations may cause temporary problems in their supply chain, requiring some form of temporary demarketing to facilitate better inventory management. In the context of the preservation of cultural heritage and the service sector in which that operates, globalization, with its attendant potential for cultural convergence, has led to the resurgence of interest in 'all things local', and it is a political, rather than organizational imperative that drives the protection of cultural traditions not only to gain the benefits of differentiating one place from another, but also to preserve heritage for future generations (Arantes, 2007: 291). Consumption of cultural heritage when involving visits to actual sites can be compared to the earlier example given of the oil and gas industry, where, similarly, the very act of consumption is what leads to the erosion, destruction or even eventual extinction of the very 'product' that is consumed. As a result, it is recognized that the tourism industry can not only 'generate serious preservation problems ... it can also contribute to the enhancement and protection' of the sites visited (Marcotte and Bourdeau, 2012: 80). Of particular interest to scholars has been the labelling of certain 'unique natural and cultural sites' as United Nations Educational Scientific and Cultural Organization (UNESCO) World Heritage Sites (WHS). Because it seems that, in some cases, to be recognized as a WHS is one factor that in itself can generate increased tourism to a particular site:

> Including the sites on a list recognizing their unique character raises their destination appeal and popularity. Perversely total protection of these sites would imply not making them known to the broader traveling public. In fact some particularly ecologically or socially sensitive heritage sites are subject to a 'demarketing' approach to reduce the number of visitors.
>
> *(Marcotte and Bourdeau, 2012: 82)*

Therefore, effective site management has become an important imperative and, since 1997, 'submission of a management plan became a prerequisite for inscription as a World Heritage Site and all sites inscribed before then were required to prepare and submit a management plan by 2005' (Wilson and Boyle, 2006: 504). However, it is also recognized that, unlike demarketing when practised by a company in the private sector, when the decision taken to demarket can usually be taken solely by the company, when considering WHS, their management, particularly for sustainable tourism objectives can involve a wide range and type of both public, private and not-for-profit organizations. A full list of 'organization types cited in implementation of sustainable tourism objectives' of UK WHS includes (ibid p508):

- advisory bodies;
- community associations;
- conservation trusts;
- education bodies;
- government departments;
- government-funded body/agency;
- local authorities;
- partnerships;
- private landowners;
- private organizations/operators;
- site managers;
- steering group;
- tourist boards;
- transport organizations.

It is therefore important that, in these cases, demarketing must be a collaborative inter-organizational activity. One example given by Wilson and Boyle of a UK WHS where high levels of collaboration are evidenced in the management plans of the site is Stonehenge, considered a 'potent and iconic symbol of England's heritage' (2006: 511). In the case of Stonehenge, Anderton (2011: 149) traces the chronic overpopularity of the site to the Stonehenge Free Festival that was first held in 1974. This festival attracted 'tens of thousands of revellers to its month-long summer solstice celebrations. It had become the pre-eminent meeting place and spiritual focal point for an increasing number of New Age Travellers'. The government at the time supported the police action undertaken in 1985 to stop the event from taking place at all, ultimately leading to 'amendments to the Public Order Act 1986 ... The measures and restrictions that it imposed largely crushed the Free Festival movement and the travelling community which had sustained it'. Although 'within the UK there is extensive legislation for site protection ... To this end there is usually a key government agency that has ownership, conservation and management responsibility for the site (Wilson and Boyle, 2006: 503), such heavy-handed techniques as were applied to conserve Stonehenge during the 1980s are not always evident in the demarketing of specific places.

Indeed, in addition to those strategies already identified of restricting access and employing price mechanisms, Medway *et al.* (2011) identify other demarketing practices that can be applied to places, these include: no marketing – either at all, or at certain times of year; diversion demarketing – involving redirection of consumers to alternative places; and informational demarketing – 'an example of this would be the way that various national governments provide ongoing advice to their citizens about which locations they should not travel to' (2011: 128).

Medway *et al.* also make the distinction between active demarketing and passive demarketing. Active demarketing would involve actively managing the demarketing mix of place (through restricting access), price (employing price mechanisms that usually involve raising prices in order to decrease demand), promotion (including informational demarketing) and product (through diversion demarketing). The strategy of no marketing can be seen to be general passive demarketing. Medway *et al.* (2011:127) also identify a strategy of selective passive demarketing that can also be followed:

> By emphasising certain place attributes to market a location to certain types of individuals or organisations, it may automatically follow that other elements that may attract alternative types of individuals or organisations are de facto demarketed.

Conceptually, however, it is difficult to see how passive selective demarketing differs in any way from what we would otherwise know as the marketing strategy where any organization of any size in any sector is simply selecting segments to serve that it believes it can serve not only well, but also better than competitors, in order to achieve its market potential.

Organizational demarketing for product elimination

Some companies may need to undertake general demarketing because the introduction of new legislation would no longer allow a company to sell a particular product or service, or because the company has chosen to eliminate a particular product or service from its portfolio due to, for example, decreased customer demand and/or because it is introducing a new product or service to replace an existing one. In all these cases, overall total demand needs to be directed to a new alternative product offering. However, in many cases, loyal customers already exist for the current product that is to be eliminated. In such cases, the company's task also therefore involves ensuring their demarketing activities do not 'create customer ill will' (Kotler and Levy, 1971: 77).

Similar to the issues raised above relating to the oil and gas industry, facing the need to find alternative energy products to replace the planet's finite natural resources upon which we currently rely, in product elimination cases, demarketing activities must be focused on:

Informing the customer as to why the product is being dropped, offering partial or full compensation to important customers who are hurt by the disappearance of the product, and maintaining a minimal stock of the product to satisfy the hard-core customers.

(Kotler and Levy, 1971: 78)

Conclusion

This chapter started by considering various perspectives on the purpose of marketing, particularly from a demand-generation perspective. Although also practised when an organization faces temporary shortages in supply so that it is unable to meet its level of customer demand, general demarketing activities are also often driven by the recognition of resource scarcity and other environmental concerns. According to Sodhi (2011: 177), the latter requires:

the development of a marketing orientation specific to this new marketing environment … This concept maintains that the marketer's task is to shape demand to conform to long-term objectives rather than blindly engineer increases in sales without regard to such objectives-sustainability in the present day context being one such objective.

(Sodhi, 2011: 177)

further recognizing that:

the consumer is also more accepting of demarketing efforts and is now willing to play along. The consumer understands his responsibility in co-creation of the environment, is willing to consume responsibly and make the sacrifices both in terms of behavior change and paying extra prices for longevity of the planet.

(ibid p183)

Indeed, this reflects the conclusion of Kotler and Levy's (1971) original article proposing the concept of demarketing. They recognize that marketing as an activity should be undertaken to 'regulate the level and shape of demand so that it conforms to the organization's current supply situation and to its long-run objectives' (1971: 80). From this perspective, the entire proposition of a concept such as 'demarketing' can be seen to be merely a contentious way of these leading authors illustrating their view of marketing as not simply an activity that is designed to generate demand, but instead as one that can affect demand either by increasing or decreasing it. However, this does point to the importance of the marketer's effective understanding of the market itself. As has been mentioned earlier in this chapter, if firms are undertaking activities to meet customer demand, then there should be no need for general demarketing at all.

References

Achrol, R.S. and Kotler, P. (2012) 'Frontiers of the marketing paradigm in the third millennium', *Journal of the Academy of Marketing Science*, 40(1), pp. 35–52.

American Marketing Association (1948) 'Report of the Definitions Committee', *Journal of Marketing*, 13(2), pp. 202–10.

Anderton, C. (2011) 'Music festival sponsorship: Between commerce and carnival', *Arts Marketing: An International Journal*, 1(2), pp. 145–58.

Andreasen, A. R. (1994) 'Social marketing: Its definition and domain', *Journal of Public Policy and Marketing*, 13(1), pp. 108–14.

Arantes, A. A. (2007), 'Diversity, heritage and cultural politics', *Theory Culture and Society*, 24, pp. 290–96.

Arlbjørn, J. S., and Lüthje, T. (2012) 'Global operations and their interaction with supply chain performance', *Industrial Management and Data Systems*, 112(7), pp. 1044–64.

Farrelly, M. C., Healton, C. G., Davis, K. C., Messeri, P., Hersey, J. C., and Haviland, M. L. (2002) 'Getting to the truth: Evaluating national tobacco countermarketing campaigns', *American Journal of Public Health*, 92(6): 901–7.

Kaur, G. and Sharma, R. D. (2009) 'Voyage of marketing thought from a barter system to a customer centric one', *Marketing Intelligence and Planning*, 27(5), pp. 567–614.

Kotler, P. and Levy, S. J. (1971) 'Demarketing, yes, demarketing', *Harvard Business Review*, 49(6), pp. 74–80.

Marcotte, P. and Bourdeau, L. (2012) 'Is the World Heritage label used as a promotional argument for sustainable tourism?' *Journal of Cultural Heritage Management and Sustainable Development*, 2(1), pp. 80–91.

Medway, D., Warnaby, G. and Sheetal, D. (2011) 'Demarketing places: Rationales and strategies', *Journal of Marketing Management*, 27(1/2), pp. 124–42.

O'Shaughnessy, J. and O'Shaughnessy, N.J. (2002) 'Marketing, the consumer society and hedonism', *European Journal of Marketing*, 36(5), pp. 524–47.

Patsiaouras, G. and Fitchett, J. A. (2012) 'The evolution of conspicuous consumption', *Journal of Historical Research in Marketing*, 4(1), pp. 154–76.

Saddik, S. M. A. (1977) 'Demarketing: An optional strategy for the oil-exporting countries', *Management Decision*, 15(2), pp. 278–87.

Sodhi, K. (2011) 'Has marketing come full circle? Demarketing for sustainability', *Business Strategy Series*, 12(4), pp. 177–85.

Wall, A. P. (2007) 'Government "demarketing" as viewed by its target audience', *Marketing Intelligence and Planning*, 25(2), pp. 123–35.

Webster, F. E. Jnr, (1992) 'The changing role of marketing in the corporation', *Journal of Marketing*, 56(4), pp. 1–17.

Wilson, L.-A. and Boyle, E. (2006) 'Interorganisational collaboration at UK World Heritage Sites', *Leadership & Organization Development Journal*, 27(6), pp. 501–23.

7

GENERAL DEMARKETING CASE STUDY

Nadio Granata and David Wyles

From Stalybridge in Lancashire to Batley in West Yorkshire, the Transpennine Real Ale Trail (TRAT) is a unique journey by train through the Pennines calling at 8 locations, each one having at least one real-ale pub within a couple of minutes' walk from the station.

Problem definition – a description of general demarketing

A situation whereby demand is flourishing, new products are being invented and profit margins are being maintained or increased would ordinarily be described as a perfect marketplace. Added to this, the general economy is either in a dip or a double-dip, depending on which politicians you listen to and the government is desperately trying to boost rural economies with grants and beneficial loans to businesses such as farm shops, rural visitor centres and farming communities. Environmentalists are demanding that we reduce our carbon footprint by swapping our preferred mode of transport from the car to the much maligned railway and health experts are actively promoting the benefits associated with leisurely outdoor pursuits such as rambling, hill walking and boating along endless miles of restored navigable waterways. What could be a better solution to our socio-economic malaise than an initiative designed to get us onto the local railways and into the countryside where we can sample culinary and, more specifically, liquid delights in the beauty of God's own county?

The following case study, The Pennine Ale Trail, a tour of track-side pubs, current and hitherto unresolved, offers the reader an insight into the complexities associated within the context of general demarketing. As Kotler and Levy state (1971), 'Marketing Management does not usually take [these] steps in isolation, but rather as part of a demarketing mix'.

What Kotler and Levy do not state in that instance is that demarketing does not necessarily take place within the auspices of one single decision-maker but often requires the strategic coming together of multiple stakeholders for mutual (though to varying degrees) benefits.

The popularity of the Transpennine Real Ale Trail has resulted in a complex and controversial dilemma that impacts on a very wide and needy set of stakeholders. Left to its own devices, the phenomenon is already displaying signs that serious injury and perhaps fatalities could possibly occur as a direct result of the lack of appropriate controls. Controls that, according to the prevailing law of the land and the ever-decreasing resources available within the public sector, are the responsibility of no single organization in particular ... or are they?

Demarketing could be described as 'the strategic use of marketing to reduce or manage demand' and, as can be seen from the response from the customer relations manager at Northern Rail, there are clearly situations where demarketing strategies are required if a company and its brand are not to be irrevocably damaged. So what exactly happened and why would anybody take the time and effort to write a letter of complaint that elicits such a contrite and considered response? What could possibly have happened to upset a resident of one of Yorkshire's most rural villages, famed for its idyllic setting amongst the sheep and rolling hillsides on the border of Yorkshire and Lancashire in northern England?

About the Transpennine Real Ale Trail

The following information is taken from one of the several websites set up to promote The Real Ale Trail.

Welcome

Welcome to the **Ale Trail**, or to give it its full title, **The Transpennine Real Ale Trail.**
The ale trail is a great day out, encompassing the best of great ales, good old fashioned pubs, interesting locations, and good pub grub, all linked together by a single rail line.

Where to find the Ale Trail

From Stalybridge in Lancashire to Batley in West Yorkshire, the ale-trail takes you on a unique journey through the Pennines calling at 8 fantastic locations, each one having a real-ale pub within a couple of minutes' walk from the station. Some even have more than one. To find the ale trail, click on the Map.

Who goes on the Ale Trail?

The simple answer is everyone. The ale trail is a popular destination for Stag and Hen parties, Pub Trips, Birthdays, or any other excuse you can think of for a great day out.
The trail's growing popularity among real ale drinkers led to it being featured in the BBC2 TV series *Drink To Britain* where Oz Clarke and James May visited three of the featured locations.

Planning your day out

The most common place to start is Stalybridge, but there are no right or wrong ways to do the trail, start at either end or in the middle and visit as many or as few of the destinations as you like. Visit half the stations on the way there, and the other half on the way back – it's up to you!

If you want to take your time, there are plenty of places to stay over.

Check out how other people have done the trail, and their advice on our feedback page.

Also featured in this guide are links to local events and festivals should you wish to plan a return trip to any single destination.

The trains

Train tickets can be purchased at Stalybridge, Greenfield, Huddersfield and Dewsbury, or alternatively on the train – but this may cost a little more.

As a rough guide, a ticket from Stalybridge to Batley cost us £10.90 (11/06/2011). This was an 'off peak day return ticket'.

The trains allow approx. 1 hour at each station, but please check with the train operators for exact times.

The complaint

The following is an exact copy of the official complaint made:

> **From:** Peter Grant
> **Sent:** 05 July 2012 12:00
> **To:** customer.relations@northernrail.org
> **Cc:** 'info@passengerfocus.org.uk'
> **Subject:** Rail service 4th July – Marsden-Manchester – 18:43
>
> I am mailing to complain about the train service yesterday evening on the 4th July 2012 departing 18:43 from Marsden to Manchester Victoria.
>
> After calling at Greenfield, the service stopped at Mossley on time at 18:55.
>
> After several minutes the driver alighted from the train and was clearly waiting around for something to happen.
>
> Shortly afterwards an inaudible announcement was made, which none of the passengers could hear due to talking, engine noise and all the doors were open, drowning out any information.
>
> After about 15 minutes it became apparent from some other passengers that an altercation between two groups of passengers at the rear of the train had occurred and the conductor had intervened and been subject to verbal abuse. I understand the conductor refused to continue until one or all of them had left the train, and they refused to leave and continued arguing.
>
> No official information was given at any point during the delay, although we were led to understand that the police had been summonsed.

After about 45 minutes, one of the miscreants who seemed to be quite drunk, came down the platform to the front of the train and began to rant at the train driver, whilst other passengers looked on, and after several minutes the ranting passenger collapsed on the platform, a couple of paramedics had just arrived and began to attend to the man who was continuing to rant and physically lash out at the paramedics, refusing their attention.

Soon afterwards, police officers arrived at this fracas and whilst they were ascertaining the situation, the drunk man had to be manhandled to control his anger and while fighting off the officers, he collapsed again.

The paramedics then managed to get him onto a portable chair and take him away apparently now unconscious.

Shortly after this, the train resumed its journey at around 19:58, over an hour after it stopped at Mossley.

The purpose of my own journey was to attend a concert by the group Roxette at the Manchester Evening News Arena, for which I missed the first part due to this delay, thus further ruining my evening.

I can only imagine the number of other trains and passengers delayed behind our train for over an hour, I am sure at least three Express trains to Piccadilly/Airport/Liverpool would have been delayed due to this moronic incident.

Until very recently, I have seen official flyers at Huddersfield Station advertising the 'Real Ale Trail', encouraging people to use local trains to visit real ale pubs on the line between Batley and Stalybridge, including Dewsbury, Huddersfield, Slaithwaite, Marsden & Greenfield. Over the last couple of years, the late afternoon and early evening local trains are full of bawdy, raucous groups of mostly male passengers who are clearly the worse for drink, having partaken in the aforementioned ale trail. Travelling on these services has become extremely uncomfortable, with drunken louts shouting, singing and using foul language. I know of a number of single women work colleagues who have been harassed by such groups, with no intervention from any of the train staff.

I would be grateful to know the full details of the incident as above and your comments and views on this culture and your staff's apparent inability to deal with it. I would encourage you to travel in particular on the Friday 16:30 service from Huddersfield to Manchester and see this for yourself.

Regards, Peter
Peter Grant
ADDRESS WITHHELD
p.grant@wherever.co.uk

Response received from Northern Rail

From: customer.relations@northernrail.org
Sent: 21 July 2012 11:19
To: Peter Grant
Subject: Northern Rail: Case 263xxx
21 July 2012
Our Reference NR/ 263xxx

Dear Mr Grant

Thank you for your e-mail, which I received recently.

I was sorry to read [sic] for the events of the 4th July when you travelled with us from Marsden to Manchester Victoria. Please accept my sincere apologies for the inconvenience you experienced.

A member of the public became abusive and aggressive and the conductor took the correct step of asking him to leave the train. When he refused the conductor contacted the British Transport Police (BTP) as per standing instructions and they were dispatched to attend the train.

It was some time before the BTP attended and the situation had escalated at that point. I understand that it took some time to resolve the on-going issue and the member of the public was arrested.

I can appreciate that this situation caused you significant delay however the conductor acted in line with all standing instructions to protect both his safety and that of other passengers.

Northern do not endorse the Real Ale Trail and feedback from our train crews has highlighted a problem on this route. We are working with the British Transport Police to try and manager [sic] the issues people who have indulged too much can cause.

Thank you for taking the time to write to Northern. I sincerely hope that your next journey is without such incident.

Yours sincerely
Andrew Talbot
Customer Relations Officer
FREEPOST RLSL-ABEC-BGUU
Northern Customer Relations
First Floor, The Travel Centre
City Railway Station
Leeds
LS1 4DY
Tel. 0123456789
Fax. 0123456789
http://www.northernrail.org

Key points

Stakeholders

The dichotomy between positive and negative aspects of the TRAT has largely focused on the Pennine villages of Marsden and Slaithwaite, which lie in the Colne Valley several miles to the west of Huddersfield.

Until the early 1970s, wealth and employment of these villages focused primarily on large textile mills, which had developed from the early nineteenth century, slowly replacing a long heritage of hand loom weaving along the valley. It was largely in response to the textile and related industries that the turnpike roads, followed by the Huddersfield Narrow Canal and railway connecting Leeds, Manchester and Liverpool, had been created.

From the mid-1980s, the decline of these communities was partially reversed by a number of factors that helped revive their status and confidence. Primary elements of this revival related to the historic environment and outstanding countryside of the valley, predominant of which were:

- Sub-regional (cross Pennine) joint working to promote the South Pennines.
- Development of the Pennine Yorkshire brand, initially by Kirklees and Calderdale councils.
- Promotion relating to the Peak District National Park.
- Restoration of the Huddersfield Narrow Canal and visitor facilities at Tunnel End Marsden, entrance to Britain's highest and longest canal tunnel, carried out by British Waterways and Kirklees Council with the benefit of substantial lottery funding, following determined campaigns for restoring the canal led by the Huddersfield Canal Society.
- Improved promotion of the National Trust's Marsden Moor estate and guided and circular walks promoted by both the N.T. and Kirklees.
- Improved publicity, including coverage, previously very limited, in national publications and media and exposure as a result of popular television programmes such as *Last of the Summer Wine* and *Where The Heart Is*.
- Increase in visitor accommodation in and around the area.
- Regeneration programmes, such as the improvement of shop fronts, hard landscaping in the village centres and along the canal corridor, and refurbishment of Marsden Mechanics Institute.
- The development and success of events such as canal festivals, National Trust plant sales and Marsden Jazz Festival, the latter attracting a UK-wide audience.

Revival over the following 25 years included investment in shops, restaurants, galleries and pubs, the TRAP venue and the Riverside pub being part of this resurgence.

Never a place to throw itself open to change,[1] with a general wariness of visitors and 'comer-inners', the community gradually adapted and, along with a growing number of commuter residents (Marsden lying roughly equidistant from Leeds and Manchester) and community activists, the visitor product became integrated into the fabric and life of the villages.

Ownership

The current problem is that the demarketing-related activities have largely focused on co-ordination by police, rail operators, publicans and community representatives to reduce anti-social behaviour, not on the root cause of TRAT's accelerating popularity. There has been little consideration of selective demarketing with the aim of retaining socially responsible consumers and their associated levels of spend, while reducing the impact of those causing much of the anti-social behaviour within the village communities.

Furthermore, while effective management involving public sector stakeholders remains a key element in helping improve and monitor the behaviour of groups arriving in Marsden and Slaithwaite, this collaboration has no impact in curbing demand from 'unwanted' consumers. One website[2] has responded to public sector concerns by including a message from Northern Rail's Response Team, British Transport Police and Trans-Pennine Express who are 'keen to deliver a firm but fair message to remind regular passengers and Real Ale Trail patrons to travel safely and sensibly'.

Efforts of this kind could be strengthened by indications that positive action by the police to deter anti-social behaviour will be taken – the zero tolerance approach similar to that implemented in certain Spanish and Greek resorts renowned for their 'loutish' behaviour. In terms of selective demarketing, this tactic may backfire. Such actions could deter responsible visitors and tourists by reinforcing the perception that the villages are not pleasant places in which to spend time. An analogy would be Malia in Crete where public disorder may have been reduced by positive action by law-enforcement agencies but the perception of the resort as a young people's party/nightclubbing town remains, and its attractiveness to other social groups, who wish to discover more authentic and scenic options on the island, is limited.

Uniqueness

A further problem in demarketing the TRAT is its uniqueness as a product. TRAT's popularity has been driven more by the consumer than by the producer. TRAT's product is managed by a somewhat diverse range of public house operators, from owner-managers to tenants, from micro-breweries to larger operators. This popularity is largely associated with the power of social media – websites, blogs, Facebook, Twitter and customer reviews on sites such as Trip Advisor. Customer power in reducing demand has been recently well illustrated by the boycott by consumers of Starbucks, following coverage of the company's failure to pay UK tax. TRAT consumers have, to a large extent, dictated demand and, given the extent to which the message is being transmitted through social media, it is difficult to relate this dynamic to assessing the continuing demand for the TRAT product. A number of bloggers have expressed concern over the growing problems associated with the trail, one site commenting, 'I've removed the TransPennine pub crawl details. ... If you're an ale drinker and know the pubs then they're all still well worth visiting, but avoid Saturdays.'[3]

Segmentation

Demarketing in this instance needs to be focused on decreasing the number of consumers who are perceived to have devalued the original concept and its values and created negative perceptions within the villages, while retaining a valuable source of income for the pubs involved and extending this value to the wider business community. Whilst Marsden and Slaithwaite are not in the position that certain Mediterranean resorts have had to face in needing to re-invent themselves, there is a case for synchromarketing the product with the wider visitor appeal of the Colne Valley area. The promotion of real ale pubs in the villages should be matched to visitor profiles, particularly the 7 per cent of visitors who stay overnight and spend proportionally larger sums. There are also the considerable benefits of the visiting friends and relatives (VFR) market to the villages. Marsden and Slaithwaite are increasingly attracting people from the South Pennine area who make key decisions when determining where to take guests. Decisions can be influenced by perceptions but, where perceptions are positive the opportunity for return visits is high. Local and district collaboration to ensure these markets are developed is essential and should evolve in parallel with measures to limit the awareness of TRAT to 'unwanted' groups. Pubs must collaborate in such marketing efforts but need a level of confidence in the latent potential of these developing markets before they can realistically be expected to withdraw their support for TRAT promotion.

Destination marketing – in practice

Positive impacts

The initial popularity of the TRAT should be considered as complementary, reflecting the development of a quality product, attracting both day and over-night visitors, defined by a broad interest in heritage, landscape, cultural events, outdoor pursuits, attractive shopping, eating and drinking facilities. In fact, destination marketers such as Albrecht would hail such progress as a resounding success. He describes destination marketing as:

> a proactive, strategic, visitor-centered approach to the economic and cultural development of a location, which balances and integrates the interests of visitors, service providers, and the community.
>
> *(Dr Karl Albrecht, and endorsed by the Destination Marketing Association International, in the report of the 2008 DMAI Futures Study, conducted for DMAI by Karl Albrecht International)*

Evidence suggests the TRAT improved both primary and secondary spend, particularly given the ease of access from railway stations to village facilities.

From comments by TRAT visitors on blogs and web forums, it is clear the overall experience and perception of the villages was positive, particularly noting the following:

- indication of multiple visits;
- positive reaction to the attractive countryside and townscape;
- indication that some wish to return for a longer stay;
- a significant number of visitors from outside the Yorkshire/Lancashire regions, some of whom clearly required overnight accommodation;
- positive reaction to the quality of locations and the welcome given.

A further benefit relates to the issue of sustainability. The TRAT is attracting large numbers of visitors to the villages by public transport, i.e. by train.

Negative impacts

The increase of car-borne visitors to rural destinations such as Marsden and Slaithwaite could have a detrimental impact on their historic and physical settings and issues of safety could become problematic at key dates such as Bank Holidays, weekends and festival periods. The issue of mid-week parking on streets around Marsden Station (used by those commuting to towns along the Trans-pennine rail corridor) has already been identified as an additional problem. The common concern that increasing numbers of car-borne visitors may destroy the very character that makes such villages special cannot, in this instance, be levelled at those on the TRAT.

Areas of concern voiced by those for whom the TRAT was a means of sampling a selection of well-thought-of beers from predominantly regional micro-breweries, heavily promoted by CAMRA, appear to be directed towards groups of people who are not specifically interested in real ale. The common view is that the trail 'has been "hijacked" by stag, hen, office and birthday parties getting tanked up on cheap lager, wine and alcopops.'[4]

These groups, comprising predominantly males, have been the cause for the majority of concerns raised by British Transport Police (BTP), rail operators and residents. The complaints primarily relate to anti-social behaviour, for which the epicentres appear to be Marsden and Slaithwaite. There are a number of reasons why these villages have become the focus of concern:

- Marsden and Slaithwaite are midway along the trail, so many TRAT visitors will have already consumed a high level of alcohol, particularly if arriving from Huddersfield, where there are clearly a number of popular pubs close to the station.
- The majority of TRAT visitors arrive in daylight hours, making their behaviour more visible.
- Most of the stag and hen party groups arrive on Saturdays when a higher pro-portion of local residents are also present.
- Such groups are seen by a wide range of age groups and families for which some activities are particularly offensive.

- The party goers tend to circulate within relatively restricted areas, within villages with relatively small populations, resulting in high visibility and a concentration of negative impacts.

Such impacts appear not so prevalent in larger centres such as Huddersfield, where a number of the above issues are dissipated as a result of its size, range of venues, predominance of the evening economy, limited population living within the centre and a relative separation of user groups within the central business area.

The issue of policing is also relevant. Huddersfield not only has more coverage by officers, PCSOs and council-employed rangers but also has comprehensive CCTV and retail radio networks. Increased policing is limited by issues of funding and priorities, with a BTP officer stating, 'on Saturdays our resources are taken up by the football matches.'[5] It may also be the case that it is more difficult to distinguish those who regularly visit town centre pubs and clubs from TRAT visitors. Although a number of real ale trails now feature on the web, the most common location for 'pub crawls' is town centres, Dublin (Temple Bar), Edinburgh and York being prime examples.

The high visibility of those associated with anti-social behaviour during daylight hours may also mask the fact that similar occurrences are prevalent during evening and night-time periods and generally caused by local residents. As one Slaithwaite resident commented, 'There's more that happens in Slawit (local pronunciation) after 9 o'clock at night than you can ever imagine on the ale trail.'[6]

Anti-social behaviour by certain TRAT visitors may also result in negative perceptions of these relatively sedate villages by day visitors and tourists. The nascent tourism industry in the area has been fuelled by those seeking attractive countryside, coupled with attractive centres with good-quality facilities. Short breaks, encouraging responsible and environmentally aware couples and families, do not sit comfortably alongside groups of rowdy party goers. A paradigm would be to compare those who holiday in Tuscany with those who prefer Malia or Magaluf. The danger is compounded by travel websites, such as Trip Advisor, and other social networks, in which interactive travel forums, reviews and opinions can have a dramatic impact on the perception of businesses and tourist locations.

For example, a reviewer on 9 October 2012 stated, 'The behaviour of some is awful – one idiot jumping on the line in Marsden because his mate threw something on the line then a bit later he decided to jump down again …'. Perhaps such behaviour would have influenced the reviewer who wrote on 17 October:

> the drive to Marsden was scenic and a delight. Standedge tunnel was amazing, the boat ride into the tunnel thrilled the younger members of our family (age range of family group 4yrs to 70years). A ten-minute walk beside the canal brought us to Marsden station and into the small but interesting town of Marsden. A very successful day out for a very mixed age group.

Further evidence of negative feelings towards the TRAT were featured in a BBC2 documentary as recently as 19 February 2013. The programme entitled

The Railway – Keeping Britain on Track featured Huddersfield train driver Jason Halstead, who said,

> I remember when it was just real ale fans. You barely noticed them. Now its stag dos and hen dos. It's a good thing in principle, bringing people and money to Colne Valley, but it's got a bit beyond control. There are limited resources, especially when it's the football season. Every week I have people urinating on my cab door and urinating off the platforms.

The profile of visitors to Kirklees indicates the tourism product appeals to affluent people within the socio-economic groups of A, B and C1. They enjoy outdoor activities, take three or more breaks a year, are over 45 with no or grown-up children, and live within a four-hour drive-time.[7] Analysis of visitors to Holmfirth and Marsden (including day visitors who account for 93 per cent of all trips) highlighted a lower age range of between 35 and 44 years old, approximately 50 per cent having young children with them. More than 65 per cent were repeat visitors. The Yorkshire Visitor Survey 2010 emphasizes the attraction of the area for these visitors. The destination is seen as 'quirky', and visitors love to experience the local and unique aspects of the area. Visitors enjoy variety, but strolling around to enjoy the local ambience, shopping for local produce – both artistic and food – and eating/drinking out were the most popular. Short walks featured highly too. It is obvious that any anti-social behaviour that becomes 'recorded' as a perception and reflection of the place visited could have substantial consequences on the number of visitors and their related level of spend.

The above case study and subsequent comments clearly highlight the complexities involved when addressing the various needs of the stakeholders. Consideration must be given to the motivation, perception and attitudes of each of the stakeholder groups if the issues are to be resolved successfully. The tensions between those that seek to profit from the increasingly popular attraction must be balanced against the needs of those who are clearly and frequently inconvenienced by the influx of the revellers.

The following section seeks to utilize some of the marketers' toolkit to analyse the complex situation and throw up some insightful solutions to the problem.

Applied marketing theory

Stakeholder analysis

Grimble and Chan (1995, pp 113–24) describe stakeholder analysis as '[a]n approach for understanding a system by identifying the key actors or stakeholders in the system, and assessing their respective interest in that system'. Ramirez (1999) rightly points out in his article 'Shareholder analysis and Conflict Management' that 'It cannot be expected to solve all problems or guarantee representation'. Indeed, he goes on to say that it is referred to as a 'range of tools for the identification and description of stakeholders on the basis of their attributes, interrelationships, and interests related to a given issue or resource'.

Conducting a stakeholder analysis would appear to be a relatively straight-forward process. However, when conducted thoroughly, certain attributes prevail to varying degrees and must be addressed accordingly. These include, but are not exclusive to:

- the relative power and interest of each stakeholder (Freeman 1984);
- the importance and influence they have (Grimble and Wellard 1996);
- the different 'hats' that they wear (Ramirez 1999);
- the networks and coalitions to which they belong (Freeman and Gilbert 1987);
- the degree to which their networks are connected.

The following six steps are adopted from Grimble *et al.* (1995):

1. identify the main purpose of the analysis;
2. develop an understanding of the system and decision-makers in the system;
3. identify principal stakeholders;
4. investigate stakeholder interests, characteristics and circumstances;
5. identify patterns and contexts of interaction between stakeholders;
6. define options for management.

The following matrix is another tool that can be used as a simple mapping exercise in identifying and positioning the different stakeholders and their influence on a given situation and has been applied to the TRAT situation:

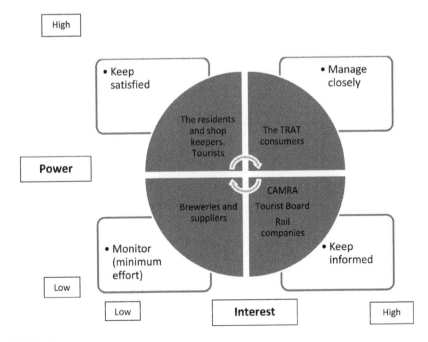

FIGURE 7.1 Taxonomy of stakeholders

The 9 Ps (Alastair Baxter)

As any qualified marketer will testify, nothing in the world of marketing makes any sense unless it starts with the letter 'P'! McCarthy's Marketing Mix classification (1960), known commonly as 'The Four Ps', has been at the root of all marketing planning ever since and is considered to be a fundamental starting point when addressing any product offering. These include:

- product;
- price;
- place;
- promotion.

Expanded to include the 7 Ps by Booms and Bitner (1981) to address the more complex needs of a service offering:

- people;
- processes;
- physical evidence,

and further expanded upon by Alistair Baxter in 1993 to further address the issues of:

- protection;
- persuasion.

Using the 9 Ps as a simple means of classifying each of the characteristics of the whole TRAT experience, Table 7.1 provides a format for quick reference:

TABLE 7.1 Mapping the TRAT experience against the 9P model

	Definition applied to the case study	Stakeholders	Issues
Product	The Transpennine Ale Trail	Service providers Residents Commuters Authorities	Ownership: if nobody 'owns' the product then who is responsible for it? What is the 'product' – who dictates?
Price	The relative costs involved in providing the service and the distribution of the profits and/or losses	Tourists Service providers Rate payers	The price the tourist pays for the products they consume is only one aspect of the whole economic impact
Place	The place at which the product is consumed.	The train stations (7) The trains The listed pubs Other venues	The destination is varied, diverse and dispersed, which causes a trail of consequences

TABLE 7.1 (continued)

	Definition applied to the case study	Stakeholders	Issues
Promotion	Any communications directly or indirectly associated with the experience.	CAMRA All media Transport partners Online: blogs; Facebook; Twitter and Trip Advisor	Managing the messages that are associated with all aspects of the experience is out of the control of any one stakeholder
People	All those involved in the consumption of the entire experience	Staff Tourists Residents Commuters Shoppers Security	The wants and needs of the widely dispersed stakeholder groups are proving to lead to conflict and misery
Physical Evidence	The physical appearance of all the touch points	Pubs Transport providers Councils Residents	The very nature of the environment is not conducive to large, unsophisticated crowds
Processes	The systems required to deliver the experience	Ticketing Food and drink dispensing Transport	The service quality experienced by those who get caught in the crowd is significantly diminished and unpredictable
Persuasion	The ability to change somebody's mind	TBD	Solutions will require highly skilled and influential interventions, often hampered by the influence of alcohol
Protection	The prevention of the loss of intellectual property and reputation	CAMRA	Unmeasurable reputational costs could be incurred by many unprotected stakeholders

Experiential marketing

Any solution to a problem must be addressed in context and the marketer is no exception to this rule. In coming to a solution or a set of solutions, the marketer must use his knowledge and skills to identify the issues and, more importantly in the long run, the cause of the issues. A good starting point, therefore, is to establish which field of marketing is the most appropriate in this instance and what are the prevailing characteristics that best define that particular field. By getting to an early diagnosis, the marketer should (in theory anyway) be able to identify the appropriate prognosis and describe the relevant solutions before the issues get out of hand; much like the patient–doctor scenario where a GP might be the first point of contact but a more specialist consultant and perhaps surgeon is required to achieve the recovery.

The TRAT case study provides us with an insight into the complexities of experiential marketing, defined expertly by Schmitt (1999) where he lists five different types of experiences, or 'strategic experiential modules (SEMs) " ... that marketers can create for customers. ... ".' He goes on to list these 'sensory experiences' (SENSE) as:

- affective experiences (feel);
- creative cognitive experiences (think);
- physical experiences, behaviours and lifestyles (act);
- social-identity experiences that result from relating to a reference group or culture (relate);
- experience providers (ExPros), i.e. communications, visual and verbal identity, product presence, electronic media, etc.

The model in Figure 7.2 is used by Schmitt to illustrate the characteristics of experiential marketing and clearly resonates with the issues discussed within our case study.

Schmitt's conclusion that experiential marketing is '[d]istinct in four ways: focusing on consumer experiences, treating consumption as a holistic experience, recognizing both rational and emotional drivers of consumption, using eclectic methodologies' provides us with a solid base from which we can analyse the characteristics of the TRAT experience and, certainly from a 'promotional point of view', is very useful to the marketer when attempting to create a marketing strategy for growth, but is not as useful when looking for demarketing solutions as it relates very little to the wider group of stakeholders and their 'demarketing' needs.

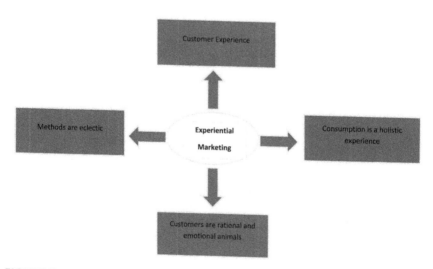

FIGURE 7.2 Experiential marketing

Product Life Cycle

Another tool commonly used by the marketer is the Product Life Cycle (PLC). The theory suggests that any product or service will pass through a series of stages (introduction, growth, maturity, decline) during its lifetime and the marketer's understanding of where the product sits in its life cycle is a key determinant as to what marketing strategies should be employed to best profit from its relative position.

This is relevant to the TRAT in so far as a risk assessment exercise would clearly identify the risks associated with any of the lead stakeholders taking any action whatsoever and, conversely, taking no action might result in the current problems escalating out of control. Understanding where the popularity curve is heading will help the marketer to strategize – if the popularity has indeed peaked, then logic suggests that natural forces of supply and demand will prevail and little or nothing needs to be done in the way of 'demarketing' as the popularity of the TRAT will wain naturally and any 'enforcement' actions will be averted. Indeed, the example of the World Heritage Sites cited by Marcotte and Bourdeau (2012: 80) suggests that the very act of containment can perversely lead to raising the issues and therefore raising popularity!

If, on the other hand, research suggests that the popularity curve is about to get steeper and is likely to go on for some considerable time, then it would be advisable that stringent measures are put in place as soon as possible to limit the damage being caused to a wide-reaching stakeholder group.

Figure 7.3 demonstrates how the PLC can be used to identify strategic marketing plans dependent on the nature of their life cycle.

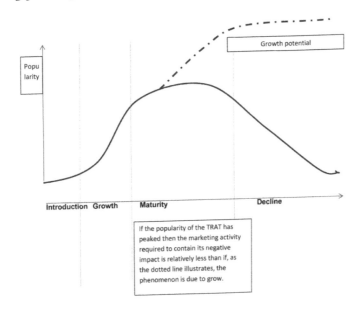

FIGURE 7.3 The Product Life Cycle

Market research should be employed to explore the life cycle of other (similar) Ale Trails with a view to determining what the typical life expectancy is and what are the signs, if any, to changes in the life cycle. Given the unique qualities of the TRAT, it would be dangerous to put too much reliance on this comparison, so some hypothesis testing would be useful in gaining a further understanding of the life cycle before any decisions are made.

Conclusions

General demarketing is a term rarely discussed in the business or academic arenas but is increasingly coming to light in the public sector where resources are being stretched and demands are continuing to rise. Social mobility, aspirational consumers, empowered interest groups and a return to traditional values are all on a collision course as modern lifestyles break down social and cultural barriers with little regard or recourse for those that get in the way.

The TRAT case study clearly demonstrates the dangers of allowing a situation, no matter how well meaning in its origins, to escalate out of control. The lack of 'ownership' means that any attempts at selective demarketing or even synchronized demarketing renders any efforts futile in the face of mob rule fuelled by sophisticated use of social media beyond the auspices of any governing bodies or would-be vigilantes. Perversely, negative publicity has only added to the appeal to a section of the community that is least welcome by those who have the greatest claim to ownership.

The head of crime management at Northern Rail said, 'I think it's about as big as it will get. Maybe this will be the novelty year but it's not going to go down and we have to be prepared for it'.

Speculation that, even if it has peaked, it is unlikely to decline in popularity indicates a need to implement actions of a diverse nature, including improved enforcement/visitor management within the villages; improved collaboration in synchromarketing the TRAT with wider area attractions; and selective demarketing by the pubs involved. Management and mitigation of risk and the evolution of new opportunities may only impact on the need to reduce the number of 'unwanted' visitors to a small extent.

Are there other means, therefore, of curtailing demand or transferring risk? Certainly, the number of real ale trails being promoted across the country is expanding. By increasing consumer choice, demand for the TRAT may decline. There has also been some development of town centre-based real ale trails. As mentioned earlier, town centres such as Huddersfield seem able to absorb and manage drinking parties more effectively than the villages. Generally, the TRAT and associated pubs in Huddersfield and Dewsbury have welcomed and benefited from TRAT-related publicity and promotion and this has recently been further developed though the 'Discover Huddersfield Real Ale Trail' featuring pubs within the town centre and produced by the town centre business partnership and other organizations. The intention is to make this trail available on the existing 'Place to Make It' website and include a Discover

Huddersfield web portal and mobile app. This will enable residents and visitors in the town centre to use the website (on their smartphones) in order to see real ale trail details, which can be posted to friends and contacts through a variety of social media. This initiative will create a popular alternative to the TRAT, and support its selective demarketing.

There are examples within the tourism industry where a policy of moving upmarket has involved both changing perceptions and increasing prices, whether through the improvement of accommodation facilities or increasing the price of food and drink. It is unlikely that selective price increases, for example by increasing the cost of lager and alcopops, would be possible and indeed such a policy within the Marsden and Slaithwaite TRAT pubs may deter core business on weekdays when TRAT visitors comprise a minority. Should the marketing of the valley area succeed in increasing visitor numbers beyond weekend periods and extending the unique appeal of its attractions, a case could be made for TRAT pubs to increase prices subject to complementary improvements in the product and positive customer reviews resulting from these changes. The TRAT again differs from other products in that demarketing should not, in the current climate, prevent the individual pubs from generating demand and their activities to meet customer demand are essential to their survival.

But the TRAT is unlike other demarketing cases. The producers, i.e. the pubs, are keen to meet increasing demand, but they are diverse and joined-up marketing is limited. Control of the product in terms of popularity has much to do with the consumer who has demonstrated a greater capacity to promote the trail.

The need for demarketing is a response to anti-social behaviour created by a certain sector of TRAT consumers and its effect, through increasingly negative perceptions, on an emerging, and potentially lucrative, visitor market to the villages.

Selective demarketing may be possible but may be limited while the demand for the product is arguably growing through coverage on social media networks.

Actions to deal with issues to deter those groups who are perceived to be responsible for creating the majority of the problems include improved management by community stakeholders and selective demarketing by reducing coverage of the village pubs on key web pages, while synchromarketing the real ale pubs in Marsden and Slaithwaite with other attractions. Diversifying the appeal to attract a greater number of overnight stays and return visits will help spread the economic benefits across the wider business community.

Reduction of market share as a result of new trails being produced and publicized and the development of specific trails within the TRAT towns, particularly Huddersfield and Dewsbury, could also offer some respite. This might, on the other hand, backfire, as the whole Ale Trail industry becomes expanded and dispersed, adding additional strain to the already over-stretched providers of public safety.

The need to ensure actions to limit the amount of undesirable visitors must not endanger the opportunity to market the villages to a wider audience whose decision on whether or not to visit the area will be influenced by acquired perceptions. This potential to seek new markets in order to sustain demand and increase profits, while retaining the core benefits of the TRAT offer, would, in an ideal world, be a perfect solution but general demarketing is likely to be the safest and therefore most appropriate course of action. Additionally, the lack of ownership and therefore control, with different stakeholders each having different agendas, calls for a general demarketing effort if the issues are to be resolved favourably in the long term.

Questions and exercises

1. Create a PESTEL analysis and discuss the usefulness of the PESTEL in the given circumstances.
2. a. Identify two key stakeholders and conduct a SWOT analysis from each perspective.
   b. Discuss the variances between the two analyses.
3. Create a poster to advertise the TRAT responsibly on behalf of one of the stakeholders.
4. Describe another general demarketing case study that contains a similar set of issues for the marketer to resolve.

Notes

1 Marsden had been the centre of the Luddite uprisings in the early nineteenth century.
2 www.ale-trail.co.uk
3 Comment on www.variousstuff.co.uk
4 *Huddersfield Daily Examiner*, 22 August 2012.
5 *Huddersfield Daily Examiner*, 8 August 2012.
6 Comment to *Huddersfield Daily Examiner* following article on 28 August 2012.
7 Kirklees *Profile report* 2008, compiled by the Yorkshire Tourist Board.

References

Baxter, A. (1993). 9P marketing toolkit by Heinemann Publishing, Oxford. *The Marketing Toolkit.*
Booms, Bernard H. and Mary Jo Bitner (1981). 'Marketing strategies and organization structures for service firms.' *Marketing of services*, 47–51.
Freeman, R. Edward (1984). *Strategic Management: A stakeholder approach.* Boston: Pitman.
Freeman, R. and Gilbert, D., Jr (1987). 'Managing stakeholder relations'. In Prakash, S. and Falbe, C., ed., *Business and society: Dimensions of conflict and cooperation.* Lexington Books, Toronto, Canada. pp. 397–422.
Grimble, R. and Chan, M. K. (1995). 'Stakeholder analysis for natural resource management in developing countries.' *Natural Resources Forum*, 19(2), 113–24.
Grimble, R. and Wellard, K. (1996). *Stakeholder Methodologies in Natural Resource Management: A review of principles, contexts, experiences and opportunities.* Paper presented at the ODA NRSP Socioeconomic Methodologies Workshop, 29–30 April, 1996, London, UK.
Karl Albrecht International (2008). *The Future of Destination Marketing.* Washington: Destination Marketing Association International.
Kotler, P. and Levy, S.J. (1971). 'Demarketing, yes, demarketing.' *Harvard Business Review*, 49(6), pp.74–80

Marcotte, P. and Bourdeau L. (2012). 'Is the World Heritage label used as a promotional argument for sustainable tourism?' *Journal of Cultural Heritage Management and Sustainable Development*, 2.1, 80–91.

McCarthy, E.J. (1960). *Basic Marketing and Basic Marketing. A Managerial Approach.* Homewood, Ill.

Ramirez, R. (1999). 'Stakeholder analysis and conflict management.' *Cultivating Peace: Conflict and collaboration in natural resource management*, 101, 126.

Schmitt, B. (1999). 'Experiential marketing.' *Journal of marketing management* 15, 1–3, 53–67.

Welcome to Yorkshire (2011). *Yorkshire Regional Visitor Survey 2010/11* (York: Welcome to Yorkshire).

Websites

www.realaletrail.net

(Fairly basic site.)

Mention of feature on BBC's *Oz and James Drink to Britain* in 2009.

Trail features pubs close to stations at 8 towns and villages in Yorkshire and Lancashire between Batley and Stalybridge – offer over 30 hand pulled beers.

Description of each pub, opening times, beers, food, etc.

www.ale-trail.co.uk

More detailed site including video of BBC2 feature (YouTube), advice on rail tickets, also phone app with train times, direction to pubs and local information. Link to Facebook and Twitter.

Also includes 'Safety First' message from rail operators and British Transport Police asking for those on the trail to act responsibly.

Mention on other websites

www.pubsgalore.co.uk

Includes mention of other real ale pubs along trail, e.g. Huddersfield (where King's Head is Real Ale Trail pub) includes Head of Steam, the Sportsman, the Grove, Rat and Ratchet. Detailed reviews and comments: e.g. from people from outside region including London, West Midlands, Shropshire, etc.

'I was quite taken with Marsden – a couple of weeks later went for a walk around the adjacent reservoir and the scenery was lovely'.

'There are more stations, pubs and route plans (especially if time to visit for a longer period)'.

Advice on rail ticket prices, etc.

www.on:yorkshiremagazine.co.uk

'The Real Ale Trail' 07/2011

www.walkinyorkshire.com

'A blog by a Frenchman walking in Yorkshire'.

www.yorkshire.com

Welcome to Yorkshire – the destination agency for the Yorkshire region. Produces 'Delicious Ale Trail' featuring pubs across region, including some TRAT and associated pubs with mention of trail in their copy, e.g. The Sportsman 'winner of CAMRA National

Heritage Award 2011' and West Riding Refreshment Rooms 'Transpennine Ale Trail pub as featured in BBC2's Oz and James Drink to Britain'.

www.leedsguide.co.uk

Article on trail.

www.imissedthetrain.com

Site for West Riding Refreshment Rooms, Dewsbury (+ sister pub, The Sportsman in Huddersfield). Link for downloading TRAT flyer + Facebook page.

Trip Advisor (www.tripadvisor.co.uk)

8 reviews: Rated No. 1 on 1 attraction in Stalybridge (!)

Most reviews mention other real ale pubs in towns/villages, e.g. 'the town of Huddersfield has to be one of the best boozing towns anywhere in the UK with half a dozen belting watering holes within 400yds of the station and several others not much further away'.

Mention on wide variety of other websites/forums, e.g. www.fellrunner.org, www.volks-zone.com, www.railforums.co.uk, www.tntmagazine.com (magazine aimed at Australian, NZ and South African expats).

www.variousstuff.co.uk

Negative review and comment: 'I've removed the Transpennine pub crawl details'.

'. ... If you're an ale drinker and know the pubs then they're all still well worth visiting, but avoid Saturdays. ... If you are a stag/hen party or other group who just want to get wrecked and behave like. ... holes I suggest you grow up and f ... off elsewhere'.

BBC News (Leeds and West Yorkshire) 15 Sept 2011: 'West Yorkshire breweries top Camra's UK league table'. 'West Yorkshire has more breweries producing more types of beer than any other county in the UK.'

Negative press commentary

BBC News 7 December 2011

'Rowdy drinkers following a real ale trail across the Pennines could be banned from the rail network, British Transport Police has warned'.

'Drunk and disorderly' passengers.

Growing number of incidents ... 'beer glasses are being carried on the trains, people are urinating on platforms, the doors on trains are being held open, disrupting services and trains themselves are being damaged'.

'Large groups of men running across the tracks and overcrowding platforms, compromising the safety of others'.

Northern Rail Press Release 18 July 2012

Northern Rail's Response Team, British Transport Police and Trans-Pennine Express 'keen to deliver a firm but fair message to remind regular passengers and Real Ale Trail patrons to travel safely and sensibly'.

Huddersfield Daily Examiner 8 August 2012

'Yesterday police, transport bosses, councillors, pub owners, villagers and local business owners met at Marsden Mechanics Hall to discuss the problems and solutions'.

The co-director of Ossett Brewery, which owns the Riverhead pub, Marsden, said 'It's been hijacked. On Saturday it's not the real ale trail'.

Head of crime management at Northern Rail said 'I think it's about as big as it will get. Maybe this will be the novelty year but it's not going to go down and we have to be prepared for it'.

Solutions: more police. BTP officer said 'on Saturday our resources taken up by the football matches'.

Other solutions suggested included volunteer marshalls, signs warning people to respect the villages and temporary street urinals.

Article ends by mentioning cost of rail ticket from Stalybridge to Batley.

Comments following Examiner article

'If people didn't visit, these pubs and other businesses would possibly be struggling in the current climate'.

'Perhaps the pubs en route should stop selling lager, alcopops and wine'.

'The pubs themselves are partly to blame as they shouldn't be selling to those who are already drunk'.

Couple of mentions of poor toilet facilities.

'Businesses have a different agenda than us residents'.

'I don't think it is right for the platform, the car park and surrounding houses to be used as an "extension" of the pubs'.

'A big thank you to The Commercial in Slaithwaite who provided temporary toilets for the Bank Holiday weekend at Slaithwaite station'.

BBC News Leeds and West Yorkshire 21 August 2012

Film footage of groups on the trail in Marsden (images of men jumping across canal lock, etc). Comments that customers are staying away from other businesses.

Huddersfield Daily Examiner 22 August 2012

Headline: 'Ale trail lager louts turn Marsden and Slaithwaite into no-go zones for villagers'.

'Now there are fears the real ale route, which includes pubs in Huddersfield and Dewsbury, has become the victim of its own success. ... '.

'The trail, originally designed to promote real ale pubs, has been "hijacked" by stag, hen, office and birthday parties getting tanked up on cheap lager, wine and alcopops'.

'Marsden and Slaithwaite have become epicentres of drunken anti-social behaviour'.

Huddersfield Daily Examiner 28 August 2012

Headline: 'All aboard the Ale Trail: Our reporter meets drinkers and a landlord to talk about recent criticism of the boozy day out'.

'A year ago, only a handful of villagers would have filed off the train. Today (Saturday) about 100 people, mostly men, spill out of the train'.

'The mood as revellers swarm onto the platform at Marsden is a little boisterous but essentially jovial'.

'The trail has brought a huge amount of business to what were primarily local pubs'.

'(A) Slaithwaite resident says "I think it's phenomenal. The trail has decent beer and it used to be rubbish".

'His son added "It's for six hours on one day of the week and on one street. 99 per cent of the people are behaving and it's money for the village'".

Also comment, 'I'm from Weymouth and we used to get taken over by tourists and you resented them. I can see why people might be a bit concerned'.

The reporter concludes, 'Today it seemed fairly civilised, if a little noisy. Had I been on another, probably busier Saturday I may have formed a different opinion'.

Comments following article

The landlady from the Shoulder of Mutton, Slaithwaite, says the trail has helped put the Pennine village on the map and, though she condemned reports of passengers urinating in public, she called on rail companies profiting from the trail to provide better platform facilities.

'There's more that happens in Slawit after 9 o'clock at night than you can ever imagine on the ale trail'.

www.westyorkshirepolice.uk

The Valley News – Ale Trail Update

> 'We have held a number of impact days where numerous officers from across the multi agencies have attended to deter anti-social behaviour. ... we continue to work with partners to improve the situation for local residents'.

8

SELECTIVE DEMARKETING

A value destruction approach

Jillian Dawes Farquhar

In this chapter, the investigation into demarketing concentrates on selective demarketing. Selective demarketing has been described as company action to reduce demand from certain classes of consumer. In spite of the strategic importance to firms of selective demarketing, the subject has attracted scant research and any research is fragmented. In this chapter, the various streams of literature that relate to selective demarketing are reviewed within the contexts of business-to-consumer, business-to-business, profit and not-for-profit. The purpose of this chapter is to develop a strategic framework for selective demarketing, drawing on service and service dominant (SD) logic research. Instead of focusing on its themes of co-creation and value-in-use, the framework integrates the idea of value destruction as the fulcrum of selective demarketing.

Introduction

The initial focus of marketing was on the attraction of customers and measuring success in market share and customer volume. More recent emphasis has been on retaining customers with a longer-term perspective of customer lifetime value (Venkatesan and Kumar, 2004), that is, customers who generate a return on any investment that the firm has made in them. Customers in a similar vein may feel that their custom with a firm is valued with this value being expressed through the granting of platinum credit cards, sitting at the captain's table on a cruise or being upgraded to business class from economy on a flight. Customers feel also in competitive markets that they may have power in any relationship that they have with a firm and that whether they stay or go is entirely their decision. It may come as something of a surprise to learn that, just as there are customers whom a firm may wish to retain, there are also customers whom a firm may wish to lose. Whilst there may be a number of reasons proffered by firms for not wishing to serve particular customers, the decision often rests on the costs of serving the customer exceeding the revenue that is generated.

The lack of cohesive research may be partly attributable to some variation in terminology that can be applied to selective demarketing, for example, abandonment, dumping, deselecting and terminating a relationship. There is accordingly a lack of consensus on how selective demarketing may be achieved particularly working within the contemporary business and marketing contexts of corporate social responsibility and stakeholder strategies. To provide a cohesive and robust framework, the chapter draws on service and service dominant literature, which focuses on the generation or creation of value for customers, as well as strategic marketing and consumer theory. The contention of this chapter is that value destruction offers a strategic approach to selective demarketing built around the concept of resource integration and so has relevance to profit-making or not-for-profit, business-to-consumer and business-to-business firms of all sizes.

This chapter opens with a discussion of selective demarketing and the literatures that contribute to a clarification and extension of this concept. The following section addresses value generation through service and service dominant (SD) logic with particular emphasis on operant resources. The next section develops a framework for selective demarketing where value destruction forms the basis a strategic approach. The chapter concludes with managerial implications and directions for future research.

Selective demarketing

The purpose of demarketing is to reduce demand by effecting a change in customer behaviour, that is, customers reduce or cease their patronage of the services of a particular firm. A firm will seek to demarket in a number of situations, for example when demand for its services/products exceeds its ability to supply, when the popularity of a particular event or attraction results in the number of visitors impacting on other visitors' appreciation of the experience or when a change in strategic direction occurs. Selective demarketing has been described as company action to reduce demand from certain classes of consumer who are referred to as 'undesirables' (Kotler and Levy, 1971). The following extract provides a particularly acute example of an institution that is struggling to accommodate the volume and diversity of visitors that it attracts.

No room in the chapel

The Sistine Chapel in the Vatican is suffering from a surfeit of visitors with over 5 million per annum and 20,000 per day queuing for entry. The sheer number of visitors is causing damage to the treasures that are housed in the chapel such as Michelangelo's frescoes. Visitors traipse sweat, dust, skin flakes and hair into the chapel. In future, all visitors will be 'dusted, cleaned and chilled'. The entrance leading to the chapel will be covered with 100 metres of carpet to clean shoes, suction vents will suck dust from clothes and temperatures will be lowered to reduce the heat and humidity of bodies. Not only is there overcrowding but a proportion of the visitors do not behave in accordance with the expectations of other visitors and the Vatican staff. The noise, heat and overcrowding make the visit a less than satisfactory experience and, in particular, disrupt the contemplations and prayers of the pilgrims and those visitors seeking a spiritual experience. Some of the visitors in particular display inappropriate behaviours for a place of worship. They ignore requests for quiet, flout the ban on flash photography and flop down for a rest wherever it suits. The Vatican staff believe that the usual measures to manage large visitor numbers at other oversubscribed venues such as art galleries and museums such as timed visits and limiting access cannot be considered. For the time being, the Sistine Chapel is no longer a place for prayer or reflection. (Adapted from guardian.co.uk/world/2012/sep/29/sistine-chapel-tourist-row; guardian.co.uk/world/2012/dec/21/sistine-chapel-tourists-vacuumed-cooled)

The demand that the Sistine Chapel is enduring could be classified as unwholesome, where certain visitors are exhibiting behaviours that damage the environment and erode the experience of others (Kotler, 1982). Not only are some of these visitors engendering unwholesome demand, but they may also be costly to serve as they take a disproportionate amount of resource in supervision and cleaning and provoke complaints from other visitors. Unlike most firms, the Vatican is not in a position, at the moment, or perhaps ever, to distinguish between visitors who are visiting the Vatican for religious or spiritual reasons and those for whom it is a stop on a tour. Whether unwholesome or not, the demand is not one that lends itself to the usual methods of management deployed by galleries, museums and other oversubscribed events such as timed visits.

Selective demarketing extends well beyond the boundaries once envisaged by Kotler and Levy (1971) as an activity of commercial companies operating in consumer markets. Any firm[1] may change the way in which it interacts with its customers and indeed with its environment, resulting in re-evaluations of customer segments, product ranges and distribution channels. Equally, customers who once displayed characteristics suggesting their capacity to generate value with the firm may no longer do so. The firm may find that the costs of serving a group of customers or an individual client exceeds any benefit derived and that the resources currently dedicated to them could be better allocated to serving other customers. Drawing on the service and service dominant logic literature (for example, Grönroos, 2006; Vargo and Lusch, 2004), firms cannot create value with these customers and who may indeed now even destroy value. The development of selective demarketing as a strategy should incorporate contemporary marketing thought where the emphasis on building relationships is accompanied by a focus on corporate social responsibility (CSR) and stakeholder networks.

Research into selective demarketing is complicated by extensive variation in terminology, which appears to all relate to similar activities. In business-to-business (B2B) marketing, research covers relationship dissolution (Pressey and Mathews, 2003), relationship termination (Halinen and Tähtinen, 2002), forced relationship ending (Helm et al., 2006) and seller-initiated relationship ending (Holmlund and Hobbs, 2009). In consumer marketing (B2C), Devlin (2002), in his study into customer knowledge and choice criteria in retail banking, refers to customer deselection, and Haenlein et al. (2006) and Haenlein and Kaplan (2011) use the term customer abandonment. In spite of the variety in this terminology, all of these studies discuss firm actions that involve the selection and elimination of customers whom the firm no longer wishes to serve. Developing a robust means of distinguishing between the customers whom the firm wishes to retain and those whom it wishes to eliminate is a prime consideration.

Customer selection for demarketing

The identification and targeting of customers has long formed a critical part of marketing strategy and planning. By dividing or segmenting the market into specific groups, firms are in a better position to understand and hence satisfy the needs of or create value for customers (McDonald and Dunbar, 2004). The processes of segmentation have been greatly enhanced by the power of technology-enabled systems. Firms have progressed from merely aggregating customers, for example according to socio-demographic data, towards what could be considered the ultimate concept in customer segmentation of one-to-one marketing (Prahalad and Ramaswamy, 2004). Profiles of individual customers are built up through customer analytics to provide a solid base for informing a range of marketing decisions (Bailey et al., 2009). Extensive research has been conducted into how to ascertain the value of a customer to a firm, producing a range of options such as customer lifetime value (for example, Venkatesan and Kumar, 2004), share of wallet (Cooil et al., 2007) and size of wallet (Kumar and Reinartz, 2006). Whatever the precise measure of value alignment the firm uses, a metric is produced that informs them of the costs of serving a customer against the value that customer brings (Kumar and Reinartz, 2006).

The problem of customers who cost more to serve than the revenue that they bring is more widespread than might be appreciated. Research has indicated that the share of customers with a negative contribution margin (revenue less direct cost and cost-to-serve) can reach up to 30 per cent in both B2C and B2B relationships (Haenlein and Kaplan, 2009). An analysis of the customer base of a leading German retail bank identified 22 different customer segments, 5 of which (accounting for over a quarter of customers) were loss generating (Haenlein et al., 2007). Not only do these customers cause losses but the firm also incurs costs in serving them, which they may then pass onto to profitable customers through raised fees and prices. Faced with raised prices, these profitable customers could decide to find another provider, leaving the original firm with a disproportionate number of costly customers and a questionable future. Smaller firms may think that they lack the technological expertise to detect unprofitable customers but this is not an excuse. The costs of not eliminating costly customers may threaten the sustainability of any firm and so systems should be reconfigured to spot them.

Returning to the example of the Vatican, a formal analysis of the visitor base should be undertaken, if it has not already been done, through the pre-booked ticket system (biglietteriamusei.vatican.va/musei/tickets). Although not all tickets are purchased this way, understanding even this partial picture of the nature of the visitor base provides an essential base for developing strategies for more effective visitor management, which may include discouraging the less committed.

Relationship dissolution

Having identified customers who are a burden to the firm, the firm is now in a position to decide what to do about them. Many firms have strived to build relationships with customers to enhance seller/performance outcomes, such as sales growth, share and profits (Palmatier *et al.*, 2006). Most of the RM research has been concerned with building and maintaining relationships (for example, Gummesson, 2002; Sheth and Parvatiyar, 1995) with only a much smaller stream acknowledging that marketing relationships may break down. As suggested in social exchange theory (for example, Cropanzano and Mitchell, 2005), relationships may be candidates for termination where the relationship costs are unevenly distributed with one partner deriving greater benefit than the other. Research into relationship ending or relationship dissolution has advanced understanding in typologies, processes and attitudes in relationship termination. Looking first at the typologies of relationship dissolution, a study proposed four relationship dissolution types. These types were developed in a matrix drawn up along two dimensions of voluntary/involuntary dissolution and of buyer/supplier action (Pressey and Mathews, 2003). The matrix is shown in Figure 8.1. According to this matrix, the third category in this typology consists of voluntary supplier action and involuntary buyer action. This configuration results in unilateral relationship dissolution from supplier to buyer or where the supplier eliminates the buyer.

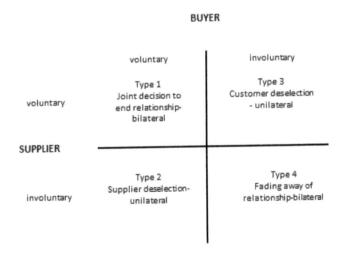

FIGURE 8.1 Categories of dissolution in buyer–seller relationships
Source: Pressey and Mathews (2003)

The matrix depicts three other categories of relationship dissolution as follows:

Type 1: bilateral relationship dissolution where both partners decide to terminate the relationship.

Type 2: unilateral decision on the part of the buyer to terminate the relationship, which might involve defection or switching to a competitor.

Type 4: where the relationship just fades away, possibly through neglect.

The research also found that the means that these suppliers used to deselect customers consisted simply of attributing blame to the customer and/or stating bluntly that the relationship was over or direct strategies (Pressey and Mathews, 2003).

The processes involved in ending B2B relationships were investigated by Halinen and Tähtinen (2002). In this research, three types of business relationship were specified – continuous, episodic and terminal, of which continuous best captures selective demarketing where the focus is usually on ending an ongoing relationship. Figure 8.2 is developed from this research to illustrate the forced or involuntary ending of a B2B relationship by the supplier, or Type 3, according to the matrix of Pressey and Mathews (2003).

The forced ending is influenced by three factors shown in the box on the left. Predisposing factors might include levels of customer risk (Cao and Gruca, 2005) or behaviour, for example the 'butterflies' described by Reinartz and Kumar (2002). The attenuating factors in the figure might include particularly strong bonds in the relationship or anxiety about attracting negative publicity. Precipitating factors would include the customer being perceived as costly (Haenlein et al., 2006) or burdensome. The final part of the figure presents the process of ending and consists of a series of stages shown in the box on the

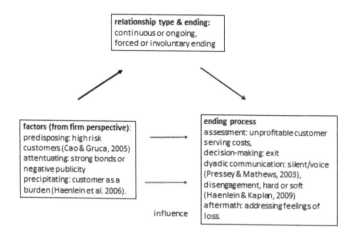

FIGURE 8.2 Process of forced relationship ending by supplier
Source: Developed from Halinen and Tähtinen (2002); Pressey and Mathews (2003)

right. In addition to the assessment and disengagement stages, which might be expected, two further stages have been added in this forced relationship-ending scenario. At the decision-making stage, management make the decision about whether to terminate the relationship or not and so may exit. This exit may be accompanied by voice, possibly endowing the termination with some potential for re-engagement at some later stage when circumstances may change again (Haenlein and Kaplan, 2011; Pressey and Mathews, 2003). During the final stage of aftermath, the former relationship partners address the losses engendered by the termination within the dyad of the relationship or within a wider stakeholder network suggested by the contextual nature of relationship ending (Halinen and Tähtinen, 2002).

In this section on B2B relationship ending, so far typologies and processes of ending have been reviewed. Now the attitudes of the suppliers in unilateral relationship termination are considered. Helm *et al.* (2006), in their study of German engineering firms operating in B2B markets, identified three clusters of firms, who engaged in what was described as forced relationship termination. These clusters were based on the attitudes held by the respondent firms and methods that they used for ending relationships with their customers.

In Table 8.1, three approaches to relationship termination are shown by the three clusters with descriptions in the second column of how each cluster conducted the forced termination. A third column has been added that summarizes the style of termination. The direct (Pressey and Mathews, 2003) or hard style (Haenlein *et al.*, 2006) captures the abrupt severance of the connection or relationship with the customer. A soft style (Bennett and Kottász, 2011; Haenlein *et al.*, 2006) consists of a weakening or reconfiguring of the relationship. A third approach of 'hesitant' has been created, which illustrates less certain termination attitudes and behaviours. The hard-line approach appears to

TABLE 8.1 Attitudes to forced endings in B2B relationships

Cluster title	Description	Style
Hard-liners	Rigorous stance in terminating unprofitable relationships, including the regular clearance of their customer portfolio. Implications such as potential loss of trust also in relationships with other customers or negative word-of-mouth do not interfere with decision-making.	Hard or direct
Appeasers	Considerate or cautious approach concerning the termination of unprofitable relationships. Due to strategic considerations such as loss of customers to competitors.	Soft or indirect
Undecided	Reluctant to terminate unprofitable relationships, mainly because they fear the costs involved in attracting new customers.	Hesitant

Source: Developed from Helm *et al.* (2006)

discount the longer-term consequences of 'clearance' or termination on a wider marketplace, which may include some of the firm's stakeholders. Short-term gains, however, can be easily demonstrated. Appeasers are concerned about what terminated customers may do. They may wish to bear in mind that the very costs that they are bearing with the unprofitable relationships can be passed onto their competitors along with the terminated customers, thus creating a potential 'win–win' situation. The final group of undecided are likely to find their current approach of hesitancy unsustainable as the costs of the unprofitable customers erode their financial viability.

In contrast to the investigation into B2B relationships work, much less investigation has been undertaken into relationship dissolution by the firm in consumer marketing. One might speculate that this is because there is less apparent investment in consumer relationships, but nonetheless a gap is revealed. As with B2B relationships, firms may choose to end relationships in three circumstances – dissatisfaction with the consumer, an unprofitable relationship or a significant change in the seller's circumstances (Hocutt, 1998). Again, there are at least two styles of termination. One example of the soft approach is to increase the costs incurred by customers whom the firm seeks to lose, thereby encouraging them to take their business elsewhere (Haenlein and Kaplan, 2009). This method, often referred to as cost escalation, need not be restricted to monetary costs incurred by the customer. The firm has the option of raising other costs that the customer incurs. The customer's physical costs can be increased, for example, by closing premises in areas where analysis suggests that revenue is poor. A firm can increase social costs by changing booking systems or opening hours as a means of discouraging certain customers. Another soft style can take the form of withdrawal by the firm, which is manifested by reducing the amount of contact or maintenance of the relationship, thus diminishing its intensity or intimacy (Haenlein and Kaplan, 2011). Financial service organizations have used this approach, for example reducing the number of mail shots, thus lowering their costs and weakening any bonds that the customer may hold with the supplier, beginning a process of customer abandonment (Haenlein et al., 2007).

Maintaining costly relationships is at least as undesirable for not-for-profit organizations as for profit-making firms. As donations diminish (*Guardian*, 2012) during the current period of economic downturn, there is increased pressure for these firms to lower their costs. As part of that process, these firms could weed out donors who are not generating sufficient value. In spite of the evident advantages to the firm's cost base, a study into UK fundraisers showed that only about a quarter of respondents implemented any form of donor profitability management. Any selective demarketing that they did carry out as part of managing donor profitability followed a soft style, where the firms sent out lower-quality materials to loss-making supporters (Bennett and Kottász, 2011). Whilst these firms may understandably have reservations about terminating relationships, they have obligations to donors, recipients and their stakeholders to maximize the benefit from the donations that they receive, which may indeed consist of focusing their resources on 'profitable' donors/supporters.

The fundraising study demonstrates the importance of developing a strategic framework to selective demarketing, which can be applied across a range of operations and activities.

Stakeholder networks and corporate social responsibility

Although much of the discussion on deselection has concentrated on the dyad between customer and firm, the RM literature suggests that relationships should be considered within the context of a range of stakeholders (for example, Christopher, Payne and Ballantyne, 2002). Stakeholder models have been variously interpreted but Freeman's definition of a stakeholder as 'any group or individual who can affect or is affected by the achievement of the firm's objective' (1984, p25) extends the number of players in strategic management beyond firm and customer. Stakeholder models vary but customers, competitors, employees and suppliers are common to most (for example, Freeman, 1997; Christopher et al., 2002). As stakeholder thinking has evolved, engaging with other stakeholders is perceived as a form of proactive partnering which, like relationships, involves similar dimensions to relationships such as trust, commitment and reciprocity (Andriof and Waddock, 2002). For firms engaged in selective demarketing, they might wonder where deselected customers fit in their stakeholder network. According to Freeman's definition (1984) above, even after the relationship has been ended, they remain a stakeholder, as they have been affected by the firm action, but, so far, they are not acknowledged in the stakeholder literature. The firm has to tread carefully. On the one hand, as it is part of a complex network mechanism, not eliminating customers who do not generate value impacts on the whole network rather than just the firm itself (Lusch and Webster, 2011). On the other hand, there is evidence that other customers within the stakeholder network, but who are not being eliminated, can penalize firms that abandon unprofitable customers. These customers may also give voice to their concerns, sharing them well beyond immediate social networks (Haenlein and Kaplan, 2011).

Linked closely to stakeholder networks is corporate social responsibility (CSR), which Carroll (1983, p604) defined as follows:

> CSR involves the conduct of business so that it is economically profitable, law abiding, ethical and socially supportive. ... Thus CSR is composed of four parts: economic, legal, ethical and voluntary or philanthropic.

CSR has emerged as inescapable for business leaders everywhere (Porter and Kramer, 2006) so the implications of terminating relationships and eliminating customers have to be considered within that context. The definition incorporates profitability so that the firm needs to demonstrate in a transparent manner the reasons for selective demarketing. The ethical element of CSR will emphasize the minimizing conflict, distress and hardship.

The customer perspective

Knowledge from customer theory on the subject of deselection is somewhat sparse. Some insight can be gained by referring to the literature on customer switching. The research here addresses reasons why customers switch their provider, thus presenting a mirror image of deselection. The relationship between satisfaction and service quality along with dissatisfaction explains at least some customer switching (Keaveney, 1995). Others factors that influenced switching intentions were extrinsic to the service itself or situational factors such as inconvenience, ethics or competition. Price also emerged as significant in customer-switching intentions (Anderson, 1996), which supports the use of cost escalation as a soft approach to deselection. In a study of on-line switching, the profile of the on-line switcher is revealed. On-line switchers are characterized as being less involved with the service, having lower usage levels, being more risk averse and having lower income and education level than stayers (Keaveney and Parthasarathy 2001). Some insight into encouraging customers to defect or switch rather than more overt deselection emerges from these studies.

Another omission in the literature seems to be investigation into how deselected customers may respond to deselection. Some insight can be gained from Exit-Voice-Loyalty-Neglect (EVLN) Model (Rusbult *et al.*, 1982). Three hypotheses were tested in the study as follows:

1. the degree of satisfaction with the relationship prior to the emergence of problems;
2. the magnitude of the individual's investment of resources in the relationship;
3. the quality of the best available alternative.

The potential of transferring these hypotheses to marketing relationships can be readily discerned. The EVLN model was developed in the context of adult romantic involvements and draws on Hirschman's (1970) EVL model, which has also been used in the context of examining the impact of current customer responses to the abandonment of other customers (see Haenlein and Kaplan, 2011). The EVLN model adds a fourth category of neglect, which contributes to this discussion with particular reference to soft or hesitant styles of deselection (see Table 8.1). This research presents the individual's responses to dissatisfaction with a romantic relationship in a matrix developed along two dimensions of active/passive and destructive/constructive. Three categories emerge from this research that might be helpful in anticipating customer responses to deselection of exit, voice and neglect. The exit category (active/negative) consists of partners separating and can be an outcome of any style of termination (see Table 8.1). Voice (active/constructive) may be an attempt on the part of the deselected to seek a compromise, to complain to the firm itself or to indulge in negative word-of-mouth amplified through digital media. The third category of neglect (passive/negative) might apply to soft and hesitant styles of relationship ending and described by the researchers as 'just letting things fall apart' (Rusbult *et al.*, 1982, p1231). The final category in this matrix is loyalty, which at first seems not to apply to selective demarketing. Interestingly though, Reinartz and Kumar (2002) describe a group of customers whom they label barnacles. This group is not profitable to the firm but as the name suggests is in the relationship for the long term!

Deselection is likely to provoke feelings of loss when consumers are excluded from the consumption patterns or experiences, which denote their identity and beliefs. Brands and consumption patterns may be associated with personality traits that provide self-expressive or symbolic benefits for the consumer (Berger and Heath, 2007). Elliott and Wattanasuwan (1998) contend that consumers bring resources to the task of identity construction and that brands can play an important role in this construction. The following extract provides an example of how a brand unwittingly became a resource in the identity construction of an entirely unexpected consumer group, completely at odds with their planned segments.

Burberry and the chav

Burberry, the luxury goods group emerged from its market of traditional garment production to become the brand of choice for A-list celebrities. They were particularly noted for a distinctive check that they used on a range of accessories as well as clothing. Quite unexpectedly, this camel-coloured check became the 'uniform' of the chav in the early noughties. Chavs were described in the press as a low-income social group obsessed with brand names, cheap jewellery and football, so a rather different market from that which the brand targeted. The check was also widely copied or counterfeited and so could be bought on market stalls at much lower prices than the company stores. The low point for the brand was a set of photographs of a soap actress called Daniella Westbrook and her daughter. Mother, daughter and pushchair were covered entirely in Burberry check! To the brand, this display of the Burberry check seemed the ultimate comedown to their elite status. Urgent action was required to preserve the brand and to bolster falling sales. Burberry responded to the problem by significantly reducing the appearance of the distinctive check pattern in their product range. Fortunately for them, the check appeared on only about 10 per cent of their range. They also took action against vendors selling the counterfeit versions of Burberry. Unsubstantiated rumours told of large bouncers turning away customers with chav characteristics from Burberry retailers. The group introduced more cutting-edge designs moving further away from their traditional range of quality coats and basics. In November 2012, Burberry reported better-than-expected half-year profits against a backdrop of global economic uncertainty.

Compiled by the author from: economist.com,
news.bbc.co.uk, telegraph.co.uk/finance

Burberry used more than one style of deselection to protect the brand. They deployed softer abandonment where they withdrew the product lines prized by and accessible to the undesired segments. They took a much harder line to extinguish counterfeit copies of the check and deter chavs from entering retail outlets – if the rumours are true.

In the first section of this chapter, several streams of literature have been reviewed that address directly and in some cases less directly selective demarketing (see Table 8.2). The review has demonstrated that most of the research has been conducted into relationship dissolution in B2B marketing with little regard to the consumer theory. Within the discussion, the implications of stakeholder networks and CSR have been considered, showing that deselected customers remain at least in the short term stakeholders in the firm network. The research so far is almost exclusively concerned with the firm's actions with little acknowledgement of how the customer may respond. The customer-switching literature indicates that there are customers who can be encouraged

TABLE 8.2 Selective demarketing: components and contribution

Component	Contribution	Author (date)
One-to-one marketing Customer value	Focus on individual customer Costs of serving customers measured against revenue	Prahalad and Ramaswamy (2004) Venkatesan and Kumar (2004), Cooil et al. (2007)
Social exchange	Mutually rewarding relationships	Cropanzano and Mitchell (2005)
Relationship dissolution (B2C)	Seller-initiated dissolution	Hocutt (1998), Haenlein and Kaplan (2009)
Relationship dissolution (B2B)	Typology, process and attitudes	Halinen and Tähtinen (2002), Helm et al. (2006), Pressey and Mathews (2003)
Deselection styles	Soft/indirect: company withdrawal, price escalation, Hard/direct: termination Hesitant unsure of the outcomes	Haenlein and Kaplan (2011), Bennett and Kottász (2011)
Stakeholder environment	Networks, value, deselected customer as stakeholder	Christopher et al. (2002), Freeman, (1978, 1984), Lusch and Webster (2011)
Corporate social responsibility	Profitable, legal, ethical and philanthropic, ethical behaviours	Andriof and Waddock (2002), Carroll (1983)
Consumer switching	Dissatisfaction and price, switching profile	Keaveney (1995), Anderson (1996), Keaveney and Parthasarathy (2001)
EVLN model	Customer responses to deselection	Rusbult et al. (1982)
Self-identity	Consumer resources	Elliott and Wattanasuwan (1998)

to switch, suggesting an important avenue for research. Table 8.2 provides a summary of the research that has been reviewed in the first section of this chapter.

The review indicates that there are thorough studies into relationship dissolution and ending in B2B but that research into consumer selective demarketing or relationship dissolution is very limited. There is therefore no evidence for drawing parallels between the two markets. The consumer literature suggests that deselected consumers may exhibit negative behaviours if deselected. This suggestion is supported by the studies into customer abandonment but again more work is needed. Reference to the CSR and stakeholder network literature connotes that selective demarketing is quite compatible as the continued vitality and wellbeing of the firm can only be assured, minimizing losses.

Value generation

In a significant step away from marketing based on the offering of goods, proponents of service (for example, Grönroos, 2006, 2008) and service dominant logic (Vargo and Lusch, 2004, 2008) propose that service is a perspective on value creation rather than a category of marketing offering (Edvardsson et al., 2011). The following extract, slightly adapted for this chapter, summarizes service logic as follows:

1. When using resources provided by the firm (typically operand) together with other resources and applying skills held by them (typically operant), customers create value for themselves in their everyday practices.
2. When creating interactive contacts with customers during their use of goods and services, the firm develops opportunities to co-create value with them and for them.

(Grönroos, 2008, p 299)

A synthesis of firm and customer resources generates value-in-use. Value-in-use refers to the way in which customers through processes of self-service create value for themselves. A key aspect of value-in-use is that it is dynamic, which calls for learning, both on the part of firm and customer (Lusch and Webster, 2011). Firstly, the organization has to gain a deep understanding of the customer experience and processes to enable the design of a co-creation and relationship experience (Payne et al., 2008) and to improve the offering to the customer (Vargo and Lusch, 2004). This learning will involve knowledge of the resources that the customer will bring to bear on the value proposition in order to gain value-in-use. Secondly, the customer also learns how to apply specialized skills and knowledge as a fundamental unit of exchange in SD logic (Vargo and Lusch, 2004) so that they can gain value-in-use. It is the relationship between the firm and the customers, which creates value for both parties, so that the choice of customer is strategically critical to the firm (Lusch and Webster, 2011).

Value, according to Vargo and Lusch (2008), can only be phenomenologically or experientially determined by the beneficiary or customer. The firm, therefore, has to understand and then facilitate how that value can be fulfilled. To achieve this mutually beneficial outcome, a great reliance is placed on the development of a robust value proposition in which to engage the participation of the customer (Vargo and Lusch, 2004), which draws on customer as well as firm resources. Once again, attention is drawn to stakeholder networks as value is not value created merely through the interaction between the customer and the firm but also through interaction between customers and other stakeholders.

A foundational premise of SD logic is that all social and economic actors are resource integrators (Vargo and Lusch, 2008), where resources are classified as either operand or operant. Customers bring together or integrate a range of operant resources such as social, cultural and physical skills and knowledge to co-create value (Arnould et al., 2006). Customers also possess operand resources such as material objects and economic assets. They perform an act with the operand resources of the firm and hence become a collaborative value-creation partner (Vargo and Lusch, 2008). Service and SD logic are both founded on the proposition that operant resources are primary in marketing as they are the producers of effects. Knowing the resources that the customer will bring to the value proposition and even supporting the refinement of these resources is an integral part of its framing. Service and SD logic is predicated on an understanding that customers learn how to derive value-in-use but, as Hibbert et al. (2012) observe, learning varies considerably according to whether it is intrinsically driven or compelled.

The firm has operant as well as operand resources and these include marketing-related capability, learning and innovativeness (Madhavaram and Hunt, 2008). Marketing-related capability consists of three elements of orientation – knowledge, skills and alignment of processes, which, according to Madhavaram and Hunt (2008), interact to reinforce each other. Learning is both an intent to learn and organizational capability in processing knowledge. Firm resources that discourage customers from engaging in value-generating processes are service failures and situational factors (Hibbert et al., 2012) and, clearly, these are learning situations for firms in selective demarketing. Creativity and innovation include competences relating to customers as well as development of new value propositions. Selective demarketing is concerned with the optimum or most beneficial allocation of resources and so draws on firm operant resources in eliminating unprofitable or undesirable customers or those customers who destroy value.

Value destruction

There are references in service and SD logic studies to customers who lack appropriate operant resources (Grönroos, 2008) and to customers who are unwilling to reciprocate the resources of the firm (Lusch and Webster, 2011). Furthermore, customers can be segmented according to their tendencies to participate in co-production (Etgar, 2008). 'Good' customers for the firms are those who provide the necessary resources to derive value in use and 'bad' customers are those who will not or cannot provide the resource. Propositions of service and SD logic may have negative value (Grönroos, 2008) in situations where the level of customer resource for gaining value-in-use exceeds any benefits that may accrue. Customers who are not able or unwilling to achieve value-in-use are therefore already destroying rather than creating value.

Recent work has explored the concept of value co-destruction from the perspective of misuse of resources (Plé and Cáceres, 2010). Value co-destruction in service and SD logic has been defined (Plé and Cáceres, 2010) as:

> an interactional process between service systems that results in a *decline* in at least one of the system's well-being.

This decline comes about from the use of mainly operant resources in a detrimental manner for one of the systems or for both. Plé and Cáceres (2010) argue that value is destroyed through misuse of resources either by the customer or by the firm whether accidental or intentional. They also point out one system or partner may intentionally misuse resources so that value may be destroyed for the other system (firm or customer), whilst creating value for the other.

Just as value can be created through the integration of resources – both operant and operand – value can equally be destroyed by these resources being poorly integrated or manipulated. It has been recognized that certain customers are not, for a variety of reasons, going to be able to create value with the firm. The 'fit' between the firm and these customers is therefore poor. In these circumstances, as has been stated throughout this chapter, a suitable policy is to deselect these customers. There are suggestions in the marketing literature of a number of ways in which this deselection can be achieved, for example through cost escalation, neglect or elimination (see Table 8.2). The focus so far on customer operand resources, that is, economic, may have narrowed horizons on customer deselection processes, whereas looking at operant resources provides some scope for more creative actions.

If the starting point is that these customers are already destroying value, then an alternative strategy through value destruction emerges. The firm may decide to offer the necessary learning opportunities or materials for these customers to gain value-in-use (Hibbert *et al.*, 2012) and monitor the situation. If the customer continues to destroy value, the firm will manipulate its own operant resources to deselect the customer through further value destruction. Given that the firm has an in-depth knowledge of the resources that the customer needs to integrate for creating value, then it should have an equal understanding of what resources, that is, its own and those of the customer, that need to be acted upon to bring about deselection.

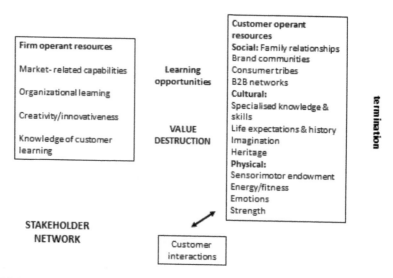

FIGURE 8.3 Value destruction as a strategic framework for selective demarketing

An integrative framework for strategic selective demarketing based on value destruction is proposed in Figure 8.3.

In this figure, firm operant resources are brought to bear in understanding which resources the customer is failing to use to create value. Once those resources are understood, then the firm can offer the customer learning opportunities, which the customer may choose or be able to respond to. If the customer does not respond to the learning opportunities, then the firm has the knowledge and capabilities to deselect through further manipulating customer operant resources. The impact of the co-consumer should also be considered where co-consumers destroy rather than create value. The figure also demonstrates, as discussed in the first section of the chapter, that CSR and stakeholder networks are entirely congruent with strategic selective demarketing.

To refer once more to the example of the Sistine Chapel, the visit is an experience where customer operant resources are integrated with the firm operand resources. Visitor operant resources may include cultural resources such as religious knowledge and physical resources such as stamina, but some visitors may not understand the need to integrate or not know how to integrate their resources in this situation. The Vatican's operand resources largely consist of tangibles such as the frescoes, the tapestries and the stonework. More recently, they have added special carpets and vacuums to clean the visitors before entry. The Vatican's problem of overcrowding can be addressed through general demarketing. It may consider the reduction of times available for all visitors including pilgrims probably unpalatable. One part of the problem of over-popularity, though, is the behaviour of some visitors, suggesting selective demarketing. To demarket selectively, the Vatican can orchestrate its operant resources (see Figure 8.3), in the first place, to provide more intensive learning or information for visitors, to develop specialist skills in the stewardship of large visitor numbers, to manage visitor expectations and to analyse the visitor base. A further dimension to the Sistine Chapel experience is the co-consumer who may be bringing a different set of operant resources to bear. Whilst Baron and Harris (2008) observe the utilization of operant resources by consumers collectively to immerse themselves in an experience, it is evident that, in this case, the collective experience and value-in-use is disrupted by incompatible customer operant resources or a failure to integrate them to be suitable for the experience.

Contribution and directions for research

The purpose of this chapter has been twofold. First, to review and synthesize the various literatures that relate to selective demarketing and these are summarized in Table 8.2. This review indicated that insufficient attention had been paid to consumer theory in selective demarketing. Switching studies in particular indicated that satisfaction/dissatisfaction and situational factors influence customer decisions to switch. Second, to appraise the service and SD logic contributions on value creation and resources to explore whether they could be manipulated in such a way as to destroy value to selected customers or customer groups. From this appraisal, a strategic framework has been developed, illustrating how the interaction between firm and customer operant resources can destroy value and bring about deselection (see Figure 8.3). This framework addresses selective demarketing in B2C, B2B, profit-making and not-for-profit organizations. The study makes a number of contributions to marketing theory. First, it expands research into service and SD logic by investigating instances of where value can intentionally be destroyed as a strategic and coherent means of selective demarketing. Second, it demonstrates how selective demarketing can be achieved through a focus on operant resources where previous efforts may have concentrated on customer's operand resources such as economic status. Third, it fuses selective demarketing with corporate social responsibility and stakeholder networks.

Managerial implications

The strategic framework does not preclude the use of direct methods in selective demarketing but suggests an alternative approach built on operant resources to destroy value for customers who do not fit the firm. Selective demarketing as demonstrated in this chapter is compatible with management concerns about CSR and stakeholder networks. By focusing on value-in-use, firms will have a much deeper understanding of with which customers they can continue to create value. Also emerging from this study is a reminder that the choice of customer rather than the volume of customers is a strategic imperative. It is a reminder that selective demarketing is costly and that firms need to be even more aware of with which customers precisely they can generate value. The onus is on the firm to develop its own operant resources as well as its operand so that it has the flexibility and capacity to address the challenges of value creations and destruction.

Further research and limitations

This study suggests a number of avenues for further research. Investigation into customer responses to being deselected will provide important information about negative behaviours, the threat of which currently deters some firms from deselecting. Allied to this suggestion is the finding that the deselected customer remains within the stakeholder network. The implications of this finding also need to be explored. The discussion has revealed the role of the other customers who destroy value rather than contributing to its creation. This has hardly been alluded to in the literature and merits further study.

Acknowledgment

Thanks to Tracy Panther for her assistance with this chapter.

Note

1 Firm is used throughout this chapter to refer to profit-making, not-for-profit, business-to-consumer and business-to-business organizations of all sizes.

References

Anderson, E. (1996), Customer satisfaction and price tolerance, *Marketing Letters*, 7, 3, 19–30.

Andriof, J. and Waddock, S. (2002), Unfolding stakeholder engagement, in (eds) J. Andriof, S. Waddock, B. Husted and S. Rahman, *Unfolding Stakeholder Thinking*, Sheffield, Greenleaf Publishing, 19–42.

Arnould, E., Price, L. and Malshe, A. (2006), Towards a cultural resource-based theory of the customer, in (eds) R. Lusch and S. Vargo, *The Service-Dominant Logic of Marketing: Dialog, debate, and directions*, NY, Armonk.

Bailey, C., Baines, P., Wilson, H. and Clark, M. (2009), Segmentation and customer insight in contemporary services marketing practice: Why grouping customers is no longer enough, *Journal of Marketing Management*, 25, 3/4, 227–52.

Baron, S. and Harris, K. (2008), Consumers as resource integrators, *Journal of Marketing Management*, 24, 1/2, 113–30.

Bennett, R. and Kottász, R. (2011), Management of unprofitable donors by UK fundraising charities, *Journal of Customer Behaviour*, 10, 4, 309–33. bbc.co.uk/news/business-19876138, accessed 11 December 2012.

Berger, J and Heath, C. (2007), Where consumers diverge from others: Identity signaling and product domains, *Journal of Consumer Research*, 34, 2 121–34. blogs.hbr.org/cs/2012/01/case_study_when_to_drop_an_unp.html

Cao, Y. and Gruca, T. (2005), Reducing adverse selection through customer relationship management, *Journal of Marketing*, 69, October, 219–29.

Carroll, A. (1983), Corporate social responsibility: Will industry respond to cutbacks in social program funding? *Vital Speeches of the Day*, 49, 604–8.

Christopher, M., Payne, A. and Ballantyne, D. (2002), *Relationship Marketing: Creating stakeholder value* (2nd ed.), Oxford: Butterworth Heinemann.

Cooil, B., Keiningham, T., Aksoy, L. and Hsu, M. (2007), A longitudinal analysis of customer satisfaction and share of wallet: Investigating the moderating effect of customer characteristics, *Journal of Marketing*, 71, 1, 67–83.

Cropanzano, R. and Mitchell, M. (2005), Social exchange theory: An interdisciplinary review, *Journal of Management*, 31, 874–900.

Devlin, J. (2002), Customer knowledge and choice criteria in retail banking, *Journal of Strategic Marketing*, 10, 273–90. economist.com/node/17963363 accessed, 31/12/2012.

Edvardsson, B., Tronvoll, B. and Gruber, T. (2011), Expanding understanding of service exchange and value co-creation: A social construction approach, *Journal of the Academy of Marketing Science*, 39, 327–39.

Elliott, R. and Wattanasuwan, K. (1998), Brands as symbolic resources for the construction of identity, *International Journal of Advertising*, 17, 2, 131–44.

Etgar, M. (2008), A descriptive model of the consumer co-production process, *Journal of the Academy of Marketing Science*, 36, 97–108.

Freeman, R. (1984), *Strategic management: A stakeholder approach*. Boston, MA. Pitman.

——(1997), Stakeholder theory, in (eds) P. Werhane and R. Freeman, *The Blackwell Encyclopaedic Dictionary of Business Ethics*, Blackwell, Oxford/Malden, MA. 602–6.

Grönroos, C. (2006), Adopting a service logic for marketing, *Marketing Theory*, 6, 3, 317–33.

——(2008), Service logic revisited: who creates value? And who co-creates? *European Business Review*, 20, 4, 298–314.

guardian.co.uk/world/2012/sep/29/sistine-chapel-tourist-row, accessed 20/10/12.

guardian.co.uk/world/2012/dec/21/sistine-chapel-tourists-vacuumed-cooled, accessed, 01/01/13.

Guardian (2012), guardian.co.uk/money/2012/nov/13/charity-donations-fall-uk-survey, accessed 31/12/12

Gummesson, E. (2002), Relationship marketing in the new economy, *Journal of Relationship Marketing*, 1, 1, 37–57.

Haenlein, M. and Kaplan, A. (2009), Unprofitable customers and their management, *Business Horizons*, 52, 89–97.

——(2011), Evaluating the consequences of abandoning unprofitable customers: A comparison of direct and indirect abandonment strategies, *Zeitschrift Betriebswirtsch* 81, 77–94.

Haenlein, M., Kaplan, A. and Beeser, A. (2007), A model to determine customer lifetime value in a retail banking context, *European Management Journal*, 25, 3, 221–34.

Haenlein, M., Kaplan, A. and Schoder, D. (2006), Valuing the real option of abandoning unprofitable customers when calculating customer lifetime value, *Journal of Marketing*, 70, 5–20.

Halinen, A. and Tähtinen, J. (2002), A process theory of relationship ending. *International Journal of Service Industry Management*, 13 (2), pp. 163–180.

Helm, S., Rolfes, L. and Günter, B. (2006), Suppliers' willingness to end unprofitable customer relationships, *European Journal of Marketing*, 40, 3/4, 366–83.

Hibbert, S., Winklehofer, H. and Temerak, M. (2012), Customers as resource integrators: Toward a model of customer learning, *Journal of Service Research*, 15, 3, 247–61.

Hirschman, A.O. (1970). *Exit, Voice, and Loyalty: Responses to Decline in Firms, Organizations, and States*. Cambridge, MA: Harvard University Press

Hocutt, M. (1998), Relationship dissolution model: Antecedents of relationship commitment and the likelihood of dissolving a relationship, *International Journal of Service Industry Management*, 9, 2, 189–200.

Holmlund, M. and Hobbs, P. (2009), Seller-initiated relationship ending: An empirical study of professional business-to-business services, *Managing Service Quality*, 19, 3, 266–85.

Keaveney, S. (1995), Customer switching behavior in service industries: An exploratory study, *Journal of Marketing*, 59, 2, 71–82.

Keaveney, S. and Parthasarathy, M. (2001), Customer switching behavior in online services: An exploratory study of the role of selected attitudinal, behavioral, demographic factors, *Journal of the Academy of Marketing Science*, 29, 4, 374–90.

Kotler, P. (1982), *Marketing for Non-Profit Organizations*, 2nd ed. Englewood Cliffs, New Jersey, Prentice-Hall.

Kotler, P. and Levy, S. (1971), Demarketing, yes, demarketing, *Harvard Business Review*, 49, 6, 74–80.

Kumar, V. and Reinartz, W. (2006), *Customer Relationship Management: A databased approach*. New York: John Wiley & Sons.

Lusch, R. and Webster, F. (2011), A stakeholder-unifying, cocreation philosophy for marketing, *Journal of Macromarketing*, 31, 2, 129–34.

McDonald, M. and Dunbar, I. (2004), *Market Segmentation*. Oxford: Elsevier.

Madhavaram, Sreedhar and Hunt, S. D. (2008), The service dominant logic and a hierarchy of operant resources: Developing masterful operant resources and implications for marketing strategy, *Journal of the Academy of Marketing Science*, 36 (1), 67–82.

Payne, A., Storbacka, K. and Frow, P. (2008), Managing the co-creation of value, *Journal of the Academy of Marketing Science*, 36, 83–96.

Palmatier, R., Dant, R., Grewal, D. and Evans, K. (2006), Factors influencing the effectiveness of relationship marketing: A meta-analysis, *Journal of Marketing*, 70, October, 136–53.

Plé, L. and Cáceres, R. (2010), Not always co-creation: Introducing interactional co-destruction of value in service-dominant logic, *Journal of Services Marketing*, 24, 6, 430–37.

Prahalad, C. and Ramaswamy, V. (2004), Co-creating unique value with customers, *Strategy and Leadership*, 32, 3, 4–9.

Porter, M. and Kramer, M. (2006), Strategy and society: The link between competitive advantage and corporate responsibility, *Harvard Business Review*, December, 1–13.

Pressey, A. and Mathews, B. (2003), Jumped, pushed or forgotten? Approaches to dissolution, *Journal of Marketing Management*, 19, 1–2, 131–55.

Reinartz, W. and Kumar, R. (2002), The mismanagement of customer loyalty-not all customers are created equal, *Harvard Business Review*, July, 86–97.

Rusbult, C., Zembrodt, I. and Gunn, L. (1982), Exit, voice, loyalty, and neglect: Responses to dissatisfaction in romantic involvements, *Journal of Personality and Social Psychology*, 43, 6, 1230–42.

Sheth, J. and Parvatiyar, A. (1995), Relationship marketing in consumer markets: antecedents and consequences, *Journal of the Academy of Marketing Science*, 23, 4, 255–71. telegraph.co.

uk/finance/2900572/Burberry-brand-tarnished-by-chavs.html, accessed 31 December 2012.

Vargo, S. and Lusch, R. (2004), Evolving to a new dominant logic for marketing, *Journal of Marketing*, 68, January, 1–17.

——(2008), Service-dominant logic: Continuing the evolution, *Journal of the Academy of Marketing Science*, 36, 1–10.

Venkatesan, R. and Kumar, V. (2004), A customer lifetime value framework for customer selection and resource allocation strategy, *Journal of Marketing*, 68, 106–25.

9
SELECTIVE DEMARKETING
Case study – Frizzell Insurance
(Daisy) Jing Tan

Introduction

The UK motor insurance industry has historically been extremely competitive with customers having very diverse needs; they shop around every time a renewal is coming in sight. To survive the competition, insurers need not only to build up awareness for recruitment purpose, but also try to retain existing customers at a higher rate. Service quality thus becomes high on the agenda. To better serve their customers and capitalize on the firms' competitive advantages, insurers pay a substantial amount of attention to whom they target and whom to let go. Changes in the general environment often lead to changes in the profitability of customer groups, such as the ageing issue of the drivers, the high risks involved with certain type of customers, and the advancement of modern technologies as well as how that would impact the distribution channels of motor insurance purchase. To ensure profitability, insurers are more interested in attracting and maintaining customers who are loyal, safety-conscious and less likely to make claims. This means certain segments in the market would be more attractive to them than the others. And it is those segments that are less promising and profitable that the insurers are trying to get rid of. Although a tough decision, insurers need to set their priorities regarding which customer group(s) they would like to serve and work out a way to reach their precise target group(s) without hurting their relationship with other customer or potential customer groups. This case study tells the story of Frizzell Insurance, a UK-based motor insurer, and how they managed to tactically expand the right type of customer base, while securing their reputation as a superior financial solution provider.

Motor insurance industry

In the UK, under the Road Traffic Act 1988, all motor vehicle drivers and passengers must be insured for liability for bodily injury and property damage. Broadly speaking, there are two types of insurance available to private motorists: comprehensive insurance and non-comprehensive insurance. Within the

UK market, there are six major players competing for the market share. They are: Admiral Group, Aviva, AXA, LV =, RBS and RSA. It has long been a highly competitive market, with players trying different techniques, fighting for customers. RBS insurance currently holds the largest market share of about 27 per cent. Aviva and LV = are competing for the second place, with a share of 11 per cent and 10 per cent, respectively. RSA and AXA have a slightly smaller proportion of 8 per cent and 7 per cent. The rest of the market share goes to some smaller players, collectively taking up 37 per cent (Mintel, 2012).

Background of the major players

Admiral Group

Admiral Group was founded in 1993. It is a financial services intermediary firm engaged in the sale and administration of private motor insurance and related products. The group is one of the top three private car insurers in the UK and holds a 10 per cent share in the UK private car insurance market, operating through its Admiral, Elephant, Diamond and Bell brands. The group also owns confused.com, one of the leading price-comparison websites in the UK. Admiral distributes its motor insurance products through price-comparison websites and direct channels including telephone and its own websites.

Relevant brands/subsidiaries:

Admiral – insurance provider launched in 1993, initially targeting people who traditionally pay higher premiums including younger drivers and those who live in cities;
Bell – launched in 1997, aimed at drivers with zero no-claims bonus;
Diamond – specialist motor insurance provider for women, launched in 1997;
Gladiator – commercial vehicle insurance broker launched in 1998;
Elephant – online-only insurer launched in 2000;
Confused.com – UK's first online car insurance price-comparison website launched in 2002.

Aviva

Aviva plc is a global insurance company that serves more than 44.5 million customers worldwide, including over 14 million in the UK. In the UK, the group offers, under the name Aviva (formerly known as Norwich Union), a range of personal and commercial general insurance products including motor, home, travel, health and pet insurance. Aviva distributes its own-brand motor insurance products through intermediaries and partnerships as well as offering them direct to customers through online and telephone channels. Aviva recently launched its 'Quote me happy' brand, a separate and distinct online service available through selected price-comparison sites and through the website quotemehappy.com.

AXA

AXA is a French insurance group that serves more than 95 million customers worldwide. In the UK, the group focuses its offerings on three major areas: wealth management, insurance and healthcare. The group's insurance business, AXA Insurance, is one of the largest general insurers in the UK and offers a range of commercial and personal lines insurance products. The group also covers brands such as Swiftcover and Bluefin. AXA distributes its motor insurance products through intermediaries as well as offering them direct to customers through its own website, axa.co.uk, and through swiftcover.com.

LV =

LV =, the trading name of Liverpool Victoria Friendly Society Limited, is the largest friendly society in the UK. The company offers a range of financial services and products including general insurance, life cover, savings and investments, financial advice and retirement plans. The group parents brands such as Highway Insurance and ABC Insurance. LV = distributes its motor insurance products direct to customers through telephone and online, as well as offering them through price-comparison websites and brokers.

RBS

Royal Bank of Scotland Plc (RBS) is a UK-based banking and financial services group that offers a range of products and services including retail and corporate banking services, private banking and wealth management services and insurance services amongst others. The group's insurance division includes a number of leading brands such as Direct Line, Churchill and Privilege. Formerly known as RBSI (Royal Bank of Scotland Insurance), the group distributes its motor insurance products through a multichannel network that varies between its brands.

RSA

RSA (Royal and Sun Alliance) is a global insurance firm that was formed in 1996 following the merger of Royal Insurance and Sun Alliance. The company's direct insurance brand, MORE TH>N, offers a range of insurance products for both personal and small business customers. RSA distributes its motor insurance products through intermediaries and affinity partners, as well as offering them direct to consumers through its MORE TH>N brand.

Consumers

Motor insurance is a widely held product: more than 70 per cent of adult Internet users have some type of cover in place. Fully comprehensive cover is held by the vast majority of policyholders. Only 10 per cent have third-party cover. Less than half of under-25s have a car insurance policy, with many put off by the high costs of car ownership and insurance. However, older drivers are accounting for a growing proportion of the motor insurance market.

Another trend in the market is that young drivers are charged substantially more than older drivers. Research has suggested that young male drivers are facing insurance premiums nearly four times more expensive than the average driver. The justification for this practice is that an 18-year-old driver for example is more than three times as likely to be involved in a crash as a 48-year-old. This is why the ABI is calling for an overhaul in how to teach people to drive, with the introduction of graduated licences. There is a gender difference in pricing insurance premiums. Generally, young females are charged significantly less than young male drivers, because female drivers tend to be more cautious and the rate of being caught in accidents is lower when compared to their male counterparts. However, starting from December 2012, insurers will no longer be able to use gender as an underwriting factor when pricing insurance premiums, following a ruling by the European Court of Justice in March 2011. This decision is expected to lead to a rise in premiums for young female drivers and could lead to an increase in premiums across the market as providers are forced to take a new approach to pricing. At the other end of the age spectrum, over-65s are accounting for a growing proportion of the car insurance market. Whether or not insurers choose to target this demographic through specialist brands or as part of their wider marketing strategy, it is clear that over-60s form an increasingly valuable sector of the motor insurance market. There is also a noticeable difference in car insurance ownership levels between households with an annual income of under £15,500 and those above this threshold.

With such a diverse market and so many players/brands competing on market share, insurers need to think very carefully regarding whom to target and whom to let go to ensure sustainable profitability. Different marketing strategies have been employed by individual players to achieve this objective.

Consumers are highly price-sensitive when it comes to arranging motor insurance. New brands offering competitive premiums are able to get a foothold in the market. Consumers also tend to shop around at renewal. Almost eight in ten car insurance policyholders shopped around at their last renewal. However, not all decided to switch. Most of the customers simply wanted to get a general view of what was on offer on the market before their next purchase. Some 43 per cent opted to remain with their existing insurer, compared to 36 per cent who chose to switch providers. Insurers appear to be having some success with retention strategies, although switching levels may not take account of some churn from within intermediary brands. Switching levels are fairly similar regardless of the level of cover, although third-party cover holders have a much higher propensity to have stayed with an existing insurer without shopping around. Car insurance switchers are more likely to be aged 35–54, although over-55s are among the most likely to have shopped around at renewal but to have decided to stay with their existing insurer, with almost 47 per cent of them have tried this approach (Mintel, 2012). Some 45 per cent of Internet users have sought quotations through direct channels, either through an insurer's website or telephony channel.

Frizzell Insurance

Company background

Frizzell Insurance was established as a UK family business in 1923. It started when Thomas Norman Frizzell was an insurance broker at Lloyds and provided motor insurance for a group of civil service motoring enthusiasts. Since its birth, Frizzell Insurance has served the members of associations and unions throughout its existence. Relationships were initially established with Civil Service and Local Government associations and in the 1930s Frizzell Insurance began associations with other major membership groups. Members of these groups were usually given a certain amount of discounts on their insurance quotes if they insured through Frizzell.

In 1992, the Frizzell family sold the entire Frizzell Financial Services group to Marsh McLennan, the US insurance broker and investment manager, for about £107 million. The Bournemouth-based financial services company Frizzell was then acquired by the Liverpool Victoria Friendly Society LV = group of companies in 1996 for about £188 million. The LV = group of companies is headed up by Liverpool Victoria Friendly Society Limited, which is authorized and regulated by the Financial Services Authority. Founded in 1843, Liverpool Victoria is now the UK's largest friendly society (Association of Friendly Societies Key Statistics – 2007 Total Net Assets). The Society does not have any shareholders and, as a mutual organization, exists wholly for the benefit of its members to provide better service and greater convenience for customers. At present, the Liverpool Victoria Life Insurance group of companies manages reportedly more than £8 billion on behalf of its members and customers. LV = are committed to providing competitive products. Frizzell Insurance has adopted exactly the same philosophy by putting the interests of their customers first. Frizzell Insurance also provides a handy chart when obtaining a car insurance quote that outlines which coverage and benefits are available. Customers can quickly compare the difference in cover between third party only and comprehensive cover. This dedication to excellence has helped the company to establish a very high customer retention rate in the general insurance industry.

Since Frizzell began working with professional organizations over eighty years ago, the number of relationships they have acquired has risen to 30 within that time. These groups cover a diverse range of professions, including teaching, electrical engineering, the healthcare and publishing sectors and leisure pursuits, such as motoring and caravanning. They offer special discounts for consumers that work in organizations and unions such as CSMA, UNISON, PCS+.

Associations

CSMA

The Civil Service Motoring Association Club is a brand of Motoring & Leisure Services Ltd. (MLS), a subsidiary of The Civil Service Motoring Association, Ltd. MLS is authorized and regulated by the Financial Services Authority. CSMA was formed in 1923 when Ministry of Labour Executive Officer Frank Edwards, who was a keen motorcyclist, was credited with being the CSMA's founder. Around the same time, a young insurance broker called Tom Frizzell had heard about the Association's proposal to offer favourable insurance terms to members and persuaded Frank that the business should be awarded to Frizzell Insurance. This relationship remained unchanged after decades of development.

UNISON

UNISON is Britain and Europe's biggest public sector union with more than 1.3 million members. Their members are people working in the public services, for private contractors providing public services and in the essential utilities. They include frontline staff and managers working full- or part-time in local authorities, the NHS, the police service, colleges and schools, the electricity, gas and water industries, transport and the voluntary sector.

PCS+

The Public and Commercial Services Union (PCS) is one of the largest trade unions in the UK, with around 270,000 members. They are organized throughout the civil service and government agencies, making them the UK's largest civil service trade union. They also organize widely in the private sector, usually in areas that have been privatized.

Most members of these associations or unions demonstrate a strong tendency towards being conservative, risk-averse and law-abiding, in terms of their character. They tend to have a secure job and lead a quiet and content life. Historical records show that, among all drivers, this group is much less likely to make claims on their motor insurance when compared to other customers.

Current performance – Motor insurance product range

At the moment, LV = offers three types of cover: comprehensive car insurance, third party, fire and theft, and third party only with a range of optional extras including £100,000 motor legal expenses cover, courtesy car, European car insurance cover and increased personal accident cover up to £100,000.

One of LV ='s related brand/ABC's motor insurance offers a product range including comprehensive and third party, fire and theft cover with optional add-ons including voluntary excess, business use and no-claim discount protection.

The motor insurance product range offered by LV's other brand High-way Insurance comprises comprehensive and third party, fire and theft car insurance, van and specialist vehicle insurance for products including classic and modified cars.

The 'When you join Frizzell, you will never want to leave' campaign

Background

The relationship that Frizzell Insurance had with membership organizations, such as CSMA, UNISON and PCS+, had given the company an unprecedented insight into the needs of their members. By sharing data with the associations, it offered Frizzell Insurance an opportunity to better understand their customers, such as their demographic background, personalities as well as other general behavioural indicators as a consumer. It enabled Frizzell to understand customers' individual financial requirements and exceed their expectations. It also facilitated more precise targeting. The company enjoyed some of the longest-serving customers in the insurance business. Generally speaking, it is found that most of Frizzell's customers demonstrate the characteristics of being conservative, loyal and risk-averse. Compared to other customer groups, they are generally safer, low-mileage drivers who are less likely to claim on their insurance. This gave Frizzell an edge in terms of financial performance. Frizzell's customers were also more likely to remain loyal; the average customer stays for over 12 years, with some being 'lifetime' customers. The motor insurance industry is known for having low loyalty rates. On average, 60 per cent of motorists shop around each year for their insurance. This number has recently climbed to 80 per cent. Only an average of 40 per cent of drivers choose to stay with the same insurer. In one survey, it is reported that only 5 per cent of motorists were unable to name either their insurer or their broker! However, research showed that the majority of Frizzell's customers would stay, even after attempts to shop around for better deals.

In the past, Frizzell traditionally tried to attract new customers with low-key advertising in civil service and teachers' journals, whose readership coincide largely with Frizzell Insurance's target group. Frizzell also kept their tradition of establishing links with staff organizations in its target markets. The new customers would remain in the same category, who tend to be civil servants, teachers and public-sector employees. Compared to the mass market where price-sensitivity is a main feature, Frizzell's customer base is more tolerant towards the company's slightly higher pricing strategy.

However, despite its close association to the unions and the advantages that come with it, it does not mean Frizzell Insurance was winning the game. In the early 1990s, Frizzell had very low market awareness of just about 16 per cent of the market beyond its stock of loyal customers. In the meantime, cheaper rivals were winning growing market share by competing on price. Competitors such as Direct Line Insurance began its first-ever TV campaign, using a direct-response telephone service to give motorists quotes on insurance.

Direct Line was established in 1985. It is the UK's first ever provider of a 'forms free' telephone claims service. Direct Line underwrote its own policies and was therefore cheaper than Frizzell. It also carried out aggressive promotional campaigns, which quickly made it one of the UK's largest insurance companies. In 1993, it achieved the status of Britain's largest insurer of privately owned motor vehicles, within a period of only nine years after being established. Although Frizzell had loyal customers, their position would not be tenable in the long run if they were unable to recruit new customers. Frizzell desired further development and a bigger market share. The company faced the problem of deciding on whom to recruit and how. They needed a clear segmentation strategy to attract the right kind of customers who would be relatively easy to serve but lucrative. At the same time, Frizzell would like to maintain and further enhance their reputation as a reliable financial solution provider. For this reason, the company decided to go for a major advertising campaign for the first time in their history. But, first of all, Frizzell needed to work out a few issues.

Target market

Frizzell Insurance understood very well their success formula within the current target market. Instead of diversifying their product portfolio and attracting other market segments, they preferred to stay within their comfort zone and offer what they do best. This was partially due to the lack of financial and human resources to expand the business further. Market research showed that Frizzell's customers regarded loyalty as the best indicator of good-quality service. They chose to remain with Frizzell simply because of the superior services they had received over the years. Therefore, customer loyalty and quality service were the main competitive advantages that Frizzell Insurance wanted to capitalize on. However, it was also apparent that, with the increase in demand, especially demand from different consumer groups, each call represented handling time. All the extra time consumed in answering calls of diverse needs would quickly escalate costs for a firm that was used to high closing rates on enquiries. It was tempting to loosen up the segmentation criteria to boost the number of enquiries, but Frizzell was not willing to sacrifice the good-quality service and customer loyalty for merely an increase in the number of calls. They were looking for something more, something beyond the pure number. Frizzell's focus was calls of excellent quality and that would generate decent profit margin. They wanted to attract people who would remain loyal and who would tend to be low-risk and therefore less likely to claim on their insurance, since this is the type of customer that the company is geared towards handling.

The company needed a strategy that is cost-effective. An internal analysis of Frizzell's customers showed that, besides being conservative, loyal and risk-averse, in terms of age, most of their customers are aged 35 and above. They work for the public sector and tend to have reliable and stable incomes. Based on the analysis, the company ruled out customer groups who are more price-sensitive, or more willingly to take risks and prone to making claims in the future, for example young adults who usually have less income and are less likely to drive safe. Consequently, the advertising objective was set up to create enquiries from people who are similar to Frizzell Insurance's current customer base that value loyalty and integrity, but, in the meantime, to actively discourage high-risk drivers or customers motivated only by cost.

Format of the ad

Since the firm was to be competing with much larger, better-established firms, the campaign needed to be imaginative rather than expensive. Frizzell's budget was small with a mere sum of only £1.7 million, while major competitors such as Direct Line had a dazzling budget of over £5 million.

BMP DDB was hired as Frizzell's agency to work on the advertising campaign. Following the trend of the time, BMP DDB proposed a strategy of using a direct-response adverts. However, the insurer rejected this strategy of their rivals because of their positioning as a slightly more expensive insurer for conservative, loyal, risk-averse drivers. Frizzell would like to differentiate themselves by being seen as offering something more for the value of money their customers are paying. Therefore, it was essential for them to establish the right image through the right type of ad. BMP DDB thus designed a TV campaign based on real case histories of long-term customers. The advertising proposition was 'when you join Frizzell, you will never want to leave'. This campaign positioned Frizzell Insurance as 'honest, expert, trustworthy and helpful' (Mortimer, 2008).

Content of the ad

As mentioned above, BMP DDB utilized real case studies that showed customers of long standing. One advert featured a pastiche of images and songs from 1960s London. There was black-and-white film footage of Beatles concerts, flashes of newspaper headlines referring to memorable events of the time and footage of slim, young men enjoying happy times in their first car. The advert had a very old but nostalgic feel and was intended to be charming to the no longer slim or young drivers who were now solid citizens of 50 years of age. The advert used news clips from the period when the customers had first insured with Frizzell, and pop music that was trendy around that time was played to help strengthen the sense of period and appeal to the target group. The advert analysed in this study shows a young man – Mr Catherall who claimed on his insurance in 1965 when his Hillman Minx was damaged. He called his insurer Frizzell in frustration. The office lady who answered his call quickly dispatched a claims form, and the claim was dealt with promptly. Mr Catherall was overall very pleased with the service. The advert ended in present time, where Mr Catherall already had grey hair, and the Hillman Minx was no longer his means of transport. However, one thing remained unchanged: the fact that he was still with Frizzell Insurance, after 29 years of relationship.

Dissemination of the ad

The ad was simply saying that Frizzell Insurance was like an old friend, always reliable in an emergency. It elicited emotional appeals from the potential customers who belong to Frizzell's target profile – the loyal, low-risk civil servants. Before the campaign was launched, qualitative pre-tests with a representative sample of customers showed that target customers found the ad charming, honest and involving, whereas the undesired customer group found the ad boring and simplistic. This, of course, was the ideal outcome. Frizzell wanted to signal implicitly that younger consumers were not the primary target audience of the firm, as some of their features do not fit well with Frizzell's product profile. Frizzell's desired market segment was older consumers who are less price-conscious and, from a car insurer's point of view, carry lower risk to ensure the firm's profitability. The ad expressed a feeling that contradicted young consumers' desired identities. Frizzell was pleased with the result from the market research. Hence, the ad went ahead. Radio advertising was used to back up the campaign. Classic FM was selected as the ideal vehicle for carrying this radio ad. A related ad was also shown in national press. In addition, a national equestrian event was sponsored by Frizzell.

Results

The results showed that, during the first year of the campaign, awareness of Frizzell went up 300 per cent at the national level, going from 20 per cent to 60 per cent of the adult population. These awareness gains appeared to be long lasting, and analysis of the enquiries received showed that the vast majority of them were in the target group that falls into the 'Careful Planners' category, who carry low risks.

Overall, Frizzell's campaign generated a return on investment of almost 25 per cent per annum. It is clearly a rewarding investment in advertising. Compared to Frizzell's competitor Direct Line who was in possession of a larger marketing budget, the return made by Frizzell over the same period was much higher. This outcome was achieved without compromising potential profit margins or increasing overall cost of the operation of the company. In addition, Frizzell managed to maintain the company's good reputation in their niche market and continued to ace in the game.

Endnote

Frizzell's 'When you join Frizzell, you will never want to leave' campaign is only one example among many others who successfully demarketed themselves from potential customer groups in a selective manner. The current development in the motor insurance industry harbours many issues that require special attention from the insurers to carefully draft their future marketing strategies. These issues include the high costs of car insurance for young adults, especially the recent increase in the young female segment, and the growing number of senior drivers aged 65+. For Frizzell Insurance, the latter issue appears more prominent. Given that their existing target market is customers who are aged 35+ and long standing with the firm, it means there is a possibility that Frizzell has a significant number of customers aged 65+. Although senior drivers tend to be cautious in driving, they carry other sets of specific risks. Whether Frizzell Insurance is ready to serve this market and how to serve (or not) these customers are still open questions.

Questions

1. What was Frizzell's purpose of carrying out the ad campaign in the mid-1990s?
2. How did Frizzell successfully increase their market share in ROI in the mid-1990s?
3. How should Frizzell approach the issue of an increasing number of senior drivers aged 65+ and the risks involved in serving this market?
4. Would there be any ethical issues if Frizzell rejected the market of senior drivers (65+)?
5. Are there any other threats to Frizzell's niche market, for example, means of distribution?

References

Blythe, Jim (2000) *Marketing*, Select Knowledge Ltd., Hertfordshire.
CSMA (2012) *About CSMA Club*, available at http://www.csmaclub.co.uk/clubinfo/aboutcsmaclub accessed 23 December 2012.
Hackley, C. (2005) *Advertising and Promotion: Communicating brands*, SAGE, London.
LV = (2012) *About us*, available at http://www.lv.com/ accessed 23 December 2012.
LV = Frizzell (2012) *About Frizzell*, available at http://www.frizzell.co.uk/ accessed 23 December 2012.
Mintel (2012) *Motor Insurance – UK –* March 2012, Mintel Group Ltd., available at http://academic.mintel.com/display/590047/, accessed 23 December 2012.

Mortimer, K. (2008) Identifying the components of effective service advertisements, *The Journal of Services Marketing*, 22(2), pp. 104–13.

PCS+ (2012) *About PCS*, available at http://www.pcs.org.uk/en/about_pcs/index.cfm accessed 23 December 2012.

Peachey, K. (2011) *New Drivers Face Motor Insurance Shock*, BBC, 14 October, available at http://www.bbc.co.uk/news/business-15277714 accessed 23 December 2012.

UNISON (2012) *Essential Information*, available at http://www.unison.org.uk/about/about.asp accessed 23 December 2012.

10

OSTENSIBLE DEMARKETING

The power of prohibition

Robin Croft

> It is agreeable with the nature of man to long after things forbidden and to desire what it denied us.
>
> *(François Rabelais 1532)*

Ostensible demarketing happens when professionals attempt to restrict or prevent the way a product, service or brand is offered: whether by accident or design, the threat of withdrawal paradoxically increases its desirability. This phenomenon was identified nearly 50 years ago by Jack Brehm who called it 'psychological reactance'. Brehm (1966) argued that, when the freedom to act in a particular way was taken away, or when it was suggested that this freedom was about to be withdrawn, consumers would invariably persuade themselves that the item in question was better than they had previously thought.

Since Brehm's classic study was published, the theory has been tested on a range of products (for example Mazis *et al.* 1973), and has provided plausible explanations for numerous marketing phenomena where consumers appear not to have acted in the manner predicted by economists. A good example was the decision by Coca-Cola in 1985 to replace their staple product line with something called New Coke: the mistake, according to Ringold (1988) and others, was not the launching of New Coke (the company spent $4 million on market research), but the decision to take the long-established original product off the market.

Psychological reactance applies to this sort of product-based demarketing, where a brand owner announces its intention to kill off an under-performing product. It is also relevant where distribution is restricted, for example by withdrawing the product from certain channels, or by restricting how much of it consumers are able to buy. There is also ample evidence to show that what Brehm described in 1966 can explain the way in which the ostensible demarketing of companies, brands, products and services actually works to their benefit.

The term 'ostensible demarketing' seems first to have been coined by Kotler and Levy in 1971, and is distinguished from other forms of demarketing by the focus on creating the appearance of trying to discourage demand as a device for actually increasing it. The problem for me in this chapter is the notion of 'creating the appearance': while there is a great deal of anecdotal evidence about products and services that appear deliberately to have been demarketed, in some cases their enhanced appeal has been an unintended consequence. Kotler and Levy's definition of ostensible demarketing is problematic in that in order for it to apply we need the certainty that a stratagem of deliberate deception was being practised.

There are many examples where demarketing a product, or having an advertisement banned, has benefited the brand, but hardly any where the marketing people have publicly admitted that this was their intention all along. This is unsurprising, as owning up to any kind of manipulation of public and media alike could easily rebound. More common is the reaction of Coca-Cola to accusations that they had deceived the public in 1985: their claim 'We are not smart enough for that' (Clifford 2009) neatly dodged the ethical questions and positioned the company as being the consumer's friend.

In order not to become diverted by a whole raft of deontological or teleological debates, it is more useful to consider ostensible demarketing, in the light of Brehm's study of psychological reactance and those that subsequently tested it, as the process by which a product, service or brand becomes more effectively marketed by being demarketed.

Similarly avoiding the tricky question of whether or not brand owners connived in 'successful' demarketing campaigns or merely benefited from them, in this chapter, I will be taking examples where a decision to restrict or prohibit some aspect of marketing appears instead to have boosted the brand in question. This means that my definition of 'ostensible demarketing' is by nature broader than Kotler and Levy's: as well as considering the strategic execution (a putative withdrawal of the product or advertising as a way of boosting its appeal), I will be looking at how this sort of outcome can emerge accidentally, often because the initiators were unaware of consumers' tendency 'to long after things forbidden and to desire what it denied us' (Rabelais). Ostensible demarketing, in this broader definition, therefore includes the attempts by different players to prevent or restrict the marketing of something: it may, for example, be practised by brand owners boosting demand by restricting supply, or by regulators banning an advertising campaign. In both cases, the ostensible aim of restricting marketing achieves the opposite.

In this chapter, I examine a number of areas where ostensible demarketing takes place: in advertising, music and publishing, creative work emerges only to fall foul of censors, regulators or other public guardians. I also show how when a government acts in the public interest to change behaviours or to withdraw services it can unwittingly create new demand; and finally I look at how taking a product off the market (or just threatening to) can dramatically boost demand and prepare the ground for a successful rebranding.

Examples of ostensible demarketing

If one takes the broad view of ostensible demarketing proposed above – where, regardless of intention, professional attempts to restrict or prevent marketing appear instead to enhance the product, service or brand – then there are two principal executions of the phenomenon. The first of these is what I will call strategic demarketing, that is where the professionals responsible take the decision to restrict or cease promotion, distribution or some other aspect of marketing. The second major category I term third-party demarketing, which refers to the attempts of others to restrict or prevent marketing – including advertising or distribution. In both cases, though, it is possible to see Brehm's principles at work, as consumers and audiences have their emotional strings pulled by the possibility of something that they may have enjoyed being withdrawn from them.

Strategic ostensible demarketing

The strategic element in this form of demarketing is the decision by an organization or its representatives to curtail or threaten to restrict some aspect of marketing (including the extreme option of taking the product off the market). What makes this ostensible demarketing is that, whatever the original intention, the net result appears to be that the marketing of the product, service or brand is enhanced. This may be an accidental outcome (we could call this serendipitous marketing), or it may be a clear choice (as per Kotler and Levy's definition) to give the appearance of demarketing as a stratagem better to achieve one's corporate objectives. The only meaningful distinction between these two types is intention, something notoriously difficult to assess.

The example of New Coke, discussed above, is a well-known and telling example of strategic ostensible demarketing. As numerous studies, popular (see, for example, Oliver 1986) and scholarly (for example, Ringold 1988), have reported, Coca-Cola's decision in 1985 to withdraw what came to be known as Classic Coke produced a very different outcome from the public relations disaster described in many entry-level marketing textbooks. Prior to the 'debacle' (Clifford 2009), when the company was forced to reintroduce Classic Coke in the USA, Coca-Cola had lost its market leadership and continued to suffer from a declining market share. Within six months of the attempted demarketing these trends had reversed, with Coca-Cola regaining the lead from Pepsi and continuing to show growth in sales and market share into the late 1980s (Ringold 1988). Whether intended or not, the company's removal of a long-established brand appeared to trigger a collective bout of national grief at the passing of a loved one, followed by a Proustian remembrance of its core qualities on the re-introduction. The extent to which an initial demarketing decision led to a reversal of a long-standing decline led to speculation that the whole exercise was indeed (in Kotler and Levy's terms) creating the appearance of a strategic marketing withdrawal with the express intention of boosting a declining brand (Haig 2011: 13). This charge was disingenuously rejected by the company, which shrugged off a threatened consumer boycott as 'a humbling experiment' (Clifford 2009). It was an example, as Ringold (1988) observed, demonstrating the classic features of psychological reactance.

Another telling example of the genre (pronouncing the death sentence on a long-established brand, only to see its fortunes revived) is that of the British staple Heinz Salad Cream in 2000. Once again, the former market leader had been overtaken by more fashionable rivals when the company threatened to take it off the market. But while in the case of Coca-Cola the consumer 'backlash' came when the product was withdrawn, Heinz was 'persuaded' to give their brand a stay of execution by the consumer campaign that followed from the announcement (Smithers 2010). A new branding strategy swung into action (Richardson 2001) with the rising tide of consumer goodwill being tapped into with an exercise repositioning of Heinz Salad Cream for a younger audience. The level of detail in this rebranding (pricing, packaging, promotion, distribution) suggests that it had been thought through in advance, in other words that that withdrawal announcement created the appearance of demarketing, while in practice the brand owner (correctly) anticipated the role of psychological reactance theory in re-awakening brand loyalty.

But while in the case of Classic Coke the threat of withdrawal was able to trigger a brand revival, Cadbury's Wispa is an example of where nostalgia for a defunct product was used to resurrect a dead brand. The chocolate bar in question had been discontinued without demur in 2003, but a social media-based campaign to bring the product back to life in 2008 'persuaded' the company that 'consumer passion' (Sweeney 2008) would support a carefully planned relaunch: in the event, the product became the company's fastest-selling product in four years, shifting 12 million bars in the four weeks following its reintroduction. The company continued to benefit and was able to extend the brand with multiple variants including an ice cream Wispa (Beckett 2011).

More tellingly is the case of BMW in the UK: in 1997, enjoying sales up 20 per cent on the previous year, the company warned that demand was outstripping supply (Smith and Nuki 1997). For good measure, towards the end of the year, BMW announced that it would henceforth be restricting sales to 60,000 a year. The rationale was sound enough: 'Exclusivity is an extremely important feature of the BMW brand,' the company told the *Sunday Times*, 'If we sold 100,000 cars next year ... we would do it at the expense of some of the values which make BMW what it is' (Nuki and Hamzic 1997). The marque was duly rewarded by an increase in sales of over 12 per cent in the following year (Burt 1999), achieved in a shrinking market and with the added bonus of a strong pound significantly increasing the profit per vehicle sold (Duckers 1999). Fast forward to 2012: BMW sold nearly 180,000 cars in Britain (Russell 2013).

A similarly inconclusive assessment of corporate motivations can apply to the music industry, where there is anecdotal evidence that parental advisory notices applied to CDs, in an ostensible demarketing way warning about profanity and other issues, often actually boost sales. The normally mild-mannered folk musician John Denver stated as much to a 1985 Congressional hearing on the subject:

> That which is denied becomes that which is most desired, and that which is hidden becomes that which is most interesting. Consequently, a great

deal of time and energy is spent trying to get at what is being kept from you.

(US Senate 1985: 65–66)

I will return to the music industry later in this chapter, where, under the heading of third-party demarketing, we can see how the efforts of regulators to ban or restrict music invariably backfires. Strategic demarketing, by contrast, involves the deliberate choices of the brand owner. Another case is that of the short-lived Death Brand cigarette in the 1990s: this item was ostensibly a branded anti-consumption message, with its owners claiming the moral high ground for its stark, graphic and paradoxical association of death and smoking (McIntosh 1996); arguably, though, the whole branding and packaging combination was a clever piece of ostensible demarketing, its nihilistic messages being part of the brand's appeal (see also Brownlie 1999:37).

Third-party demarketing

Third-party demarketing happens when an outside agency (for example, a regulator, a moral arbiter or the legal system) attempts to curtail or terminate the marketing of a product, service or brand, only to find that the very threat of restriction has the opposite effect and actually increases demand. This phenomenon is common in music, publishing and in advertising. Third-party demarketing shares the same problem with strategic intention that I discussed earlier: in some cases, the attempt to ban a product or advertisement seems a genuine one, but in others it is possible to detect the manipulating hand of brand owners, provoking the media or other moral guardians into actions designed to heighten the brand's appeal. Once again, though, it is difficult to find actors prepared to own up to this sort of deception.

In third-party demarketing, the original protagonist can include government. One example of how a statutory regulator's attempted demarketing decision seemed to have played into the hands of the brand owner is that of Virgin Rail in 2012: the company had lost out to a competitor in the bidding to retain its franchise to run trains on the west coast lines in Britain, but mounted a highly successful rear-guard action via social media highlighting to its customers what life would be like without Virgin. Despite Virgin Rail being the country's second most complained-about operator (Osborne 2012), users rushed to its defence and demanded that the government's decision to award the contract to First Group be reversed. This came to pass in the autumn of 2012, although ostensibly the reason had nothing to do with the public backlash (Topham 2013).

It is possible, of course, that the social media campaign was a spontaneous one, unconnected with Virgin or its PR advisers: what is not in doubt is the connection between a threatened withdrawal of a service and the emergence of significant numbers of users who claimed not to be able to do without it. A similar story is recounted by Goldacre (2012: 138–40) concerning the blood-pressure drug Midodrine. This had been approved by the FDA, the US regulator, in 1996, but with only limited clinical data to support its therapeutic claims. Fourteen years later, the original manufacturer had still failed to provide this evidence (although the company disputed this) and the FDA announced that the drug's licence would be withdrawn. This provoked a public outcry from some of the 100,000 US users of the drug, triggered in part by anecdotal evidence from patients published in the national and international press. Backing up the stories of patients desperate that something that, regardless of the trials, worked for them (there was no other clinically proven alternative on the market) was a Facebook campaign, which helpfully linked supporters to their representatives in Congress. When the FDA reversed its decision after just a month of lobbying, some of the same publications that had earlier criticized the FDA for ignoring the voices of patients (for example, Miller 2010) now derided the same agency for ignoring its own stated principles of evidence-based decision making. More bizarrely, Shire (the original manufacturer and patent owner of Midodrine), which had announced that it was to cease manufacturing in any case, changed its corporate mind and decided to continue to market the drug (*Star Tribune*, citing Associated Press 2010). Echoes of Coca-Cola, perhaps, and a suggestion that this should be considered as strategic demarketing?

But there is another form of third-party demarketing where the brand owner provokes the regulators into threatening a ban, sometimes in order to enhance the brand's visibility, at other times in order to boost sales. One example where the execution of this strategy has been described by those involved is George Shaw, the PR specialist responsible for the notorious 2001 'Ditch the bitch' advertising campaign for London divorce lawyers Brookmans. Shaw fell just short of admitting to deception: 'Experience has taught us that the press are more likely to cover stories that have been leaked or they have unearthed for themselves' (Shaw 2013). The client in this case was able to leverage a minute advertising budget into a campaign worth in excess of £1.5 million by carefully and covertly orchestrating viral marketing to give the impression to national media that the public was outraged by the slogans 'Ditch the bitch' and 'All men are bastards' (Clarke 2001). Shaw's strategy seemed to be to leak details of two otherwise obscure posters to moral guardians (women's groups) and regulators (the Advertising Standards Authority and the Law Society). When the media storm had died down, it became clear that, far from being outraged, nobody from the general public had complained (Dyer 2001), so there was no ban and no investigation.

Another unusually frank admission about the use of this kind of third-party demarketing comes from 1996, courtesy of what was then a start-up airline. easyJet was opening a new Luton to Aberdeen route, but, with an established competitor in British Airways, and short of funds to finance a major promotional push, easyJet instead booked advertising spots close to BA's check-in desk at Aberdeen Airport (Anderson 2010). They then designed a poster in BA colours and typeface warning 'Beware! Thieves operate in this airport'. This provocative execution, which tied in with easyJet's wider PR message about BA's fares, predictably was vetoed by the airport authority: what followed was what easyJet's marketing director at the time called 'a strategic leak' to the local *Press and Journal* (Anderson 2010), which obligingly gave the offending poster front-page coverage. Advertising bans have become something of a staple of the now fiercely competitive airline industry, with easyJet as likely to be complained about as to make complaints (see, for example, Farey-Jones 2011, 2012). A new strategy seems to be emerging with this form of attack advertising: in making a complaint, the rival travel company positions itself as the consumer's friend; however, in defending it, the original company is able to generate publicity by attempting to substantiate the claims made.

The phenomenon of producing advertising with the express purpose of generating headlines through stimulating controversy has been extensively discussed in relation to the Benetton poster campaigns of the 1980s and 1990s (see, for example, O'Donohoe and Turley 2000). Despite the conspiracy theories in Benetton's case, though, the company resolutely defended the artistic intent in the creative execution, denying that there was any cynical exploitation of media controversy. Far from saving on cost of advertising (as was the case with easyJet in 1996), Benetton's spend on above the line advertising ran into the millions (Brown 2004: 126).

A more recent example of a brand courting controversy is Paddy Power. Like the early easyJet campaigns, it picked strategically placed billboards on which to make provocative gestures (see, for example, Sale 2013). Provocation seemed to define the Paddy Power brand, although one would be hard pressed to find the company admitting to deliberately deceiving the public and media. Brown had earlier (2001) described how the fruit juice brand Tango had been censured in 1994 for duping an estimated 30,000 people into calling a bogus customer help line. Paddy Power, though, seemed to adopt the approach advocated by George Shaw (above), leaking the story and allowing the press to find it for themselves. In 2012, the Advertising Standards Authority (ASA) ruled on seven formal complaints about Paddy Power, upholding six and rejecting one. It also informally resolved five cases featuring Paddy Power marketing, including sales promotions, web pages and emails. Dutifully, Britain's national and trade press reported the complaints and judgments: obligingly, Paddy Power made the banned material available to the public via social media and the worldwide web.

The company's own YouTube pages included the boast 'Paddy Power Blind Football – Most complained advert in 2010' – although ironically this was the sole complaint that the ASA rejected from that year. Paddy Power's YouTube presence includes 900 videos, which at the time of writing had been viewed nearly 14 million times. These were fed by 125,000 followers on Twitter and 730,000 fans on Facebook.

When regulatory bodies intervene in marketing programmes the unintended consequences are often a boosting of brand equity and sales. Titanium drivers in golf, full body suits in swimming, energy-absorbing basketball shoes, steel baseball bats – all have been accused of giving competitors an unfair advantage, and many have been banned by the sports' governing bodies (see, for example,

Garside 2013). Online retailers of Nike Air Jordan basketball shoes have not been slow to exploit the notoriety of some products, helpfully adding the description 'banned' in red type to some of the items that had fallen foul of the sport's governing body.

The attempted imposition of bans by regulators, backed up by the calls of moral guardians, are the stuff of legend in the music industry also. One of the early arbiters of public taste was the BBC and its infamous Dance Music Policy Committee, whose archives date back to the 1930s. Leigh's excellent 2007 study of these shows how the corporation objected to innuendo and direct reference to sex, drugs, brand names, blasphemy and other taboos. Nor was this merely a pre-war phenomenon: 'Relax', the début single from Frankie Goes to Hollywood, was banned shortly after its release in 1984 by the BBC, the single going on to reach number one and stay there for five weeks (Grundy 2011). It was a similar story for other classic pieces, not just ones censored by the BBC: the Evil Dead, Serge Gainsbourg, the Sex Pistols, Louis Armstrong, Frank Zappa, the Beatles, Billie Holiday and Pink Floyd all succeeded despite – or perhaps, because of – officious regulators or censors (Spencer 2005). What better way to be noticed in a crowded marketplace, what more effective way of establishing the cutting-edge credentials of a piece of culture than to have it withdrawn? (See Brown 2001.)

The marketing message 'The one they tried to ban' is a potent one, not only exploited by the music business but by publishers also. When ex-spymaster Peter Wright attempted to publish his memoirs in 1985, he came up against the might of the British Government, which went to court in an attempt to suppress publication (Norton-Taylor 1988). Despite the fact that there was little in the book that was not already in the public domain, the notoriety generated by the attempted gag on publication ensured the book's success (Zuckerman 1987). It is not just governments and official censors that can boost the popularity of a book through exploiting its non-availability: Flaubert, DH Lawrence, Salman Rushdie, Nabokov and many other authors appear to have benefited from being denounced by moral guardians. Dan Brown's *The Da Vinci Code* was hardly in need of a publicity boost ahead of being made into a film in 2005, but sales were not noticeably harmed when the world's press learned that the Vatican had appointed a Cardinal officially to debunk the heresies it saw in the book (see, for example, Pauli 2005). Similarly, sales of JK Rowling's Harry Potter books were buoyed by regular media reports that it was the most banned book in America (Capon and Scott 2013): Rowling's publishers have also been adept at exploiting other aspects of psychological reactance theory – in particular carefully withholding information from the media and giving the appearance that there would be restricted supplies of the books available (Brown 2001).

Benefits of ostensible demarketing

The examples above show how it is possible to choose to restrict aspects of the marketing of a product, service or brand in order to enhance its desirability.

Ostensible demarketing, in summary, demonstrates a range of possible benefits, whether or not those responsible are able to admit to the fact that their actions merely 'give the appearance' (Kotler and Levy) of demarketing. These include:

- free or cheap publicity (Paddy Power, Tango, easyJet, Brookmans);
- positioning the product on the cultural cutting edge (Benetton, most of the musical numbers listed);
- creating desire for something unavailable (Coca-Cola, Wispa, Heinz Salad Cream, Virgin Rail, BMW, Midodrine);
- creating desire through aroused curiosity (Harry Potter);
- enhancing the product's appeal through conspiracy theories (*The Da Vinci Code*);
- offering users the unfair advantage of banned technologies.

Most of these benefits are predicted both by psychological reactance theory and its more limited extension into studies of consumer behaviour (for example, Brown's Marketease analyses of 2001, or Gerstner *et al.*'s differentiation strategies of 1993). What these authors are able to demonstrate is that ostensible demarketing is a long way from being an obscure theory from behavioural psychology, but instead has long been in the marketing tool chest of retailers, hucksters, salesmen and brand entrepreneurs. Brown (2001) goes further than considering this sort of ostensible demarketing as a peripheral set of actions outside the marketing mainstream: under the heading 'retromarketing', Brown describes how the savvy brand owner 'eschews the modern marketing proposition by deliberately holding back supplies. You want it? Can't have it. Try again later, pal.' Moreover, as the words of Rabelais at the start of this chapter demonstrate, the underlying principles are understood by writers and other artists.

Brown also alludes to the process of scaling up a small advertising budget through amplifying the communication process, restricting information and creating desire through anticipation and expectation. Similarly, producing advertising that seems expressly designed to be banned was described thus: 'There's nothing like a little outrage to attract attention and turn a tiny advertising spend into a megabudget monster' (Brown 2001). This principle has been exploited effectively in the examples here including easyJet and Brookmans. The processes are modelled in Figure 10.1, which shows how a brand owner can manipulate media and public opinions in order to provoke regulators into considering an advertising ban (or, in the case of Midodrine, to prevent the de-licensing of a product). It shows how the creative execution (deliberately provocative) can be strategically leaked to the mainstream media and taste guardians (for example, conservative politicians, civic leaders, religious authorities) in order to generate the adverse publicity needed to make a regulator consider a ban. Whether or not this comes to pass, the resulting publicity is exploited via social media as 'the one they tried to ban'.

What I have also hinted at in this chapter is that the process controlling information – rationing or withholding news, for example – can have similar

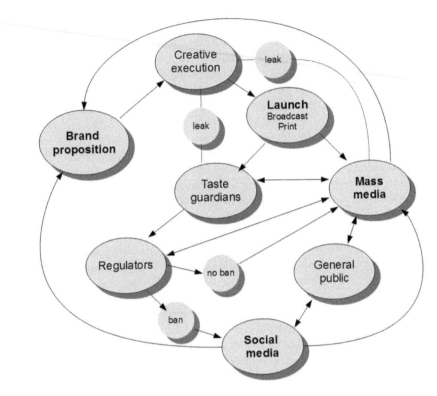

FIGURE 10.1 Model of third-party demarketing to provoke an advertising ban

consequences in enhancing the message, often in a manner unforeseen by those originally responsible for the decision. Once again, there is an ostensible element: JK Rowling's publishers were able to heighten media speculation about forthcoming Harry Potter novels by restricting information (Brown 2001), while Shaw found it useful to place elements of a story in different places in order to allow journalists to discover the story themselves. However, the most disruptive new arrivals in the communications environment were social media from about 2007 onwards (Croft 2013). These technologies, particularly blogs and microblogs like Twitter, put a range of mass communication tools in the hands of what originally was an audience; it is outside the scope of this chapter to do anything more than touch on this area, but it is sufficient to say that the processes for managing the brand narrative, in particular public relations, have needed a fundamental overhaul to take into account a new constituency of opinionated, sceptical and, above all, connected, consumers. I have already alluded to this in the examples of Virgin Rail, Midodrine, Wispa and others in the context of using social media to amplify a message when a product or service is withdrawn. What Paddy Power managed, though, was to amplify its brand proposition online precisely because it had been withdrawn. A similar strategy was used by *The Guardian* newspaper in 2007: by printing a news story (Leigh 2009) that tantalizingly talked of 'Legal obstacles, which cannot be identified, involve proceedings, which cannot be mentioned, on behalf of a client who must remain secret'. Withholding the story became the story itself, and Twitter became the medium by which the legal instruments that had been used to protect the reputation of an international oil trader were effectively undermined, and as a consequence the company's corporate brand was seriously damaged. As the WikiLeaks phenomenon shows (see Leigh 2011), governments, celebrities, politicians, companies or brand owners can no longer rely on the legal system to suppress inconvenient truths or scandalous untruths: indeed, in a process that mirrors the theory of psychological reactance discussed in this chapter, restricting, rationing or withholding information will often give that data the very energy it needs to disseminate widely. And, once again, there seems to be a category of strategic withholding of information, as well as third-party censorship.

The chapter opened with a brief discussion of the difficulties of applying Kotler and Levy's definition of ostensible demarketing, due to the near impossibility of being certain that a deliberate strategy of deception (giving the appearance of demarketing) had been employed. The easyJet example cited above is a rare, unambiguous case where those involved in the creative process candidly admitted that the intention from the outset was to have a piece of advertising banned in order to exploit the headlines that the ban would generate. In most cases, publicly at least, those responsible for campaigns described here as ostensibly demarketing would claim that their intentions were transparent, and that any branding benefits either represented a teleological justification, or was merely evidence of the action of the law of unintended consequences.

The fact that Kotler and Levy's definition of ostensible demarketing is problematic is unsurprising: as late as 1993, Gerstner *et al.* were reminding scholars that the original authors themselves had highlighted the need for empirical testing. In this chapter, I have proposed two categories of ostensible demarketing, strategic and third party. The examples used in turn could suggest further categories – for example, prohibition demarketing where the intention is to provoke an advertising ban or product withdrawal, or execution demarketing where, like many brand revivals, the termination of a brand is the trigger for a consumer resurgence. Coca-Cola's experience of finding one's decline reversed by accident rather than design could be termed serendipitous demarketing, where the assumption is made that there was no deception attempted. Perhaps the most surprising element of this debate is not so much the problematic nature of Kotler and Levy's definitions, but the comparative lack of conceptual development in this area, in the field of marketing and consumer behaviour at least (a rare example being Gerstner 1993). By contrast, Brehm's original 1966 writings have been challenged, tested and reworked extensively, and the principles of psychological reactance – key to any discussion of demarketing – are widely known (if not widely accepted) in the field of social psychology (see also Pettigrew's treatment of Lacan, 1996).

Withholding, rationing or restricting information, products, services or brands, whether deliberately undertaken or giving the appearance of demarketing, can be a highly complex and unpredictable process. However defined, however articulated, its use is widespread in marketing, the cultural industries and the mass media. More importantly, though, the very phenomenon we imperfectly understand is now subject to disruptive change with the widespread dissemination and democratization of digital media. However, it is worth remembering that when Francois Rabelais was writing the words quoted at the opening of this chapter the printing press was a relatively new, disruptive phenomenon in the communications environment. However, the ideas on desiring that which is unattainable or forbidden are just as relevant in the digital era.

References

Anderson, Tony (2010), *Gorilla Marketing*, London: Grosvenor House Publishing Ltd.

Beckett, Alex (2011), 'Wispa to hit freezers as Cadbury serves up an ice cream variant', *The Grocer*, 5 March.

Brehm, J.W. (1966), *A Theory of Psychological Reactance*, New York: Academic Press.

Brown, Stephen (2001), 'Torment your customers (they'll love it)', *Harvard Business Review*, October.

——(2004), Free Gift Inside!!: Forget the customer. *Develop Marketease*, London: John Wiley & Sons.

Brownlie, Douglas (1999), *Rethinking Marketing: Towards critical marketing accountings*, London: Sage Publications.

Burt, Tim (1999), 'Britain: BMW 's Rover offshoot suffers near-20% decline', *Financial Times* 8 July.

Capon, Felicity and Catherine Scott (2013), 'Top 20 books they tried to ban', *The Daily Telegraph*, 1 March.

Clarke, Anna (2001), 'Legal firm attacked over "ditch the bitch" ad campaign', *PR Week*, 16 May.

Clifford, Stephanie (2009), 'Coca-Cola deleting "Classic" from Coke label', *New York Times*, 31 January.

Croft, R. (2013), 'Blessed are the geeks: An ethnographic study of consumer networks in social media', 2006–2012 *Journal of Marketing Management* May 8, 2013.

Duckers, John (1999), 'The Birmingham Post: Call For car firms to drive down prices as sales fall', *The Birmingham Post*, 7 December.

Dyer, Clare (2001), 'Divorce lawyers' posters attacked', *The Guardian*, 16 May.

Farey-Jones, Daniel (2011), 'EasyJet business ad banned after Ryanair complaint', *Campaign*, 27 April.

——(2012), 'EasyJet complaint leads ad watchdog to ban train ad', *Campaign*, 9 May.

Garside, Kevin (2013), 'Consultation period ends over use of controversial anchored putters', *The Independent*, 1 March.

Gerstner, Eitan, James Hess and Wujin Chu (1993), 'Demarketing as a differentiation strategy', *Marketing Letters*, 4:1, pp. 49–57.

Goldacre, Ben (2012), *Bad Pharma: How drug companies mislead doctors and harm patients*, London: Fourth Estate.

Grundy, Gareth (2011), 'Frankie Goes to Hollywood's Relax "banned" by the BBC', *The Guardian*, 11 June.

Haig, Matt (2011), *Brand failures: the truth about the 100 biggest branding mistakes of all time*, London: Kogan Page Publishers.

Kotler, Philip and Sidney Levy (1971), 'Demarketing, yes, demarketing', *Harvard Business Review*, November–December, pp. 74–80.

Leigh, David (2009), 'Guardian gagged from reporting parliament', *The Guardian*, 12 October.

——(2011), *WikiLeaks: Inside Julian Assange's War on Secrecy*, London: Guardian Books.

Leigh, Spencer (2007), 'Unfit for Auntie's airwaves: the artists censored by the BBC', *The Independent*, 14 December.

McIntosh, Alastair (1996), 'From Eros to Thanatos: Cigarette advertising's imagery of violation as an icon into British cultural psychopathology', Occasional Paper, Centre for Human Ecology, Faculty of Science and Engineering, University of Edinburgh.

Mazis, Michael B., Robert B. Settle and Dennis C. Leslie (1973), 'Elimination of phosphate detergents and psychological reactance', *Journal of Marketing Research*, 10, pp. 390–95.

Miller, Henry I. (2010), 'Agency dithers, reputation withers – Ditsy decisions make for dizzy bureaucrats', *The Washington Times*, 29 September.

Norton-Taylor, Richard (1988), 'Newspapers win Spycatcher battle', *The Guardian*, 14 October.

Nuki, Paul and Edin Hamzic (1997), 'BMW rations cars to keep its cachet', *The Sunday Times*, 9 November.

Oliver, Thomas (1986), *The Real Coke, the Real Story*, New York: Random House.

O'Donohoe, Stephanie and Darach Turley (2000), 'Dealing with death: Art, morality and the market place', in Stephen Brown and Anthony Patterson (eds) (2000), *Imagining Marketing: Art, aesthetics and the avant-garde*, London: Routledge.

Osborne, Hilary (2012), 'Virgin Trains v FirstGroup: Which is best?', *The Guardian*, 15 August.

Pauli, Michelle (2005), 'Vatican appoints official Da Vinci Code debunker', *The Guardian*, 15 March.

Pettigrew, David (1996), *Disseminating Lacan*, New York: State University of New York Press.

Rabelais, Francois (1532), *Gargantua and Pantagruel*, translated by A. Screech, London: Penguin Classics (2006).

Ringold, Debra Jones (1988), 'Consumer response to product withdrawal: The reformulation of Coca-Cola', *Psychology and Marketing*, 5(3), pp. 189–210.

Richardson, Belinda (2001), 'Kitchen classic: Salad cream', *The Daily Telegraph*, 7 July.

Russell, Jonathan (2013), 'Britain in the driving seat as car sales leap to four–year record', *The Daily Telegraph*, 8 January.

Sale, Charles (2013), 'Cheeky Torres poster outside Stamford Bridge puts Chelsea in a paddy', *The Daily Mail*, 27 February.

Shaw, George (2013), *Brookmans Case Study, Avocado Media*, London, via www.avocadomedia. co.uk/Pages/case.html, accessed February 2013.

Smith, David and Paul Nuki (1997), 'Boom is official as the Porsche yuppie rides again', *The Sunday Times*, 17 August.

Smithers, Rebecca (2010), 'Dressing fancy: after 96 years, Heinz Salad Cream gets a new flavour', *The Guardian*, 1 September.

Spencer, Neil (2005), 'The 10 most x-rated records', *The Guardian*, 22 May.

Star Tribune (2010), 'FDA backs off plan to withdraw Shire low blood-pressure drug midodrine from market', *Star Tribune* citing Associated Press, 6 September.

Sweeney, Mark (2008), 'Cadbury calls on Wispa fans for ad help', *The Guardian*, 5 November.

Topham, Gwyn (2013), 'MPs blame west coast mainline fiasco on "complete lack of common sense"', *The Guardian*, 26 February.

US Senate (1985), *Record Labelling: Hearing before the Committee on Commerce, Science, and Transportation*, Ninety-Ninth Congress, First session on contents of music and the lyrics of records, Washington: US Government Printing Office.

Zuckerman, Laurence (1987), 'Press: how not to silence a spy', *Time Magazine*, 17 August.

11
OSTENSIBLE DEMARKETING CASE STUDY

Sally McKechnie

British Airways tells Britons 'Don't Fly'

The aim of this case study is to focus on one part of British Airways' integrated marketing communications plan for London 2012. It reviews the main advertising campaign, 'Don't Fly', which actively discouraged demand for outbound air travel by British nationals during the period of the Games so that they would stay and support the athletes in Team GB and Paralympics GB instead. The airline had just undergone its first major brand overhaul for a decade and was seeking to appeal to a wider audience especially in the increasingly commoditized short-haul market, where it had been losing market share to low-cost airlines. As a national Olympic sponsor, British Airways took a huge gamble with this bold demarketing campaign. Using traditional and new media platforms for the advertising campaign, BA was able to engage with a wider audience around the concept of boosting the 'home advantage', which would help to increase positive sentiment towards the brand.

Background

British Airways plc (BA) is the UK's largest airline by turnover (£9.99bn in 2011) and national flag-carrier (Key Note, 2013). Based near London Heathrow Airport, it is a leading global premium airline operator and member of the oneworld global airline alliance. The airline industry has undergone a period of consolidation. Having formed a transatlantic joint business with American Airlines and Iberia in 2010, BA recently merged in January 2011 with Iberia, to create the holding company International Airlines Group (IAG).

Since the terrorist attacks of 9/11, the airline industry has had to cope with a very turbulent environment. There have been severe periods of disruption caused around the world by pandemics, extreme weather and political instability, as well as concerns about soaring oil prices and the global economic downturn (Massey, 2011). Even so, air travel has continued to grow worldwide. According to the International Civil Aviation Organization (ICAO), 2.7 bn passengers travelled by air in 2011, representing a 5.1 per cent increase from the previous year (Matthews, 2012). The outlook, however, has not been so promising for the UK airlines industry, which experienced a year-on-year decline in passenger numbers between 2008 (131.4 m) and 2010 (122.4 m). This drop was largely a result of the onset of the UK recession in 2008/09, together with flight delays and cancellations brought about by the volcanic ash cloud following the eruption of Eyjafjallajökull in Iceland in 2010 and adverse winter weather conditions in 2010/11 (Key Note, 2013).

In May 2010, BA reported its second consecutive year of record financial losses (£531m at financial year ending March 2010 compared to £401m in 2009) (BBC News, 2010), and to add to its woes the airline's cabin crew had already begun strike action over pay and conditions, which marked the beginning of what proved to be a bitter eighteen-month-long dispute (Milmo, 2011). A further problem for BA was that, while UK airline passenger numbers were declining between 2008 and 2010, there had been an increase in the share of passenger numbers for the low-cost airline easyJet (from 28.7 per cent to 34.7 per cent) yet negligible variation for BA, which was the more established legacy carrier (from 24.2 per cent to 24.4 per cent). Changing public sentiment towards BA was succinctly captured on YouGov's BrandIndex, which measures overall brand health. Figure 11.1 shows how BA's Index score of +25 in December 2009 experienced a triple dip (twice into negative numbers following bouts of strike action) before managing to

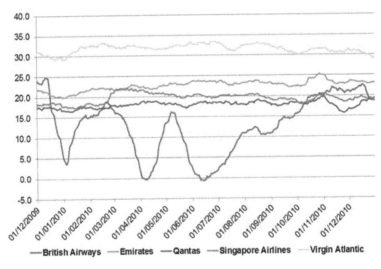

FIGURE 11.1 YouGov BrandIndex Scores for Airlines (Dec 2009–Dec 2010)
Data from YouGov BrandIndex, which is compiled by 2,000 respondents rating brands daily either positively or negatively on brand perception across 7 values (quality, value, reputation, impression, advocacy, satisfaction and buzz). Then, for each value, the proportion giving a negative answer is subtracted from those giving a positive answer to produce a single score ranging from -100 to +100.
Source: Shakespeare (2012a)

make a fairly steady recovery a year later to an Index score of +17 (Shakespeare, 2012a).

Recommitting to the core service ethos

Clearly, BA was suffering from a branding crisis, but its fortunes steadily began to be revived following the appointment in January 2011 of Frank van der Post (formerly Chief Operating Officer of the Jumeirah Group) as Managing Director of Brands and Customer Experience. He headed up a major rebranding exercise, which provided a timely opportunity to clarify the core values of the brand both externally and internally. Given the ongoing industrial strife at the time, it was important to consult employees as part of a company-wide improvement programme and increase staff engagement.

After revisiting the airline's British origins to decode the brand's DNA, it was clear that a sense of pride, passion and belief in the national carrier had to be restored rather than inventing something new. Indeed, the last thing BA needed was another marketing disaster like the huge outcry caused in 1997 when the Union Flag design on aircraft tail-fins was replaced with a variety of ethnic designs, which resulted in BA making a highly embarrassing U-turn two years later (Marketing Week, 1999).

The company motto 'To Fly. To Serve', which features on BA's coat of arms, uniform and was last seen on aircraft livery in the late 1980s, consists of four words that captured the essence of the airline's core service ethos. It was then used by their advertising agency Bartle, Bogle and Hegarty (BBH) to spearhead its first major global integrated brand campaign for a decade (Bacon, 2012). By replacing the airline's former corporate strapline 'The World's Favourite Airline' with 'To Fly. To Serve', BA was able to reaffirm its commitment to the core service ethos of the brand in the hope that this would help to increase brand engagement and renew belief in the core brand promise.

September 2011 saw the launch of a 90-second centrepiece TV advertisement titled 'Aviators', which celebrated the airline's 92-year history and heritage and articulated the strength of the brand promise. Keith Williams, CEO of British Airways, announced at the time: 'It represents the opening of a new chapter for British Airways' (Massey, 2011). BA also uploaded an Internet version of the commercial (YouTube, 2011a), along with two short videos. One of them features what the brand promise means to a range of BA employees (YouTube, 2011b) and the other shows how the commercial starring employees was made (YouTube, 2011c). At the same time as this launch, BA publicized a five-year programme to invest £5bn in improving the 'customer experience' that would cover new aircraft (such as Airbus A380) and improvements to cabin interiors, catering and other services (Bacon, 2012; Massey, 2011). According to Abigail Comber, BA's Head of Brands and Marketing, this investment would 'show that everything we do underpins that promise' (Marketing Week, 2012a). By November 2011, this included the relaunch of BA's Executive Club loyalty scheme and the debut of Avios points to replace AirMiles (Johnson, 2011).

the message, which is painted in white, is preceded by the ribbon symbol from BA's corporate logo (also in white) but there is no mention of the company name. Basically, this outdoor advertisement was relying on the principle of closure from Gestalt psychology to encourage people to participate in the advertisement so that they would fill in the gaps and make sense of it (Evans *et al.*, 2009). In doing so, BA would then be able to build awareness that it was the official airline partner of London 2012 and through inclusion of the hashtag #HomeAdvantage trigger a buzz on Twitter about garnering support for the national team.

With London Heathrow being the world's busiest airport in terms of passenger traffic (Key Note, 2013) and around four-fifths of all Games visitors expected to pass through it (*London Evening Standard*, 2012), this advertisement's reach was enormous. Luisa Fernandez, BA's sponsorship manager, commented that: 'Whether you're a Brit coming home, or an athlete arriving in for the London 2012 Games, this celebratory message reminds us all of the power of the home crowd and how important it is to get behind Team GB and ParalympicsGB' (Chapman, 2012). As for Ennis, she hoped that: '... it brings excitement to homecoming Brits, and reminds international athletes that we're ready and prepared' (Hanna, 2012).

The following week, BA uploaded a teaser version of the London 2012 commercial on BA's Facebook page before the full 60-second television version made its debut on national television later that day (YouTube, 2012d). Like 'The Race', the tone of voice in this commercial is light-hearted, and was described by Van der Post (YouTube, 2012c) as 'very tongue-in-cheek'. It features a scenario where passengers board a BA aircraft, which instead of taking off from a runway continues to taxi through the streets of London and across Westminster Bridge (see Figure 11.3) passing famous landmarks on its way to the Olympic Park. When the passengers disembark and hear the roar of the crowd as they head towards the Olympic stadium, the slogan 'Don't Fly. Support Team GB' appears with the hashtag #HomeAdvantage underneath. Finally, there is an aerial view of the stadium with a centrepiece BA logo flanked on either side by the logos of Team GB and the oneworld alliance. For the soundtrack, the commercial uses the iconic song 'London Calling' by the British punk rock group The Clash to serve as a rallying cry for the nation to get behind the national team and grow the home advantage for London 2012. While television advertising was used to spearhead the 'Don't Fly' campaign, it was supported by press advertising and outdoor posters bearing the same slogan 'Don't Fly. Support Team GB. #HomeAdvantage'. Once the Olympics were over (12th August), this supplementary advertising was repeated for the Paralympics (29th August to 9th September) with the wording of the slogan in press and outdoor advertising revised to 'Don't Fly. Support ParalympicsGB #HomeAdvantage.'

As one of the official domestic Olympic sponsors, BA was keen to get positive results from all of its paid media activities for London 2012. Through a carefully planned public relations strategy, BA had already attracted favourable media coverage of its experiential pop-up proposition on Shoreditch High

FIGURE 11.3 British Airways 'Don't Fly' commercial
Source: © British Airways. Reproduced by permission

Street in April (Cross, 2012; O' Ceallaigh, 2012), and of the arrival of 'Firefly', the BA aircraft delivering the Olympic flame in April from Athens to Royal Navy Air Station Culdrose in Cornwall (Mower, 2012). With these Games being labelled as 'the first social media Olympics' (Bell, 2012), driving social media activity was equally important. By prominently featuring the hashtag #HomeAdvantage in the guerrilla marketing stunt and then in the slogan of the 'Don't Fly' campaign, BA was hoping this would generate Twitter followers, who could then read and send messages that tapped into the sense of national pride that was being fostered not only by the Olympics, but also by the celebrations surrounding the Queen's Diamond Jubilee in June. This is not to say that BA ignored other social media platforms, because online versions of the TV commercial were made available on BA's Facebook page and on YouTube as well. Although users posted comments on these particular platforms, they were encouraged to join the conversation about the campaign using the hashtag #HomeAdvantage on Twitter.

In addition, on Facebook, the commercial was accompanied by an application (also available on another site taxi.ba.com), where users could watch the BA plane featured in the commercial taxiing down their street. This only worked for users with UK-based postcodes, but was a highly original way of reaching out to a broader UK audience to grab their attention and encourage buzz about the campaign. Another very clever social media application was BA's online social barometer, which captured the volume and nature of social media chatter about the home advantage campaign to support Team GB and Paralympics GB. All messages of support created through tweets, updates or blog posts were integrated with bespoke software, so that they could be used to produce a visual and audible sound wave called a 'Social Symphony' (British Airways, 2012). By being able to create online 'the sound of the #HomeAdvantage', BA was able to reflect the volume of user interaction with the campaign at any point in time before, during and after the Games (see Figure 11.4). Richard Bowden, British Airways' digital marketing innovation manager, commented that: 'The social barometer allows users to not only to see, but also hear the home support behind Team GB via ba.com or on the airline's Facebook and Twitter pages. We think it's a unique way of doing it which will inspire people to get involved via #HomeAdvantage' (British Airways, 2012). Besides, apart from the site giving a daily overview of message counts and top mentions, the sound could be filtered according to athlete, sport or venue being discussed and individual messages could be read by clicking on sound particles.

When the 'Don't Fly' campaign broke, one of the leading travel trade magazines described it as a campaign that 'risks upsetting the outbound travel

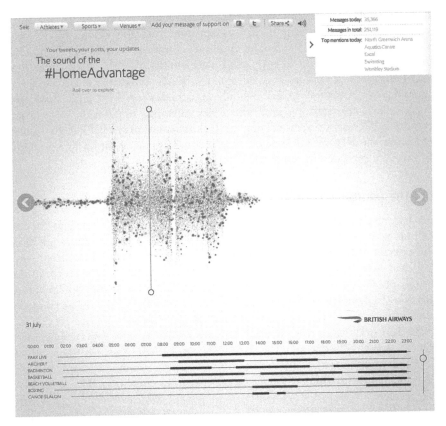

FIGURE 11.4 Social Symphony
Source: © British Airways. Reproduced by permission

industry' (Travel Weekly, 2012a). Its readers posted comments about it, such as 'it is outrageous' (Travel Weekly Reader) or 'The lunatics have finally been taken control on the asylum!' (Travel Weekly Reader) to voice concerns over the damage it could do to their business. With bookings already down while the Games were taking place, the 'Don't Fly' message was also perceived as 'a great own goal!' (Travel Weekly Reader) for the travel industry. Marketers, on the other hand, had praise for the campaign. For example, one creative consultant commented: 'Unlike so many of the other sponsors, BA found a way to make their London Olympics campaign not only eye-catching, but refreshing in content and tonally bang on' (Kershaw, 2012).

Consumer reactions to the 'Don't Fly' commercial were somewhat mixed as could be seen from reading the content of 431 comments posted on YouTube between the time of its launch up till mid-December. Consumers fell into three categories. First, there were many people who admired and understood the campaign; then there were those who were confused by it because it did not make sense to them; and finally there was a small minority who were negative and interpreted hidden meanings or took issue with the appropriateness of the choice of song for the soundtrack because of its lyrics. Throughout the five-month period of observation, it was apparent that the airline was closely monitoring these comments and posting consistent responses from Fly-BritishAirways to explain to users who were confused by the commercial that the campaign's intention was meant to be 'a tongue-in-cheek way of encouraging the nation to get behind our athletes for the Games', and, for those who were unhappy with the lyrics, that the soundtrack was chosen because it '... makes a great rallying cry for the nation to get behind the Games and boost the #HomeAdvantage!' A selection of some of the early comments by users are provided in Table 11.2.

Did the gamble pay off?

BA had taken a huge risk with the 'Don't Fly' advertising campaign for the Olympics. It could have gone horribly wrong for the airline. Although they had control of how the campaign would be executed, they did not have control over how such a bold and patriotic campaign would be perceived by the British public, particularly when they were trying to boost support for Team GB and ParalympicsGB through the 'home advantage' concept on social media platforms.

BA had nothing to fear, as the following results recently reported by Marketing Week (2012b) indicate: BA had the highest press coverage of all Olympic sponsors with 3,387 articles (Precise, media monitoring agency); there was an increase in BA's Olympic sponsorship awareness from 18 per cent to 54 per cent (Millward Brown data); and 86,000 Twitter users engaged with #HomeAdvantage (BA in-house data) meaning that not only did these users engage with the cause of supporting the national athletes, but they also engaged with the brand.

TABLE 11.2 Illustrative comments posted by YouTube users about 'Don't Fly'

Positive	I think it's incredibly brave and very patriotic. Well done to ALL involved! (YouTube User)
	Excellent ad! I love the "tongue in cheek" "don't fly" ! Great Work! (YouTube User)
	Britain Lets show The World What we can really do at London 2012 GO TEAM GB!! (YouTube User)
	Amazingly British!!! As only BA could do!!! (YouTube User)
	Well Done British Airways for this Advert! The best ever yet. And you just keep making them better. Talk about being creative and entertaining WOW! This is Fantastic. Awesome. Superb. Brilliant. Never thought I Would see a Boeing 777 Taxiing down my road. (YouTube User)
	Absolutely wonderful advert! It screams British Airways and a lovely ending. #Homeadvantage all the way … (YouTube User)
	Amazing. Quality … Brilliant … BA at it's Best … Proud to be British … BA Flying Us To Glory …. @TeamGB @ParalympicsGB #OurGreatestTeam #HomeAdvantage GoGB (YouTube User)
Confused	Isn't it a bit weird for an airline to say 'don't fly'? Otherwise great ad. (YouTube User)
	Strange line: "Don't Fly. Support team GB." Why the "don't fly" bit? Stunning ad by the way, superbly done! (YouTube User)
	Love it, But don't get it (YouTube User)
	So your encouraging 62 million potential customers to not fly?? (YouTube User)
Negative	Am I missing the point or an AIRWAYS company just told us NOT TO FLY ? (arround) the games timeframe ? #conspiracy anyone ? (YouTube User)
	Errmmm there seems to be a mistake in this ad...the Crew are smiling and have actually turned up for work....unusual! (YouTube User)
	Sorry, but London Calling was a poor choice of song. It's over-used by /anything/ to do with London and I think BA could have done a lot better. (YouTube User)
	Has anyone actually listened to the full lyrics of London Calling by The Clash? London's Calling is a song with lyrics that include references to violence, nuclear war, floods, famine, police violence and contains the line 'the engines stop running'. (YouTube User)
	Why would anyone fly with an airline that advertises that "Engines stop running but I have no fear"? (YouTube User)

Source: YouTube (2012a) (accessed June to December 2012)

According to Ritson (2012): 'While most brands are doing everything they can to avoid being lost in the clutter of modern marketing communications, the sponsors of 2012 are creating their own little cluttered environment and spending millions to achieve it'. Indeed, to appreciate just how cluttered the marketing communications environment was in the run-up to and during

London 2012, Timo Lumme, Managing Director, IOC Television and Marketing Services (IOC, 2012a, p. 47), commented: 'The sheer volume of London 2012 sponsor activities was staggering, with more than double the number of activations than for Beijing in 2008.' Setting aside the sponsorship from eleven Worldwide Olympic Partners, the Domestic Sponsorship Programme alone raised a total of £764 million (Beard, 2012). On top of this, there were the inevitable attempts by non-official sponsors at ambush marketing (Sweney, 2012). Therefore, during the Games, the onus was very much on brands being able to cut through all of this Olympics-themed clutter to get their message across to their target audience. The 'Don't Fly' campaign was innovative and enabled BA to do exactly this.

The first part of the 'Don't Fly. Support Team GB' slogan was disruptive to say the least. The message took the audience by surprise for this was not what anyone would normally expect an airline to say in its advertising. By comparison, the second part of the slogan indicated a pairing between the brand and the national team of athletes. By finishing off the slogan with the hashtag #HomeAdvantage to drive the social media side of the 'Don't Fly' campaign, BA was able to make an emotional connection with a much broader audience than normal. As the national flag-carrier, official airline partner of the London 2012 Games and also the official airline of the British team, there was a very good fit between the airline, the event it was sponsoring and the cause it was supporting. This congruence was critical for the campaign to be able to strike a chord with Britons so that they would get behind Team GB and ParalympicsGB.

By the end of the Games, medals for the home nation were in abundance (see Table 11.3) with the British team coming third in both the Olympics and the Paralympics. This represented the best performance by the team as a whole

TABLE 11.3 London 2012 Medal Table

Position	Olympic Team	Gold	Silver	Bronze	Total
1	United States of America	46	29	29	104
2	People's Republic of China	38	27	23	88
3	Great Britain	29	17	19	65
4	Russian Federation	24	26	32	82
5	Republic of Korea	13	8	7	28
	Paralympics				
1	People's Republic of China	95	71	65	231
2	Russian Federation	36	38	28	102
3	Great Britain	34	43	43	120
4	Ukraine	32	24	28	84
5	Australia	32	23	30	85

Source: Compiled by author from final medal tables available at
http://www.london2012.com/medals/medal-count/
http://www.london2012.com/paralympics/medals/medal-count/

for 104 years (IOC, 2012a). With London 2012 over, it was back to business as usual for BA's advertising campaigns. Straight after the Games, as a way of rewarding those who had delayed travel and stayed at home to support the nation, the airline ran a 'Thank you Great Britain sale'. IAG, BA's parent company, reported in early October that the sale had resulted in an increase in passenger numbers for premium and leisure travel (Travel Weekly, 2012b).

In mid-October, BA launched a new advertising campaign created by BBH, aimed at repositioning the airline in the short-haul market where it is ultimately seeking to increase its market share. Once again, the executions employed were light-hearted in nature, but sought to differentiate the airline from its low-cost rivals in terms of clarity over services included in the ticket price. The 'To Fly. To Serve' strapline was used at the end. Additionally, following the success of the 'Don't Fly' campaign, traditional media spots and spaces were supported by activity on social platforms as well (Eleftheriou-Smith, 2012). Time will tell how successful BA will be in increasing its share of short-haul business; however, in the meantime, the icing on the cake for 2012 was that BA was shortlisted for The Marketing Society's Brand of the Year 2012 award. Although BA did not win the award, in December its advertising agency BBH was named Marketing's Ad Agency of the Year. This bodes well for future collaborations.

Conclusion

Overall, the 'Don't Fly' campaign was able to tap into the emotions of the nation in the run-up to and during the Games in a very creative manner. According to Chiarelli (2012) at the Future Foundation, the 'Don't Fly' advertising campaign is an example of 'brave, disruptive advertising, with messages that make consumers think "huh?" on first glance and which seem to be anti-advertising but which are intended to work at on a subtler level'. The strategy behind the campaign can be interpreted as a clever piece of ostensible demarketing.

In their seminal paper on demarketing, Kotler and Levy (1971, p.80) argued that 'Marketing inevitably has a role to play in the face of excess demand: the challenge is to demarket thoughtfully and skillfully'. In the case of 'ostensible demarketing', they stated that 'Sometimes an establishment goes through the motions of demarketing in the hope of achieving the opposite effect. By creating the appearance of not wanting more customers, it hopes to make the product even more desirable to people'. This is exactly what BA did. The 'Don't Fly' campaign successfully managed to cut through the clutter of London 2012 marketing communications activity, grab attention through its disruptive message and enable BA to engage with a wider audience than usual through traditional and new media platforms. Not only did the bold and patriotic campaign help to boost the home advantage in an innovative and very creative manner, it has also worked to the airline's advantage to help it to broaden its customer base.

References

BBC News (2010), 'British Airways in record £531m loss,' 21st May, available from: http://www.bbc.co.uk/news/10135112 (accessed 12th December, 2012).

——(2009), 'T5 check-in reopens after glitch,' 29th June, available from: http://news.bbc.co.uk/1/hi/uk/8123273.stm (accessed 7th January, 2013).

——(2008a), 'BA to sponsor London 2012 Games,' 5th May, available from: http://news.bbc.co.uk/1/hi/england/london/7228007.stm (accessed 12th January, 2013).

——(2008b), 'Fresh baggage woes at Terminal 5,' 5th April, available from: http://news.bbc.co.uk/1/hi/uk/7331954.stm (accessed 7th January, 2013).

Bacon, J. (2012), 'Flying the brand flag for British Airways', *Marketing Week*, 8th November, available from: http://www.marketingweek.co.uk/trends/flying-the-brand-flag-for-british-airways/4004567.article (accessed 10th December, 2012).

Balmer, N.J., Nevill, A.M. and Williams, A.M. (2003), 'Modelling home advantage in the Summer Olympic Games', *Journal of Sports Science*, 21: 469–78.

Beard, M. (2012), 'We'll break even on £2.4bn Olympics bill, says locog', *London Evening Standard*, 9th November, available from: http://www.standard.co.uk/news/uk/well-break-even-on-24bn-olympics-bill-says-locog-8300378.html (accessed 10th December, 2012).

Bell, E. (2012), 'Lessons to be learned from the first social media Olympics', *The Guardian*, 5th August, available at: http://www.guardian.co.uk/media/2012/aug/05/lessons-learned-social-media-olympics (accessed 11 January, 2013).

British Airways (2012), 'British Airways' social barometer measures the mood of the nation', Press Release, 31st July, 090/AA/12.

Chapman, M. (2012), 'BA psyches out overseas athletes with giant Jessica Ennis image', *Campaign*, 15th June, accessible at: http://www.marketingmagazine.co.uk/news/1136715 (accessed 10 December 2012).

Chiarelli, N. (2012), 'Don't buy my product: the new wave of brave advertising', *Get Real*, available from: http://trendsgetreal.blogspot.co.uk/2012/08/dont-buy-my-product-new-wave-of-brave.html (accessed 9 January, 2013).

Cross, T. (2012), 'British Airways announce the launch of flight BA 2012', Conde Nast Traveller, 4th April, available at: http://www.cntraveller.com/news/2012/april/british-airways-pop-up-in-shoreditch (accessed 28 December, 2012).

Eleftheriou-Smith, L. (2012), 'BA looks to distance itself from no-frills airlines', *Marketing*, 17th October, available at: http://www.marketingmagazine.co.uk/news/1155240/BA-looks-distance-itself-no-frills-airlines/ (accessed 28th December, 2013).

Evans, M., Jamal A. and Foxall, G. (2009), *Consumer Behaviour*, Wiley, Chichester (2nd ed.).

Hanna, L. (2012), 'Faster ... higher ... bigger ... Huge Jessica Ennis picture will welcome visitors to Olympics', *Mirror*, 15th June, available at: http://www.mirror.co.uk/news/uk-news/giant-jessica-ennis-picture-will-welcome-884034 (accessed 28 December 2012).

IOC (2012a), *International Olympic Committee Marketing Report* London 2012, available from: http://www.olympic.org/Documents/IOC_Marketing/London_2012/LR_IOC_Marketing Report_medium_res1.pdf (accessed 15th December 2012).

——(2012b), *IOC Marketing: Media guide* London 2012, available from: http://www.olympic.org/Documents/IOC_Marketing/London_2012/IOC_Marketing_Media_Guide_2012.pdf (accessed 11th November 2012).

Jobber, D. and Fahy, D. (2012), *Foundations of Marketing*, 4th edition, McGraw-Hill Higher Education, Maidenhead.

Johnson, B. (2011), 'BA Executive Club loyalty scheme relaunches', *Marketing Week*, 16th November, available at: http://www.marketingweek.co.uk/ba-executive-club-loyalty-scheme-relaunches/3031910.article (accessed 4th January, 2013).

Kershaw, S.S. (2012), 'Creative strategy: British Airways unfurls a new way to fly the flag', Media Week, 13th September, available at: http://www.mediaweek.co.uk/news/1149860/CREATIVE-STRATEGY-British-Airways-unfurls-new-fly-flag/?DCMP=ILC-SEARCH (accessed 10th December, 2012).

Key Note (2013), *Airlines Market Report.*

Kotler, P. and Levy, S.J. (1971), 'Demarketing, yes, demarketing', *Harvard Business Review*, Vol. 49 (6), pp. 74–80.

London Evening Standard (2012), 'A giant of sport … Jessica Ennis from the air', 14th June, available at: http://www.standard.co.uk/olympics/olympic-news/a-giant-of-sport-jessica-ennis-from-the-air-7851142.html (accessed 8 January 2013).

Marketing Week (2012a), 'Q& a: Abigail Comber, British Airways head of brands and marketing', 7th November, available at: http://www.marketingweek.co.uk/opinion/qa-abigail-comber-british-airways-head-of-brands-and-marketing/4004638.article (accessed 10th December, 2012).

——(2012b), 'BA and Olympic sponsorship: how being bold paid off', 7th November, available at: http://www.marketingweek.co.uk/sectors/travel-and-leisure/ba-and-olympic-sponsorship-how-being-being-bold-paid-off/4004639.article (accessed 10th December, 2012).

——(1999), 'Heads you win, tail-fins you lose', 24th June, available at: http://www.marketingweek.co.uk/heads-you-win-tail-fins-you-lose/2041848.article (accessed 11th January, 2013).

Massey, R. (2011), 'To fly. To serve: British Airways relaunches itself with new slogan that nods to its imperial origins', MailOnline, 21st Sept, available at: http://www.dailymail.co.uk/news/article-2039678/British-Airways-relaunches-new-slogan-nods-imperial-origins.html (accessed 1st January, 2013).

Matthews, D. (2012), 'Travel: Will it still fly?', *The Marketer*, May/June, p. 34.

Milmo, D. (2011), 'BA and Unite reach deal to end cabin crew strikes', *Guardian.co.uk*, 12th May, available at: http://www.guardian.co.uk/business/2011/may/12/british-airways-crew-strike-deal (accessed 3rd January, 2013).

Mower, J. (2012), 'Olympic Torch: Top pilot's 'most precious cargo', *BBC News UK*, 18th May, available at: http://www.bbc.co.uk/news/uk-18006750 (accessed 11th January, 2013)

Nevill, A.M. and Holder, R.L. (1999), 'Home advantage in sport: An overview of studies on the advantage of playing at home', *Sports Medicine*, 28, 221–36.

O' Ceallaigh, J. (2012), 'British Airways' Olympics-themed Shoreditch pop-up project', *Telegraph*, 5th April, available at: http://www.telegraph.co.uk/travel/destinations/europe/uk/london/9188877/British-Airways-Olympics-themed-Shoreditch-pop-up-project.html (accessed 28th December, 2012).

Ritson, M. (2012), 'Olympic sponsors stuck in the slow lane', *Marketing Week*, 5th July, available at: http://www.marketingweek.co.uk/opinion/olympic-sponsors-stuck-in-the-slow-lane/4002546.article (accessed 10th December, 2012).

Shakespeare, S. (2012a), 'Steady climb to the top for British Airways', *YouGov – BrandIndex*, 4th January, available at: http://www.brandindex.com/article/steady-climb-top-british-airways (accessed 5th January, 2013).

——(2012b), 'British Airways shows firms can recover ground', *YouGov – BrandIndex*, 25th July, available at: http://www.brandindex.com/article/british-airways-shows-firms-can-recover-ground (accessed 4th January, 2013).

Sweney, M. (2012), 'Non-Olympic brands push ambush marketing rules to the limit', *The Guardian*, 25 July, available at: http://www.guardian.co.uk/media/2012/jul/25/non-olympic-brands-ambush-marketing (accessed 10th October, 2013).

Travel Weekly (2012a), 'BA launches 'Don't fly' campaign for London Olympics', 19th June, available at: http://www.travelweekly.co.uk/staticpages/404.html?aspxerrorpath=/Articles/2012/06/19/40814/ba+launches+dont+fly+campaign+for+london+olympics.html (accessed 14 November, 2012).

——(2012b), 'BA enjoys London Olympics boost', 4th October, available at: http://www.travelweekly.co.uk/Articles/2012/10/04/41823/ba+enjoys+london+olympics+boost.html (accessed 12th January, 2013).

YouTube (2011a), *British Airways Advert 2011: To Fly. To Serve.* (HD). Uploaded on 19th October 2011, available at: http://www.youtube.com/watch?v=XozHLoqwp_4

——(2011b), *British Airways Advert 2011: To Fly. To Serve.* Uploaded on 20th September 2011, available at: http://www.youtube.com/watch?v=x_G4MV_DG2Q

——(2011c), *British Airways-The making of our advert.* Uploaded on 20th September 2011, available at: http://www.youtube.com/watch?v=chjN5SerNeQ

——(2012a), *British Airways – Our Advert 2012: The Race.* Uploaded on 8th February, available at: http://www.youtube.com/watch?v=1n-9-6ULjHY

——(2012b), *British Airways Home Advantage (UK).* Uploaded on 21st June, available at: https://www.youtube.com/watch?v=S-G7ayhPetQ

——(2012c), *British Airways – Behind the idea of our London 2012 AD.* Uploaded on 19th June, available at: https://www.youtube.com/watch?v=Elp2cabTkU0

——(2012d), *British Airways–London 2012 AD (K).* Uploaded on 19th June, available at: https://www.youtube.com/watch?v=M6VzhDE1Wso; http://www.london2012.com/medals/medal-count/; http://www.london2012.com/paralympics/medals/medal-count/

12
UNINTENTIONAL DEMARKETING
Theresa A. Kirchner

Introduction

> A fourth type (of demarketing), unintentional demarketing, is also impor-
> tant but does not need to be considered here. So many abortive efforts to
> increase demand, resulting actually in driving customers away, have been
> reported in recent years that the dreary tale does not need to be told again.
>
> *(Kotler and Levy 1971, p. 75)*

While a body of academic work exists on the topic of demarketing, the lack of
academic focus on the concept of "unintentional demarketing" or unintended
consequences of marketing/demarketing which can result in unintentional
demarketing effects, is striking, and no qualitative/quantitative research studies
address these specific topics. Kotler and Levy (1971) identified unintentional
demarketing as one of four types of demarketing but, at the same, dismissed the
need for further discussion of it. While their intention was likely to limit the
scope of their article, the effects of unintentional demarketing are so common,
and can be so detrimental and expensive for organizations, that they bear closer
examination and empirical research.

This chapter, then, is an initial attempt to explore the various interpretations
and manifestations of the concept of "unintentional demarketing" as well as its
consequences and implications for both marketers and academicians. Given the
paucity of prior literature and need for future concentration on the topic, it
concludes with opportunities for future research and related questions.

Definitions

The concept of "unintentional demarketing" must be defined and assessed in the
context of its "parent" terms: marketing and demarketing. Kotler and Levy
(1971), who appear to have coined the phrase, defined marketing as

> the business function concerned with controlling the level and composi-
> tion of demand facing the company. Its short-run task is to adjust the
> demand to a level and composition that the company can, or wishes to,

handle. Its long-run task is to adjust the demand to a level and composition that meets the company's long-run objectives.

Although the idea of "demand" is central to Kotler and Levy's definition of "marketing" (the word occurs three times in the definition, the current American Marketing Association definition of marketing does not include the word "demand" or any other word which could be considered a strong synonym: "Marketing is the activity, set of institutions, and processes for creating, communicating, delivering, and exchanging offerings that have value for customers, clients, partners, and society at large."

In its definition of "demarketing," however, the American Marketing Association does include the concept of demand (and the related idea of consumption): "(1) (economic definition) A term used to describe a marketing strategy when the objective is to decrease the consumption of a product, and (2) (social marketing definition) The process of reducing the demand for products or services believed to be harmful to society."

The question of whether or not demand is an inherent component of marketing and/or demarketing is important for this chapter, because much of the literature on marketing, in general, and demarketing, in particular, involves a discussion of demand. Kotler and Levy (1971) and Kotler 1973 defined "demarketing" as an aspect of marketing used in an overfull demand state that deals with discouraging customers in general or a certain class of customers in particular, on either a temporary or permanent basis. It is used in cases where "demand exceeds the level at which the marketer feels able or motivated to supply it," or to reduce demand from "undesirable segments" (Kotler and Levy 1971 p. 78).

A term that is closely related to demarketing is "countermarketing" (also termed "unselling"), which Kotler defined as trying to destroy the demand for a service or product by attempting to portray it as intrinsically unwholesome or undesirable. Kotler viewed demarketing and countermarketing as distinct concepts, but a review of the literature on demarketing shows that authors use the term "demarketing" to apply to situations that Kotler would classify as countermarketing or unselling, generally involving social demarketing. Regardless of the term used, the strategy often backfires, since, as Kotler noted, for some demographic groups, portraying something forbidden (e.g. X-rated movies and drugs) may actually increase desire for the product (Kotler 1973) – a phenomenon that might be described either as "unintentional marketing," or as "unintentional demarketing" of the intended campaign.

How is "unintentional demarketing" defined? It isn't. Neither the American Marketing Association Dictionary nor the Marketing Association of Australia and New Zealand Glossary provides a definition for "unintentional demarketing," and a review of the academic literature finds no definition for the term. The glossaries of the Canadian Marketing Association and the UK's Chartered Institute of Marketing do not define either "demarketing" or "unintentional demarketing."

How might "unintentional demarketing" be defined? Doing so based simply on the Kotler and Levy (1971) view of the concept, which looked at

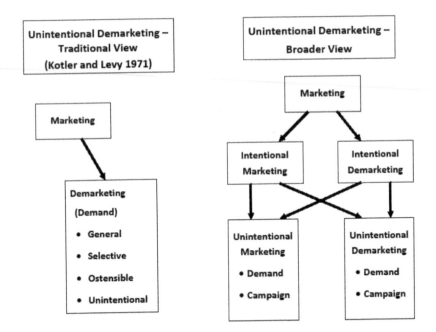

FIGURE 12.1 Views of unintentional demarketing

unintentional demarketing as a type of marketing "gone wrong" (as depicted in Figure 12.1), one might define it simply as "a decrease in demand resulting from an abortive effort to increase demand." However, reading the term literally, it cries out for a broader definition, as depicted in Figure 12.1. As discussed later in this chapter, either intentional marketing or intentional demarketing can have unintended consequences (which may, or may not, involve demand), which can have the effect of either unintentional marketing or of unintentional demarketing. Unintentional demarketing, in this context, might be defined as: "(1) an unanticipated decrease in demand resulting from unanticipated consequences of a marketing or demarketing effort, or (2) unanticipated results of a marketing or demarketing campaign which have the effect of demarketing it in terms of meeting intended objectives."

Unintentional demarketing in the context of marketing/demarketing

Understanding the relationship of demarketing to marketing is important in understanding unintentional demarketing. Kotler (2011) views the two concepts as not only related but also as virtual opposites, defining marketing in terms of demand expansion, and demarketing in terms of demand reduction or anti-consumption. An example is that of electricity companies, which, from a marketing perspective, could logically encourage people to use more electricity, but, from a demarketing standpoint, now commonly encourage people to conserve electricity, not only from a relatively abstract environmental stewardship perspective, but also because they and local/regional/national governments may fear that electrical grids may become overloaded.

Though, as Kotler maintains, it may seem logical to view demarketing as simply the reverse of marketing, Medway and Warnaby (2008) make the case that the two are not mutually exclusive, and Beeton and Benfield (2002), among others, propose that demarketing should be viewed as an inherent working component of marketing, which provides a set of tools that should be used by marketers to achieve optimal demand on an ongoing basis. This view contrasts with Kotler's, since unintentional demarketing would not logically be included as a type of demarketing in this context – it certainly is not a tool that would purposely be used by marketers.

Kotler and Levy (1971) proposed four high-level types of demarketing situations: (1) general, (2) selective, (3) ostensible, and (4) unintentional. While the fourth type clearly produces unintended consequences, the first three types can be either intentional or unintentional, and produce either intended or unintended consequences, which can be either positive or negative. General demarketing involves managed temporary or permanent discouragement of overall demand. Intentional general demarketing may involve managing demand to deal with either temporary or ongoing shortages of goods/services, for example, to deal with expected/unexpected popularity or with cyclical peaks/ valleys of availability and demand. In the services industries, in particular, demand fluctuations can result in cost, operations, and quality control issues associated with resource availability. Unintentional general demarketing may occur when general demand for a product is inadvertently lowered due to problems and unanticipated impacts resulting from planned marketing or demarketing efforts.

Selective demarketing involves partial discouragement of demand, for example from certain market segments. When employed intentionally, it uses a variety of tools for managing demand, for example, leveraging relationship management tools to target market segments judged to be unprofitable or unsuitable. An example of unintended consequences of selective demarketing involves airline frequent flyer and hotel frequent stayer reward systems, which reward customers who achieve specified levels of purchase, but also may delete points or accounts of customers who do not achieve minimum levels of pur- chase within certain time periods. Although the intent of the rewards program manager may be to demarket low-level customers and the impact of carrying rewards points associated with those customers, an unanticipated result of that approach may be that the customer may initiate activity to maintain the rewards program relationship (a flight purchase or a hotel stay) in order to avoid deac- tivation of the account and preserve the points already earned (Suh *et al.* 2012), which may, if unanticipated, be considered a case of unintentional marketing. From another perspective, such aggressive demarketing of inactive customers may have unintentional demarketing effects beyond the intent of the campaign, if otherwise good customers, who, potentially for reasons beyond their control, neglect to do business with the organization during a single calendar year, may be antagonized by the loss of points and abandon it for other rewards programs that are less stringent in their demarketing efforts.

Ostensible demarketing involves an approach in which the organization appears to act in ways that appear to discourage demand but that actually purposefully function to increase it. As an example, in the 1950s, Durgin Park, a 200-year-old Boston restaurant, decided to capitalize on its issues and began to promote itself as an establishment featuring rude waitresses who wear unattractive uniforms, provide poor service, and serve old-fashioned food at uncomfortable, crowded communal tables. While a typical restaurant with those traits could be viewed as having serious marketing/customer relationship issues that could cause its ruin, Durgin Park thrives, with diners flocking to it to experience the unique atmosphere. However, this type of approach can also have unintended consequences. Hypothetically, an organization that sets out to purposely provide rude and poor service could face lawsuits if patrons and/or employees perceive that the line has been crossed between attempted humor and harassment/discrimination, and resulting unfavorable publicity could cause unintentional demarketing. Ultimately, unintentional demarketing could also result from the unique ostensible demarketing approach if patrons or employees terminate the relationship due to satiation (the novelty wears off), dissatisfaction, the determination that an alternative is superior (the restaurant down the street treats them better), or conflict (Sheth and Parvatiyar 1995).

Marketing and demarketing, both intended and unintended, can also be classified as "internal" or "external." While external marketing/demarketing focuses on lowering or eliminating consumer demand for a product or service, internal marketing/demarketing focuses within the organization, on the employees. Ideally, intentional internal marketing/demarketing, in the form of actions, decisions, and behaviors of managers, will positively affect both performance and productivity. However, while unintentional results may affect employees either favorably or unfavorably, negative reactions can translate into negative employee perceptions, satisfaction, motivation, functionality, operations, and efficiency (Vasconcelos 2011).

In summary, marketing or demarketing practices may, when implemented, turn out not to apply and/or work as intended. The results may be mixed, differing demographically or by market segment, and may have both positive/negative and intended/unintended consequences. An interesting intellectual question is how to characterize those results. For example, if unintentional demarketing happens to result in increased business due to unintended effects of the demarketing effort, should that be categorized as "unintentional marketing," based on the increase in demand, or "unintentional demarketing" (or, possibly, "de-demarketing"), based on the failure of the campaign to achieve the intended demarketing results. Great minds may disagree on how to answer this type of question.

The nature and characteristics of unintentional demarketing

Kotler and Levy (1971) appeared to view unintentional demarketing as simply an unintended, negative result of marketing to increase demand gone awry. However, when analyzed more thoroughly, unintentional demarketing is a more complex concept than might be assumed at first glance. Examined logically, it may be viewed both (1) as a type of demarketing (as proposed by Kotler and Levy 1971), and (2) a potential consequence of either intended marketing or demarketing, as depicted in Figure 12.2. Intended marketing may result in either the intended results (which, logically, would be positive), or unintended results (either positive or negative.) Kotler and Levy's view of unintentional demarketing centered on the unintended consequences (positive and/or negative) of intended marketing.

However, unintended marketing can also have either positive or negative consequences, and negative results can result in de facto unintentional demarketing. In addition, demarketing, itself, whether intended or unintended, can have either positive or negative consequences, and negative results can include further unintended demarketing. Finally, interactions of various marketing/demarketing strategies and results may result in complex interactions, producing a variety of unintended consequences. (Due to the difficulty of diagraming this last dynamic, it is not included in Figure 12.2.)

Consequences of unintended/intended marketing/demarketing

As discussed earlier, it is important for marketers and academicians to understand that, although the concept of "unintentional demarketing" has been classified as a subset of demarketing (Kotler and Levy 1971), it also can, from a practical standpoint, result from any type of marketing or demarketing effort. Unintended consequences of intended marketing can result in unintentional

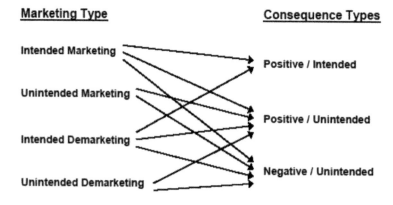

FIGURE 12.2 Marketing types and consequences

demarketing (Kirchner *et al.* 2012). Unintended consequences of intended demarketing can result in negative or undesired effects and result in additional demarketing in unintended areas. Finally, unintended demarketing can result in further demarketing – for example in a situation in which the marketer does not realize that demarketing is taking place and/or fails to recognize the consequences, resulting in a "snowball effect" of further demarketing.

The characteristics of unintentional demarketing are, understandably, complex, and, unfortunately, understudied.

- The **scope** of unintentional demarketing, as described above and outlined in Figure 12.1, is very broad.
- From a **typology** standpoint, unintentional demarketing applies to products, services, and behavioral adjustment situations (e.g. public policy attempts to discourage "undesirable" behavior). It can manifest itself in a variety of different contexts: corporations, small businesses, non-profit organizations, and governments. It can involve unintentional demarketing of an organization's own products or services, or unintentional demarketing of another stakeholder's products and services. It can involve demarketing of social behaviors at various levels (the organization, the organization's value chain, and/or the local, national, or world societal communities; customer/ social or another organization's behaviours.
- The **importance** of unintentional demarketing and its results can range dramatically, from relatively minor to devastating.

Unintentional demarketing in the context of social marketing/ demarketing

Much of the existing literature on demarketing concentrates on social marketing/ demarketing, which some authors term "countermarketing." Kotler and Zaltman (1971) defined social marketing as "the design, implementation, and control of programs calculated to influence the acceptability of social ideas and involving considerations of product pricing, planning, communication, distribution, and marketing research" (p. 5) and a "framework for planning and implementing social change" (p. 3). Social marketing/demarketing is often used by nonprofits, non-governmental organizations (NGOs), and governments, at the local, regional, or national level, to either promote (market) products, services, or behaviors that are considered socially desirable or to discourage or prohibit (demarket) those which are considered socially undesirable. Examples of academic writing on the topic of social marketing include examinations of the campaigns involving smoking (Teel *et al.* 1979; Shiu *et al.* 2009), national health services (Mark and Elliott 1997), paper/plastic shopping bags (Sharp *et al.* 2010), and the environment (Kotler 2011).

Methods of social demarketing (countermarketing) include increasing taxes (or providing tax incentives for avoiding socially undesirable purchases or behavior), promoting positive alternatives, restricting availability or consumption (e.g. age restrictions), decreasing product attractiveness, increasing prices, decreasing consumption/distribution spaces/opportunities, impeding purchases, education/public relations, controlling or decreasing advertising, mandatory warning labels, etc. (Mark and Elliott 1997; Shiu *et al.* 2009; Sharp *et al.* 2010; Kotler 2011).

Implementation of social demarketing efforts and/or requirements without considering the unintended effects of such demarketing on businesses, consumers, and governments can be problematic. Unanticipated consequences can include economic impacts that are significant and counterproductive to society's dependence on a healthy economic environment. As an example, an otherwise successful social demarketing campaign may result in lower tax incomes or fines than expected for a government, affecting its income. Another case in point is that of environmental demarketing. Reducing emissions through controls, for example, is often deemed an example of desirable demarketing, but it may have the unintended effects of reducing alternatives for reasonably priced sources of energy and increasing energy prices for low-income customers who have no alternatives. These results can be particularly problematic in fast-growing areas that have energy shortages. These types of unintended effects of intended demarketing, which could affect both the target audience and other entities that were not anticipated to be affected, could be viewed as unintentional demarketing. The question, in this kind of case, is whether the campaign should be modified to mitigate unanticipated negative effects.

The issue of national healthcare typically involves both intentional and unintentional social marketing and demarketing. Mark and Elliott (1997) assess the case of the UK National Health Service, which has tended to address the problem by reducing supply rather than increasing resources to address demand, in terms of Kotler and Levy's (1971) categorization of demarketing modes (general, selective, ostensible, and unintentional). They examine two examples of unintentional demarketing in the context of the National Health Service: (1) "inappropriate or insensitive provision of treatment or care" (Ahmad 1993) and (2) the use of waiting lists, which can result in either negative outcomes or, in some cases, recovery from a condition without intervention, albeit with some negative effects on mental/physical quality of life.

These types of issues affect countries around the world to varying degrees. To avoid or minimize them, governments, non-profit organizations, and business organizations should work together to achieve joint goals, or, at least, minimize effects, rather than acting arbitrarily and without considering implications for the wide range of stakeholders.

Unintended consequences of unintentional demarketing

In 1971, the USA implemented a ban on cigarette advertising in broadcast media. The rationale for the ban was that it would result in declines in both the total number of smokers in the population and the number of young people adopting the habit of smoking. However, the statistical results showed the opposite.

In the five years following the ban's implementation, the percentage of adult smokers actually rose slightly. Per person cigarette consumption increased significantly. The number of young adults who adopted smoking did not fall; in fact, an increase in 18–24-year-old-smokers occurred, especially young women (Teel *et al.* 1979).

Why did the mandated demarketing of cigarettes yield these unexpected results? Teel *et al.* (1979) proposed several possibilities:

- The tobacco industry redesigned its product mix to include low-tar, low-nicotine cigarettes, which were considered safer than its previous products.
- The tobacco industry's promotional themes ignored, discounted, and refuted the health hazards of smoking.
- Print media advertising by the tobacco industry was still reaching current and potential smokers, and served as a practical substitute.
- Anti-smoking advocates no longer had tobacco industry broadcast media ads to react to as a focus of their efforts.

It is also possible that, in the case of young people, an anti-smoking campaign may actually increase interest in smoking among young people who are in the rebellious stage, are attracted to something that is forbidden, and are not interested or impressed by the extolled health risks. Assessments of the effectiveness of anti-smoking campaigns on the attitudes, intentions, and behaviors of young people show mixed results (Pechmann and Reibling 2006).

As a demand management tool, demarketing is typically used to address unintended scarcity or oversupply, but it may also unintentionally exacerbate those problems or create new ones. For example, demarketing may be implemented too successfully (Medway *et al.* 2011), e.g. over-reducing short-term demand (Kotler and Levy 1971). At the other end of the scale, demarketing also may do irreparable harm to long-run demand, for example, alienating current customers. Another possibility is that demarketing that is intended to be temporary may become long term or permanent. Demarketing may also result in the unanticipated need for remarketing, either to the same consumers and segments or to others – in which case it can be viewed as an example of planned demarketing that misses the mark, resulting in unintentional demarketing that must be corrected.

Resistance is a normal human response to change (Carrigan *et al.* 2004) Consumers are therefore likely to resist demarketing efforts that may be seen as manipulative or "Orwellian." A perception that they are being dominated my lead to resentment, particularly when consumers are being asked to change their routine, habitual behavior (Kotler and Zaltman 1971).

When demarketing or countermarketing is used as a tool to change social behavior, education and positive persuasive efforts alone may not be sufficient to achieve desired results. Demarketing campaigns may not be able to achieve widespread behavioral change with positive messages alone. Negative reinforcers (e.g. significant regulations, penalties and outright bans) may be necessary to achieve widespread behavioral change (Sharp *et al.* 2010), and they may result in unintentional demarketing if they are not well received.

Demarketing may be viewed as problematic by stakeholders at large, who may view it as alarmist, counterproductive, and harmful to other stakeholder organizations that are not competitors. In the same way, unintended marketing/demarketing results may include significant consequences for both internal external parties, for example, lower tax incomes than expected for governments, affecting stakeholders and increasing the difficulty of managing them (Medway *et al.* 2011).

Any demarketing efforts may have different effects for different demographic groups (age, gender, income, social status, political, and product/service-specific sub-groups). Results may also vary depending on attitudinal support or resistance to the specific product or service that is being demarketed (Sharp *et al.* 2010). Feelings of being forced into an undesired behavior rather than being positively encouraged to change behavior can result in resistance or refusal.

Finally, Kotler (1973) noted that there is danger in failing to realize that every effort to unsell something may also be viewed as an effort to sell something else. Therefore, there is a need to evaluate the entire context of every marketing effort to understand what is, by intention or default, being sold. "Unselling" a product in order to sell another product may, in fact, also result in selling a competitor's product. As an example, Kotler (2011) gives the example of electricity companies that encourage people to waste less electricity (turn off lights; unplug devices when not in use). While that may be a noble goal, and an electricity company can certainly use it in its advertising and public relations campaigns as an example of its commitment to sustainability of the environment, it may result in unintended demarketing consequences: (1) people may simply use more of other types of power, in effect, switching the demand to competitors who may be less environmentally responsible, and (2) the organization's revenue may decrease, affecting its bottom line. The revenue decrease may result in higher rates for consumers if governments allow them to rise so that the electricity companies can achieve a mandated floor revenue – which may have unintended negative consequences in terms of consumer satisfaction. Consumers may, for example, switch to less environmentally friendly alternatives, a clear case of unintentional demarketing.

Marketing/demarketing perspectives and drivers

Marketing/demarketing strategies and results can be examined from a variety of perspectives. In general, unintended consequences of those strategies generally involve not achieving expected results or experiencing results that are different in nature or in degree from those that were expected. Examples of those marketing/demarketing perspectives include: (1) the traditional perspective of undersupply/oversupply of demand, (2) the economic (external) environment (Dadzie 1989) perspective, (3) the stakeholder perspective (both horizontal and vertical), including customers, investors, employees, suppliers, governments and governmental agencies, communities, media, trade associations, special interest groups, etc., (4) the Customer Relationship Management (CRM) demarketing perspective (Suh *et al.* 2012), (5) the psychological perspective, including psychological resistance, non-cooperation, unanticipated responses, and dealing with customers who receive demarketing stimulation but do not voluntarily elect to exit (Suh *et al.* 2012), (6) the internal perspective, involving internal organizational/employee-related issues and consequences, (7) the demographics perspective, and (8) the environmental/green perspective

Demarketing tools and potential unintended consequences of their use

Kotler and Levy (1971) proposed that demarketing utilizes the same 4 Ps (Product, Price, Place, and Promotion) as those leveraged in traditional marketing efforts. However, demarketing requires that those factors be utilized in the ongoing effort to identify, monitor, and evaluate unintended consequences, since too much demarketing can, either temporarily or permanently, destroy the customer base. Fine-tuning the marketing mix becomes particularly important in dealing with demarketing, since it involves being able to quickly stop or reduce demarketing efforts, and/or balance them with marketing or remarketing efforts. Otherwise, additional unintentional demarketing is likely to result.

Examples of specific tools that are valuable in the context of demarketing, but can sometimes result in unintended consequences include:

- **Price increases.** High prices can be viewed as indicators of luxury and prestige to consumers and increase demand, but may be seen as discriminatory to lower-income groups. They may also reduce perception of value for money, especially in price-sensitive contexts, which can cause unintentional demarketing of price-sensitive middle-class and upper-class customers.
- **Elimination of discounts.** Reducing or eliminating discounts can result in the loss of customers who patronize the organization because of them.
- **Distribution/availability reduction or service reduction.** Hard-to-get items/services may be perceived as more valuable and increase demand.
- **Restriction controls/guidelines.** Restrictions on the numbers of people who are given access to a special museum exhibit or allowed into a store at a peak period (e.g. the day after Thanksgiving, which is the largest shopping day in the USA) may actually increase demand and result in long lines.
- **Educational programs.** While educational programs can be powerful tools, they need to be carefully crafted and tested in order to avoid ineffective or unanticipated results.
- **Purposely accentuating the negative aspects of a product/service to reduce demand, or deflecting interest from a particular product/service.** This approach may actually raise the profile of the organization and

its products/services and increase demand (unintentional marketing) for unanticipated reasons, if those negative aspects actually are seen as positive by potential consumers (Medway and Warnaby 2008). "Dark tourism" actually attracts people – consider the Pont de L'Alma tunnel where Princess Diana died, which has become a significant tourist attraction. Government warnings to avoid an area of danger (e.g. a volcanic eruption, a tornado path, or a tsunami) may not only affect desired tourism to that area but may also attract the very people whom the warnings are intended to discourage – adventurers who are drawn to danger or want to experience the effects of tragedy.

Addressing unintentional demarketing in the context of the strategic planning process

Demarketing and its unintentional results are not typically outlined in specific elements of an organization's formal strategic plan, but a demarketing strategy should be carefully planned, ideally in the context of the organization's strategic and tactical planning processes. By definition, unintentional demarketing is unplanned, but assessment of its results should involve circling back through the strategic plan components (vision, mission, goals, and objectives) to determine how the organization should react to them.

While both marketing and demarketing may focus primarily on the consumer/client/customer, an organization's strategic/tactical planning and marketing/demarketing strategies and implementations must also be assessed in the context of the organization's range and breadth of stakeholders. Demarketing, both active/passive and intended/unintended, is not always simply the result of the organization's efforts. It may be externally driven by the organization's stakeholders (Medway and Warnaby 2008). Many unintended consequences of marketing/demarketing programs stem from failure to predict adequately how stakeholders will react.

Potential demarketing strategies include (Medway *et al.* 2011):

- no marketing;
- redirection/marketing of alternatives;
- informational demarketing;
- restricting access/making access difficult;
- pricing mechanisms, e.g. tourism, exclusivity;
- environmental deterring.

More than one strategy may be used at a time. Doing so could heighten the risk of overshooting the goal, and/or it could leverage alternatives that could allow more control in terms of achieving an optimal result. Monitoring and evaluation of results, and communication/consultation with stakeholders are critical. Those processes should be iterative and substantial. What is attractive to one consumer may be unattractive to another, and differing consumer responses must be anticipated and addressed quickly, or unintended consequences may result.

From a strategic and tactical planning perspective, an organization should identify and evaluate alternative strategies when demarketing is necessary. Synchromarketing involves fine-tuning marketing/demarketing efforts using multiple strategies to manage demand fluctuations (Krentler 1988). Each of those multiple strategies should be examined both independently, and as part of the package of strategies, to assess potential unintended consequences. For example, if a bookstore handles the issue of unexpectedly not having enough personnel (sales clerks and customer service representatives) to handle the number of store customers, it could handle the situation with a number of concurrent strategies: (1) allowing long queues to build up, (2) giving preferential treatment to the "best" customers, (3) encouraging others to come back during a less busy time, (4) sending customers to other queues, and (5) not answering the telephone or returning calls. While one of those strategies, used briefly, might address a temporary resource shortage, the cumulative effect of using multiple strategies might be to quickly drive the store's customers to the competition – Amazon, for example. Even brief use of one or a combination of these strategies may result in a long-term loss of business, a case of unintentional demarketing.

Using place demarketing (Medway and Warnaby 2008) as an example, if a museum which is already at capacity from an attendance perspective, determines that it needs to close one of its wings for maintenance for a year, it might consider two alternatives – active and passive. The passive alternative might involve simply not actively marketing the museum as much as normal, counting on the lower level of advertising and public relations activity to suppress attendance to the level that the smaller space can accommodate. The active alternative might involve a combination of demarketing visitation at the physical museum location and actively creating and marketing museum alternatives in other locations (e.g. moving art to vacant retail stores for display, lending pieces of the affected collection to other non-competitor or out-of-town museums). While the second alternative is tactically more complex, it might prove to be more financially attractive than simply downsizing attendance at the museum.

From a strategic/tactical perspective, an organization should:

- Recognize that any marketing effort has the potential to result in unintended consequences, which can have the effect of unintended demarketing to some or all customer segments.
- Recognize that any demarketing effort may have unintended consequences (positive or negative).
- Identify all current and potential consumers and stakeholders.
- Analyze the current marketing/demarketing strategy in terms of (1) demand, and (2) beliefs, attitudes and norms that may affect that demand, and (3) potential reactions of all market segments and stakeholders.
- Anticipate unintended negative and positive consequences, and develop alternative strategies, as necessary, to address them.

- Investigate the alternatives to uncover potential errors in assumptions that can result in unintentional demarketing.
- Develop a revised marketing/demarketing plan that incorporates the alternative strategies.
- Establish an iterative process of monitoring, measurement, assessment and evaluation, and adjustment, based on both anticipated and unanticipated results.

Managerial implications

The managerial implications of both the negative and positive impacts of unintentional demarketing have a wide range, since it is difficult to imagine a national environment, industry, sector, or organization in which they would not manifest themselves. From a practical standpoint, it is important for organizational leaders, strategic/tactical planners and marketers to evaluate the potential for the occurrence of unintentional marketing to occur, not only to anticipate potential issues but also to leverage positive unintended effects of marketing and demarketing.

This analysis is also important from a value/distribution chain perspective, since both upstream/downstream and horizontal unexpected effects of marketing/demarketing may impact an organization's stakeholders (manufacturers, distributors, retailers, etc.) as well as simply its customers. There is, therefore, a need for organizations and their managers to evaluate their entire networks of exchanges and relationships in terms of impacts on all stakeholders (Polonsky et al. 2003), since communities, organizations, and other stakeholders are likely to have different and conflicting interests and agendas.

In the arena of social marketing and public policy, those involved in campaigning against undesirable demand for goods and services may not realize that they are actually engaged in demarketing/countermarketing, as described by Suh et al. (2012), and fail to anticipate and plan strategies to address unintended consequences.

Managers at all levels must realize that the interactions among marketing/demarketing strategies and applications are complex and may be difficult to assess, analyze, and address. They need to develop detailed strategies to identify, troubleshoot, and resolve unintentional demarketing results.

Academic implications/opportunities for future research

At this point, the limited body of literature and research on the general topic of demarketing and the specific topic of unintentional demarketing raises more questions than it answers, such as:

- How can marketers and academicians determine the interaction effects of marketing/demarketing elements?
- How can they anticipate unintentional demarketing (unintended consequences of marketing/demarketing)?

- Is the overall result greater than "the sum of the parts"? Is a combination of marketing/demarketing approaches more effective, ineffective, or harmful than individual strategies or elements?
- How do these concepts translate across countries, cultures, and markets?
- What are the potential ethical issues associated with unintentional demarketing?

What we do know is that the general topic of unintentional marketing/demarketing and its consequences is both important and under-researched, as outlined below:

- Empirical assessment of demarketing in domestic and global markets is lacking (Dadzie 1989).
- Empirical assessment of unintentional demarketing appears to be non-existent, which presents a huge opportunity for academic researchers.
- There is a need for standardization and general acceptance of terms (e.g. demarketing vs. countermarketing).
- There is a need for expansion of demarketing research from the non-profit sectors to the business sector, especially in the context of CRM (Suh *et al.* 2012).
- Hypothesized assumptions can be dangerous, as shown by Shiu *et al.*'s (2009) excellent quantitative research on demarketing tobacco through governmental policies. Less-than-rigorous qualitative/quantitative research can also be dangerous. Results can be highly situational. For example, channeling smokers into smoking rooms could actually be perceived as a "reward" for smokers, who have had an increasingly difficult time finding comfortable places to smoke in workplaces and other locations, and may, from an implementation standpoint, actually encourage smokers to continue to smoke – an example of de-demarketing.
- Care must be taken in generalizing. Manifestations and consequences of unintentional demarketing may vary widely, depending on the organization(s), stakeholders, type of product/service involved, etc. For example, unintentional demarketing related to smoking cessation involves a very different situation from unintentional demarketing for an automobile dealership.

Conclusion

Circling back to where we began this chapter, with Kotler and Levy's dismissal of unintentional demarketing to concentrate on the other types of demarketing, the aim of this chapter is to make the point that the topic is broad and complex, and it needs further study.

There is an implied assumption that all marketing results in positive outcomes, whereas we know that this is not the case – not only do marketing campaigns frequently fail to deliver anticipated outcomes, but they also frequently deliver negative outcomes. This may have more important consequences for the initiating organization than would be the case if the campaign were successful – an increase in business is a fine thing, but a substantial decrease could spell disaster. There is a need for an initial comprehensive, in-depth examination of the nature of the relationships between the related concepts of marketing and demarketing and their unintended consequences, beginning with a clarification and standardization of terminology. The theoretical aspects of those topics and sub-topics should be explored and conceptualized. Finally, the practical aspects, implementations, and assessments of unintentional demarketing should be assessed – an effort in which both managers and the academic community have roles to play. From a practical standpoint, how can it be identified? What are the potential results? How can they be assessed? How should they be handled? The bottom line is that demarketing needs to be planned and leveraged intelligently, either in its traditional role as a constraint on marketing or for other logical reasons, and that unintentional demarketing and its results deserve much more attention than they have previously received.

References

Ahmad W.I.U. (ed) (1993). '*Race' and Health in Contemporary Britain*, Open University Press, pp. 247.

Beeton, S. and Benfield, R. (2003). Demand Control: The case for demarketing as a visitor and environmental management tool. *Journal of Sustainable Tourism*, 10(6), 497–513.

Carrigan, M., Szmigin, I. and Wright, J. (2004). Shopping for a better world? An interpretive study of the potential for ethical consumption within the older market. *Journal of Consumer Marketing*, 21(6), 401–417.

Dadzie, Kofi Q. (1989), Demarketing strategy in shortage marketing environments. *Journal of the Academy of Marketing Science*, 17(2), (Summer), 157-165.

Kirchner, Theresa A., John B. Ford, and Sandra Mottner, (2012). *Arts Marketing: An International Journal*. 2(1), 70-90.

Kotler, P. (1973). The major tasks of marketing management. *Journal of Marketing*, 37(4), 42–49.

——(2011). Reinventing marketing to manage the environmental imperative. *Journal of Marketing*, 75(4), 132–35.

Kotler, P. and Levy, S. J. (1971). Demarketing, yes, demarketing. *Harvard Business Review*, 49(6), 74–80.

Kotler, P. and Zaltman, G. (1971). Social marketing: An approach to planned social change. *Journal of Marketing*, 35(3), 3–12.

Krentler, K. (1988). Maintaining quality control in the 'Crunch' in service firms. *Journal of Services Marketing*, 2(1), 71.

Mark, A. and Elliott, R. (1997). Demarketing dysfunctional demand in the UK National Health Service. *The International Journal of Health Planning and Management*, 12(4), 297–314.

Medway, D. and Warnaby, G. (2008). Alternative perspectives on marketing and the place brand. *European Journal of Marketing*, 42(5/6), 641–53.

Medway, D., Warnaby, G. and Dharni, S. (2011). Demarketing places: Rationales and strategies. *Journal of Marketing Management*, 27(1/2), 124–42.

Pechmann, C. and Reibling, E. T. (2006). Antismoking advertisements for youths: An independent evaluation of health, counter-industry, and industry approaches. *American Journal of Public Health*, 96(5), 906–13.

Polonsky, Michael Jay, Carlson, Les and Fry, Marie-Louise (2003). The harm chain: A public policy development and stakeholder perspective. *Marketing Theory*, 3(3), 365–387.

Sharp, A., Stine, A. and Wheeler, Meagan. (2010). Proscription and its impact on anti-consumption behaviour and attitudes: The case of plastic bags. *Journal of Consumer Behaviour*, 9(6), 470–84.

Sheth, J. N. and Parvatiyar, A. (1995). Relationship marketing in consumer markets: Antecedents and consequences. *Journal of the Academy of Marketing Science*, 23(4), 255–71.

Shiu, E., Hassan, L. M. and Walsh, G. (2009). Demarketing tobacco through governmental policies – The 4Ps revisited. *Journal of Business Research*, 62(2), 269–78.

Suh, M., Taeseok, R. and Greene, Henry. (2012). Relationship behavior between customers and service providers in demarketing situations: What makes customers try to improve their relationships? *Database Marketing and Customer Strategy Management*, 19(1), 39–55.

Teel, S. J., Teel, J. E. and Bearden, W. O. (1979). Lessons learned from the broadcast cigarette advertising ban. *Journal of Marketing*, 43(1), 45–50.

Vasconcelos, A. F. (2011). Internal demarketing: Construct, research propositions and managerial implications. *Management and Marketing Challenges for the Knowledge Society*, 6(1), 35–58.

13

"UNINTENTIONAL DEMARKETING" IN HIGHER EDUCATION

Nnamdi O. Madichie

There have been so many abortive efforts to increase demand, resulting actually in driving customers away – this epitomizes "demarketing" and it is, by all means, "unintentional". This chapter presents the developments in a sector where the consequences of such "unintentional demarketing" have often been overlooked. It highlights the "demarketing" consequences that were not envisaged by the HEI sector, which according to Levy, equates to "marketing myopia" arising from the unintentional demarketing initiatives by those institutions that should have known better. In their bid to embark upon *ostensible demarketing* (or sometimes strategic demarketing), HEIs have only ended up "cannibalizing" their flagship brands and/or services. Typical examples considered in this chapter include (i) the rampant revised editions of best-selling textbooks with very little value-added; (ii) polycentric misunderstanding of regionally adapted texts in order to appeal to erroneously perceived new frontiers (e.g. Asia and the Middle East); and (iii) the launch of inappropriate programmes and/or courses, which are little more than "a flash in the pan" with no sustainable basis for achieving medium- to long-term goals.

Unintended demarketing in higher education

While unintentional demarketing alluded to in the opening section may have been more prominent when it comes to fast-moving consumer goods (FMCGs), the purveyors of tools and techniques of marketing such as higher education institutions (HEIs) may be just as guilty as their clients. Unlike the over-reported *Global Financial Crisis*, there is a new wave of crisis, but this time it's in the Ivory Towers – i.e. the higher education (or HE) sector. In this chapter, the *Global Ivory Tower Crisis* is presented in the form of a series of marketing (or, better stated, demarketing) case studies in the HE sector – revised editions (with outrageously short product lifecycles, PLCs – best suited for high-tech products such as smartphones); regional adaptations of leading textbooks, and the "unintended consequences" of scrambling to launch new courses and/ or programmes to leverage marketing opportunities without due regard for the organizational capabilities in place. These are discussed in turn in the following sub-sections of this chapter.

The revised edition dilemma

In the first case illustration, it is worth pointing out that there are many (mostly marketing) higher education textbooks currently in the market where some publishers either churn out revised editions or some regional adaptation of a bestseller for some inexplicable reason. This often leads to confusion in the eyes of the target markets as to what edition may be best suited to their teaching needs. For example, while some marketing professors, lecturers and instructors tend to have a preference for Kotler and Armstrong's 13th Edition of *Principles of Marketing* text, there have been two additional variants of the text within two years (the 14th Edition and an Arab world edition in 2012 alone) – the latter in particular being nothing more than what could have been achieved within the classroom, as case studies.

This raises the question as to why HE textbook publishers resort to thinking that revised editions (as demonstrated in the marketing of the new edition), and regional adaptations (such as the Arab world edition) are actually market driven. Under these kinds of circumstances, what may have been planned to be a temporary deflection and/or deferral may well become permanent as alternative publishing houses are sought. The glut in HE textbook publishing is nothing new. The Second Edition of *Marketing* by Elliott, Rundle-Thiele and Waller (2012) has been described by Wiley, its publishers, as "the ideal text for the undergraduate introductory marketing course in the Asia-Pacific region. Significantly, it is an original work rather than being an adaptation of a US text". This ultimately meant that, rather than being an adaptation, the plan was to update the text in a revised form. However, it is difficult to understand the need for a revised edition so soon considering also that "the 1st edition of this text was the most successful 'ground-up' Introductory Marketing text ever released in the local market".[1]

Furthermore, Wiley, the publishers, went on to specify that the revised text built upon "… the strengths of the popular 1st edition […] and its extensive accompanying digital resources are designed to engage students in the study of marketing. A diverse range of organisations, goods and services from Australia, New Zealand and the Asian region are featured to illustrate key concepts, coupled with detailed coverage of the latest marketing theory, research and thinking". From this there are some leanings towards adaptation to the Australia, New Zealand and the Asian region – a topic that is covered in our next section.

Regional adaptations

In the second illustration, two events are evident. First is that of "unplanned obsolescence". The second is about the glut for "throwing away the baby with the bath water" by embracing regionally and "politically correct" versions of leading texts for specific regions. An example in the case of this latter practice is sub-titles like "First Arab Edition" of a leading Anglo-Saxon textbook. It's even more problematic to see supposedly "global marketing" or "international business" texts adorning such labels. What makes these global or international remains food for thought. As practitioners and/or publishers grapple to balance the act of standardization versus adaptation of business and management textbooks, the tilt towards the latter may have little relevance for the real needs of consumers. This exploratory study presents the debate based on a mini-survey from the Arab world context. The perceived gaps between the expectations and perceptions of publishers and the students/faculty, respectively, on the suitability of Western textbooks for the Arab world are a problem akin to "unintentional demarketing". This raises two central questions:

1. Is there a danger of "polycentrism" in adapted Anglo-Saxon textbooks for Arab university students?
2. Can undergraduate students undertake real-life marketing research?

Perhaps after reading this case study, you may be able to provide a confident response to these nagging questions. Based on preliminary findings from a mini-survey undertaken by undergraduate students in an Arab university regarding the relevance of Western business and management textbooks for their context, some interesting issues have emerged – these are presented in our next section. In their attempt to tackle the two questions above, and to understand the reality behind the contention that "Western business and management textbooks may not be suited to the Arab world context", the students set themselves three research questions seeking to understand the what, why and how:

1. What benefits are Western textbooks for undergraduate business and management students in the Arab world?
2. How satisfied are students with the current provisions (pedagogical tools) of Western textbooks?
3. To what extent is there an urgency for context-relevant (i.e. adapted) textbooks to the Arab world?

The tentative results of these are presented in Table 13.4 in the next section of this chapter.

New programmes

In the third and final illustration, a typical example in this regard would be that of launching new courses, programmes and/or departments without in-depth cost-benefit analyses, which often results in duplication and overlaps, and thereby stretching resources wide and thin and subsequently realizing how unsustainable these may have become.[2] Most often than not, such activities tend to result in the severance and/or merging of courses, departments or both; and the attendant severance of lecturers and professors (especially Deans and HODs) as schools or departments merge, etc. There have been instances of universities offering courses on international marketing, as well as global marketing, which seems to make no sense at all. Other examples may be seen by the surge of universities launching sports marketing and/or management programmes in the run up to mega sporting events such as was the case in the period prior to the London 2012 Olympics. We shall return to this topic in the next section.

Case discussions

Revised editions

A quick search of the McGraw-Hill online catalogue revealed over 100 marketing titles split into the categories in Table 13.1. This is in addition to the best-selling text by David Jobber; *Principles and Practice of Marketing*, which arguably "sets the benchmark for achievement in introductory marketing courses". As part of the promotional material for this best-selling text, it was opined that his "... clear writing style, engaging examples and comprehensive coverage of all the essential concepts combine to make this book a trusted and stimulating choice to support your course".[3] Furthermore, this sixth edition was described as having been "fully updated to offer a contemporary perspective on marketing, with the latest digital developments and ethical accountability emphasised throughout [and] packed with examples of marketing practice in well-known companies, brought to life through real print, video and online advertising examples". With such glowing reviews, one would or should expect that the text should have a longer lifespan than just a few months prior to the release of an updated version. Is this the case? Shouldn't it be the case? From Table 13.2, it can be seen that the same authors released both *Essentials of Marketing* and *Basic Marketing* simultaneously.

Pearson is another culprit in this demarketing exercise with regional adaptations spanning Asia, Sweden and the Arab world (see Table 13.3). Indeed, going by the promotional material for the Arab world edition of Kotler and Armstrong's best-selling *Principles of Marketing* text, it was suggested that the

TABLE 13.1 McGraw-Hill marketing text portfolio

Titles	No. of books	Titles	No. of books
Advertising & promotion	30	International marketing	6
Advertising principles	10	Internet marketing	19
Consumer behavior	9	Marketing management	20
CRM	12	Marketing principles	26
Database marketing	2	Marketing research	4
Direct marketing	8	New product management	3
e-commerce	6	Product management	7
e-commerce strategy	3	Strategic marketing	8
Total	80		93
Grand Total	173		

Source: http://catalogs.mhhe.com/mhhe/viewNode.do?node_type=c&catid=924296

TABLE 13.2 McGraw-Hill marketing text portfolio

Author/Year	Title	ISBN/Edition
Perreault, Jr., Cannon, and McCarthy (2012)	*Essentials of Marketing*	ISBN-13 9780078028885 (13th Edition, January 2012)
Perreault, Jr., Cannon, and McCarthy (2011)	*Basic Marketing*	ISBN-13 9780073529950
Fahy and Jobber (2012)	*Foundations of Marketing*	ISBN: 0077137019 (4th Edition, January)
Jobber and Ellis-Chadwick (2012)	*Principles and Practice of Marketing*	ISBN: 0077140001
Jobber (2009)	*Principles and Practice of Marketing*	ISBN: 9780077123307 (December 2009)
Grewal and Levy (2010)	*Marketing*	ISBN-13 9780073380957 (2nd Edition)

Note: See the Confusion on McGraw Hill *Principles of Marketing* titles. Online at: http://catalogs.mhhe.com/mhhe/viewProductList.do?cnt=26&catid=924435

TABLE 13.3 Kotler and Armstrong regional adaptations (in 12 months)

Author	Title/Region	Year/ISBN
Parment, Kotler and Armstrong (2011)	*Principles of Marketing*	(Swedish Edition, September 2011) ISBN13: 9780273735960 ISBN10: 0273735969
Kotler, Tolba, Habib and Armstrong (2011)	*Principles of Marketing*	(Arab World Editions, December 2011) ISBN13: 9781408289075 ISBN10: 1408289075

adaptation seeks to "discover what makes a marketing campaign successful in this rapidly developing region through the Arab edition of this widely acclaimed textbook".

Kotler and Armstrong's hugely successful approach has been adapted specifically for the Arab world, using Arab world business examples, case studies and statistics as well as cultural and demographic insights. "Emphasis is placed on making marketing ideas and concepts come alive by encouraging readers to apply established marketing principles to real companies in real situations".[4] Additional features specially designed for students in the Arab region included what the publishers deemed to be of importance, notably, "An English-Arabic Glossary–translation of key terms; Adapted vocabulary throughout the book to be sympathetic to students whose first language is not English; and a Slight reduction in length to 17 focused chapters, to meet the demand for a resource which is easier to handle and to cover in the time available". While the shortened number of chapters may be a welcome development, the Arabic glossary seems a bit polycentric in orientation.

For the Swedish Edition of *Principles of Marketing*, this has been described as the "ideal introductory text for undergraduate students and practitioners alike" amongst other unique selling points such as:

1. This, the first Swedish edition, is true to Kotler and Armstrong's classic conceptual framework, which has proved itself as an exceptional introduction to marketing and has been used by millions of students all over the world.
2. The book outlines and discusses concepts and ideas that help students and practitioners develop an effective marketing strategy for today's markets. Cases and examples are written to reflect current best practice in Swedish, Scandinavian and European companies.
3. The book describes and explains how these companies deal with challenges in domestic and international markets.
4. It is set in a Swedish context but is global in scope and is very relevant for modern marketers.

Furthermore, the product description for Kotler and Armstrong's Global Edition (published April 2011) reads thus:

> The Editorial team at Pearson has worked closely with educators around the world to include content which is especially relevant to students outside the United States.

With such a positioning statement, one begins to wonder why the need for regional adaptations such as the Asian Perspective, Arab world edition and the Swedish Edition (with Anders Parment) amongst others. Today's marketing challenge is creating vibrant, interactive communities of consumers who make products and brands a part of their daily lives. Learn how to create value and gain loyal customers. The pitch is also interesting and very similar to that presented by McGraw-Hill in relation to David Jobber's bestseller. In the case of Pearson, the text by Kotler and Armstrong was described as "a comprehensive, classic principles text organized around an innovative customer-value framework [that teaches] students … how to create customer value, target the correct market, and build customer relationships". The pitch, which now sounds a bit ironical, also acknowledged "the changing nature of consumer expectations means that marketers must learn how to build communities in addition to brand loyalty".

Regional adaptations

This case illustration is based upon a mini-survey of 55 respondents using a convenience sample of faculty and students in an Arab world university within a two-week period in the Fall 2009/2010 semester. The sample was split into 48 business students (i.e. n = 48) and 7 faculty members (n = 7). The participants were conveniently selected from around the college of business (or business school) spreading across majors and departments (i.e. accounting and finance, management, marketing and MIS). It is also worth stating that the survey was put together by a group of undergraduate students (straddling majors) as part of their marketing research group project for the Fall 2009/2010 semester, where they were initially required to develop a marketing research design/framework for investigating the suitability of Western textbooks to their specific needs in the region. The findings may be useful fodder for relevant stakeholders in the Middle East and North African (MENA) region, as they weigh the options of developing/adopting textbook adaptations with extensive local content.

The results of the survey seem to suggest that students were not disposed to reading enough of their textbooks, even though many had the conviction of the relevance of such textbooks (almost exclusively Western) to their needs. It was also found that certain students were faced with difficulties in 'comprehending' the content of Western textbooks (especially the expressions used) and contexts (e.g. case examples and other illustrations) in these largely 'Americanized' or 'Europeanized' textbooks. This partially explains the 'lack of commitment' towards the use (i.e. reading) of such texts for general knowledge development and preparation for examinations and other forms of assessment. Consequently, any attempt to verify whether the texts were either useful or to what extent they may require adaptation may be jeopardized by what Malhotra and Binks (2007) ascribed to as "inability to answer".

However, any prospects of introducing fully adapted textbooks with local content that includes cases and examples from within their own "Arab" environment seems appealing to some of these students as evidenced in the paradox illustrated in Table 13.4, where we see mean scores of above three in both extremes – general understanding (3.31) and difficulty in comprehending illustrations and/or examples (3.06), as well as the relationship to the fact that students hardly read their textbooks (2.50).

From the figures in Table 13.4, a sample mean of 3.31 suggests that students don't find it very difficult "understanding" materials from their current "Western" textbooks. However, with a mean of 3.06, there is also a suggestion that there were some difficulties experienced. Another readily observable problem arising from this is the duality of opinions. On the one hand, there are students who were concerned that there aren't much cases and examples from the Arab world context to illustrate the workings of different concepts in business and

TABLE 13.4 Summary statistics

Variable	Mean Score	Total Weighting
General understanding of Western texts	3.31	5.00
Challenges using Western texts	3.06	5.00
General reading (irrespective)	2.50	5.00
Partial adaptation of Western texts	3.00	5.00
★ Standardization of Western texts	4.14	5.00
★ Adaptation of Western texts	2.57	5.00

Note: ★ Results from the sample of faculty members

management in the region. For others, on the other hand, there was a perception that Western textbooks tended to cover many different topics and issues in a simple and clear manner to the appreciation of some students. However, certain other students may not be well versed in noting this as they do not even seem to bother with reading their assigned textbooks (as indicated by the mean of 2.50) but tended to rely exclusively on the lecture slides.

Responses from the faculty members suggest a consensual level of satisfaction with the current Western textbooks provision. Indeed, faculty members expressed reservations over the appeal of adapted textbooks and locally inspired case studies (both with mean scores of just above average at 2.57). They also found Western textbooks to be very useful for their teaching needs. Furthermore, regarding the observation of "tailor-made textbooks" for the region, faculty members, while appreciating that it wouldn't be hard to develop such textbooks, still seemed to argue that there was not an urgent need for this as the current textbooks still seemed to "get the job done". For the business faculty members, this group seemed more satisfied than their students in terms of the current coverage of Western textbooks. For those faculty members who were receptive to adapted editions of Western textbooks, they were more likely to welcome "only marginal modifications" in the form of updated case studies for local fit rather than going for the full adaptation option anticipated by some publishers – notably Pearson Education. This is very instructive for all concerned parties.

New programmes

While there is a persuasive argument for the launch and development of new courses, programmes and/or departments in higher education, doing this without in-depth cost-benefit analyses would often result in duplication and overlaps; overstretched resources; quality implications; and unsustainable outcomes. The result is often one of a return to the status quo, or perhaps even further back where merging of departments/courses, severance of lecturers and professors (especially Deans and HODs) have often been the case.

However, it seems very likely that most post-1992 universities in the UK may be reconsidering a return to the status quo. Evidently, it seems like the policy of ridding these former polytechnics of vocational courses such as NVQ, HNCS and/or HNDs may have impacted on their relationship with industry and perhaps even the government. Unintentionally, the demarketing of the HEI provisions in the 1990s has brought about a widened gap between academia and practice where a new tagline "entrepreneurship" or "enterprise" has become the future of most universities (both older universities and their post-1992 siblings) as they continuously gravitate towards the old guard (vocational studies). Indeed, there is hardly any business school anywhere in the world without either a Centre for Entrepreneurship and/or business incubation – or with plans to set up one in the near future.

Under sports management studies, a student is exposed to a variety of subjects like advertising, event promotion, facility management, public relations, sports administration, coaching, recruitment, health and safety measures for athletes, etc.[5] After a post-graduation degree in sports management from any of the following renowned universities of the UK and effective workplace training, one can make a career in sports and leisure, facility management, sports development, education, research, consultancy, policy making, planning and strategic management. According to an Expert website on studying in the UK, there is "top-10 list" of universities known for sports management in the UK – University of Loughborough, University of Bath, Durham University, University of Exeter, University of Birmingham, Edinburgh University, and the University of Leeds amongst others.[6]

However, many other me-too universities with questionable resources to run such specialized programmes have mushroomed – especially, but not always exclusively (see Box 13.1 and Table 13.5), in the run-up to the London 2012 Olympics.

BOX 13.1 Elite sporting success at the University of Nottingham

Olympic feel-good factor in UK higher education

While it makes a great deal of sense that "An Olympic feel-good factor is clearly helping inspire those who wish to aspire", can this be achieved without launching new sports degrees or courses? The experience of the University of Nottingham may provide a good insight.

The University of Nottingham might not have any sports-specific post-graduate courses, but nonetheless offers opportunities for sports specialisms for those training in vocations such as medicine or physiotherapy. In addition, they're also very proud of their sporting roll of honour.

According to Nigel Mayglothling, assistant director of sport and physical recreation at the University of Nottingham pointed out that "Most of our elite sporting success is built around supporting academics who also play sport rather than study sport..."

The University of Nottingham gives bursary support to around 30 athletes a year from a wide range of sports. This includes mentoring, free physiotherapy, specialist instruction and close liaison with local sports clubs.

It is also hopeful that admissions will continue to rise as Nottingham capitalizes on its own "legacy games" – an event hosted this summer across the university's multiple campuses as the Olympic torch passed through the city. Recent reports suggests that recruitment was looking quite healthy in 2012 with increased numbers at the university's "open days" coupled with a good range of performance athletes again seeking to study and train at the university.

Source: Adapted from Carrie Dunn (*The Guardian*, 13 November 2012) Universities benefit from Olympic feel-good factor. Online at: http://www.guardian.co.uk/education/2012/nov/13/postgrad-sports-courses

Perhaps not surprisingly, even Pearson, the major international publisher and education firm, has become a for-profit private higher education provider in the UK.[7] The firm is even reported to be opening a Pearson College, teaching a degree course validated by existing London universities. The business and enterprise degree, taught in London and Manchester, will have about 40 places in 2012. The college says it will be for "students who are serious about succeeding in business". Pearson says this will be the first time a FTSE 100 company has directly delivered a degree course. It will be seen as a significant symbolic step into UK higher education from a major player in the education market – the Quality Assurance Agency (QAA) implications is beyond the scope of this chapter.

In Table 13.5, the *Guardian* league table for sports science education in the UK ranked 68 universities of which about 18 had scores of 3 or less out of 10 in terms of value-added. The question remains as to whether there was really any sense in continuing such programmes in the light of these scores.

Conclusions

This chapter on unintentional demarketing has highlighted three different, but connected case illustrations from the higher education sector. While not a lot can be plucked from the concept of "unintentional demarketing", these can be inferred from the literature. In the first illustration, the number of textbooks (mostly marketing) currently in the market defies the logic of the concept. Indeed, most publishers (notably McGraw-Hill and Pearson Education) have been observed to be overly reliant upon either churning out revised editions (sometimes twice a year) or some form of regional adaptation of their supposed "bestseller" titles. This may lead to the cannibalization of the leading texts (which they may have hoped to demarket) in their portfolio, as it more often than not leads to confusion of their target markets as to what edition best suits their teaching needs. For example, while some instructors and students may be more comfortable with Kotler and Armstrong's 13th Edition of *Principles of Marketing* text, there have been two additional variants of the text within two years (the 14th Edition and an Arab world edition). To the publishers, the thinking might be that the Arab world may be interested in simply "Buying Arab". Under these kinds of circumstances, what may have been planned to be a temporary deflection and/or deferral may well become permanent as alternative publishing houses are sought.

In the second illustration, an attempt at understanding the extent of the suitability of Western textbooks for business and management in the Arab world higher education sector, the mini-survey found mixed results. While some students appreciated the relevance of Western textbooks for their local contexts, they found the idea of textbooks with cases, examples and illustrations from their own local culture equally appealing. On the part of faculty members, however, most seemed quite satisfied with the current textbook provision, and tend to believe that the development of 'region-centric' texts (i.e. adaptations

TABLE 13.5 Winners and losers in value-added

Rating	Name of institution	Guardian score /100	Satisfied with course (%)	Satisfied with teaching (%)	Satisfied with feedback (%)	Student: staff ratio	Spend per student (FTE)	Average entry tariff	Value-added score /10	Career after 6 months
2	Exeter	98.2	94	95	74	26.9	7	397	9	62
6	Bath	91.1	89	91	69	18.7		357	9	54
7	Salford	90.8	89	91	83	13.0	5	289	8	
8	Bournemouth	87.9	91	90	80	22.3	6	321	10	53
12	Liverpool John Moores	83.9	84	84	71	17.7	5	301	9	54
18	Coventry	81.6	76	84	59	18.7	4	286	9	73
21	Southampton Solent	80.4	90	90	87	6.5	3	260	1	
23	Plymouth	79.9	46	74	44	18.6	10	272	10	49
24	Cardiff Met	79.0	88	89	76	19.4	4	267	8	51
25	Gloucestershire	78.5	90	87	66	24.1	4	310	10	50
26	Sheffield Hallam	78.3	85	83	67	24.0	4	328	8	58
27	Cumbria	77.4	87	92	62	17.5	8	262	3	56
29	Oxford Brookes	76.0	88	96	72	33.2	5	318	8	
31	Nottingham Trent	75.2	83	82	55	20.6	6	270	8	54
35	Chester	72.8	75	78	67	19.5	7	270	2	69
38	Middlesex	71.9	73	81	66	29.5	7	210	8	
39	Lincoln	71.8	87	89	71	22.7	7	295	2	53
40	Robert Gordon	71.6	72	77	60	14.9	4	314	3	
43	Hull	70.8	78	89	63	24.9	7	263	3	60
47	Bedfordshire	67.1	70	80	52	19.7	5	214	8	48
47	Roehampton	67.1	65	71	56	25.4	7	226	8	68
49	Stirling	66.3	93	87	70	28.6	4	355	2	
50	London South Bank	66.2	94	90	67	18.8	4	209	2	41

TABLE 13.5 (continued)

Rating	Name of institution	Guardian score /100	Satisfied with course (%)	Satisfied with teaching (%)	Satisfied with feedback (%)	Student: staff ratio	Spend per student (FTE)	Average entry tariff	Value-added score /10	Career after 6 months
56	Marjon (St Mark and St John)	61.0	81	88	69	19.9	2	199	3	47
57	Newman University College	60.8	85	91	69	20.6	3	230	3	
58	Manchester Met	59.2	72	84	69	19.9	3	251	2	
60	Leeds Trinity University College	56.0	79	82	64	28.1	2	239	2	61
61	Canterbury Christ Church	55.7	91	85	72	24.5	3	175	3	40
62	Bolton	55.6	72	77	60	18.7	3	212	2	46
62	East London	55.6	91	90	78	37.8	3	179	3	50
66	West of Scotland	48.1	83	84	64	38.0	3	283	2	39
67	Newport	44.4	88	83	73	41.4	2	192	2	36
68	Bucks New University	36.6	62	60	54	25.9	4	199	2	33

Source: *The Guardian* (Tuesday, 22 May 2012) University league table for sports science in the UK online at: http://www.guardian.co.uk/education/table./2012/may/22/university-guide-sports-science

Note: For a detailed description of the rankings, see Judy Friedberg (*The Guardian*, 22 May 2012) Key to the university guide subject tables 2013: What does each column mean? Online at: http://www.guardian.co.uk/education/2012/may/22/key-to-university-guide

to the Arab world context) was not an urgent requirement. This seems consistent with the observation made by Pitt *et al.* (2009, p. 297) that "[…] most university professors can identify with the hours spent searching for the appropriate textbook just to find that nothing is suitable for their course". In the end, the "inconclusiveness" of this survey is suggestive of the need for a much broader, more in-depth study drawing upon a more representative sample size – especially one that includes students from the natural sciences as well as the social sciences, arts and humanities disciplines. This case illustration has two broad implications – first, from a practical point of view, textbook publishers, on the one hand, may need to exercise some caution in their engagement more with their target markets in order to establish the "real needs" of the latter prior to commissioning regionally adapted texts. On the other hand, faculty members need to be more creative in their teaching using Western textbooks by providing regionally inspired case illustrations in a pastoral capacity. This proposition is consistent with the findings of McChlery and Wilkie (2009) as their contribution to the student support debate in learning and teaching, that it should be focused "primarily at improving retention and progression metrics" through pastoral support (p. 23). Second, and from a pedagogical stand point, considering that the study was originally inspired by student researchers getting acquainted with the tools of the marketing research trade, the case study not only contributes to the student support debate advocated by McChlery and Wilkie (2009) but also the motivation of students by rewarding achievements through showcase events such as student conferences.

In the third and final illustration, it is arguable that the concept alludes to a situation where marketers, in a bid to embark upon ostensible demarketing (or sometime strategic demarketing), have only ended up cannibalizing their product offerings. A typical example in this regard would be the case of unnecessary new course launches (or new product development, NPD in the case of traditional/conventional products), which often imply the stretching of resources "wide and thin" before realizing how unsustainable these initiatives might have been (sadly only as an afterthought). Often, such myopic approaches to marketing lead to the merging of courses or complete withdrawal of these courses, with attendant spill-over effects on departmental mergers (post ante), severance of lecturers and professors (especially deans and department heads) in a bid to cut costs and rein in redundant financial outlays. Furthermore, looking back at most post-1992 universities in the UK today, most of which have had to rid themselves of vocational courses (such as HNCS/HNDs and NVQs), whilst they sought to transform from the old polytechnic garb to universities, only to revert to the status quo – where most universities are navigating towards the old guard (vocational studies) in the name of Centres for Entrepreneurship with business incubation units amongst others – are these measures truly intentional?

Questions

1. What might be the drivers for producing regional editions of textbooks?

2. Why might regional editions be counter-productive in terms of sales?
3. What are the pitfalls of offering revised courses?
4. Why would a publisher like Pearson seek to establish its own teaching facility?

Notes

1 See the product information on the Second Edition of *Marketing* by Elliott, Rundle-Thiele and Waller (2012) online at: http://eu.wiley.com/WileyCDA/WileyTitle/product Cd-1742467210.html
2 See *Enterprising Matters*. Online at: http://www.isbe.org.uk/entrepreneurialUniversity
3 http://www.mcgrawhill.co.uk/html/0077123301.html
4 http://www.pearsoned.co.uk/bookshop/detail.asp?item=100000000446201
5 See http://www.studyinuk.co.in/tag/sports-management-courses-in-uk/
6 This analysis is based on student satisfaction, research assessment, entry standards and graduate prospects by complete university guide.
7 Sean Coughlan (*BBC News*, 3 August 2012) Publisher Pearson launches UK degree course. Online at: http://www.bbc.co.uk/news/education-19245788

References

Dunn, C. (2012) *Universities benefit from Olympic feelgood factor*. The Guardian, Postgrad Supplement 2012 (13 November 2012). Online at: http://www.guardian.co.uk/education/2012/nov/13/postgrad-sports-courses

Elliott, G., Rundle-Thiele, S. and Waller, D. (2012) *Marketing, 2nd Edition*. Wiley.

Guardian, The (22 May 2012) *University League table for sports science in the UK* online at: http://www.guardian.co.uk/education/table/2012/may/22/university-guide-sports-science

Kotler, P. and Armstrong, G. (2011) *Principles of Marketing*. Upper Saddle River, NJ: Pearson Education. Thirteenth Global Edition.

McChlery, S. and Wilkie, J. (2009) Pastoral Support to undergraduates in higher education. *International Journal of Management Education*, 8(1): pp. 23–35.

Malhotra, Naresh and Birks, David (2007) Marketing Research: An applied approach: 3rd European Edition, Harlow, UK, Pearson Education, 835pp.

Pitt, L., Nel, D., van Heerden, G. and Chan, A. (2009) Global text project: new horizons in textbook marketing. *Marketing Intelligence and Planning*, vol. 27 No. 3, pp. 297–307.

14

DEMARKETING AND MARKETING

A conceptual discussion

Jim Blythe

Because demarketing has been virtually ignored in the half-century since Kotler and Levy first coined the word, there have been few attempts to develop a working conceptual framework for its study, and (perhaps more important) its applications to practice. Marketing practitioners are certainly familiar with the general idea of what demarketing is – either because they are actively engaged in discouraging unwanted customers or because they have made a marketing gaffe, which has resulted in lost business – but the terminology is not in current use in the same way as (for example) segmentation or branding, which are of course critical concepts in marketing management. We even lack a clear typology of demarketing – the one provided by Kotler and Levy was a good starting point, but still lacks a rigorous definition for each type.

Therein lies one of the biggest conceptual problems in considering demarketing: that of deciding where the boundaries lie. This was explored to some extent in Chapter 1, but most of the authors who have contributed chapters to this book have wrestled with the problem of definition, and therefore of setting boundaries: where does general demarketing end and selective demarketing begin? Does a campaign to reduce the use of illegal drugs fall within counter-marketing, or within general demarketing, or even within selective demarketing (since the use of illegal drugs is confined to fairly well-defined groups of the population). The case study chapters have further served to flag up the difficulties in recognizing the boundaries in the 'real world'.

Marketing, as an academic subject, is plagued with problems of definition: even the boundaries of marketing itself are often unclear because marketers use different definitions of what is, and is not, marketing. Most of the definitions currently in popular use imply that marketing is about increasing demand, either for profit or for the general welfare of humanity, yet much marketing activity (as we have seen in the case study chapters of this book) has been aimed at reducing demand in some way.

In fact, the strands of demarketing comprise a potential new way of looking at marketing as a discipline. In our second chapter, María Pilar Martínez-Ruiz expounded the theory that marketing should be redefined, moving away from the current definitions, which centre around facilitating profitable exchange, and considering marketing as being more about matching supply and demand. For traditional marketers, matching supply and demand would revolve around increasing demand in order to match growing production capacity, but in the twenty-first century this is not always possible. Environmentalism, restrictions on raw material supply and other factors may mean that supply cannot meet demand efficiently, in which case demand will need to be reduced or deferred until such time as production can handle the task. This is especially true for service industries, which often cannot increase production to meet seasonality and have expensive personnel who are idle (or at least underworked) during periods of lower demand.

Traditional marketing thinking has usually approached this problem by considering ways of increasing demand during quiet periods, usually by offering incentives to some segments of the market. Others have sought to reduce supply during quiet periods by laying staff off or employing seasonal staff to handle busy periods. Synchromarketing seeks to look at the demand side, but, if we are to take a rounded view of the whole problem, there is a case for redefining marketing. Perhaps an appropriate new definition might be:

The management process that seeks to match supply and demand in order to create efficient and satisfying exchanges between producers and customers.

This definition may require refinement as this chapter progresses and we consider other types of demarketing.

In Chapter 4, Nigel Jones, Paul Baines and Steve Welsh looked at another aspect of demarketing, that of counter-marketing. This is the use of marketing techniques to reduce the demand for a product which is not supplied by the demarketer, and is typical of social marketing campaigns such as the reduction in demand for cocaine, which our authors use as an example. In this case, Jones, Baines and Welsh examined counter-marketing in the context of wicked problems. A wicked problem is one that has no solution without creating more problems – which is substantially the case in counter-marketing, since the marketer has no control over the organization making the supply. If counter-marketing is considered in this context, the problem for social marketers becomes acute because there are too many variables to consider in formulating a viable campaign. Marketing therefore becomes an aspirational activity rather than one that deals with certainties: although no reasonable marketing practitioner would ever believe that there are certainties in business, marketing theory is not quite so pragmatic. There seems to be an inherent assumption in the current definitions of marketing that planning that is carefully carried out will provide the intended results. Demarketing theory, such as it is, continually refutes that view.

Counter-marketing implies opposition to an existing marketing activity by another organization. In the case of cocaine, the organization is quite large, although it is composed of many self-employed distributors, so counter-marketers may find themselves having to combat a large number of marketing approaches and separate channels of distribution.

Our redefinition of marketing therefore may need to include the concept of wickedness (in the problem-solving sense) when considering counter-marketing. The definition might now read as:

> *The management process that seeks (sometimes unsuccessfully) to match supply and demand in order to create efficient and satisfying exchanges between producers and customers, whether the customers are those of the marketer or not.*

The definition is beginning to look a little clumsy now, which is of course a consequence of dealing with a wicked problem.

General demarketing is concerned with discouraging customers in general, in other words, reducing demand across the board. This may be necessary when excess demand is present in the entire economy: economists tell us that this will lead to inflation and eventually unemployment as economic disruption occurs. Heather Skinner's chapter on this subject seeks to differentiate between general demarketing and other forms of demarketing – no easy process, since there is a lack of definition in the field, and the intentions of marketers are not always clear to an outsider. Skinner points out that it would be difficult to imagine a circumstance where a profit-making company would actively seek to reduce demand for its own products across the board (although it is easy to see where reducing demand from some groups would be desirable – this, however, is selective demarketing, not general demarketing). The point is also well made that general demarketing implies a deliberate act on the part of marketers, not an accident or an omission. This raises the question as to whether general demarketing exists 'in the wild' in the case of commercial organizations, or whether it is the prerogative of governments who are seeking to control the level of demand in the economy – in other words, is general demarketing part of marketing at all, or should it be considered as a central tool of macroeconomics?

If general demarketing is in the domain of macroeconomics, that may not entirely absolve marketers from responsibility, since the techniques used to reduce demand would still be within the realm of not-for-profit marketing, which marketers have already staked out as their own. For example, campaigns conducted during the Second World War to reduce demand for almost every consumer good including food certainly used typical marketing techniques, and were in fact quite sophisticated. Jingles, rhymes and cartoon images encouraged people to mend clothes rather than buy new; to eat less wheat; to save metal; and to recycle newspapers instead of using new paper. The boundary between general demarketing and counter-marketing is a narrow one, but counter-marketing implies an active marketing campaign acting in opposition to the demarketing campaign. In the case of (for example) government water-conservation efforts, the campaign is not matched by a campaign from the water companies encouraging people to use more, and is therefore general demarketing rather than counter-marketing.

Our new definition of marketing should include the concept of a deliberate reduction across the board, therefore, whether we are considering overall demand in the economy (macroeconomics) or demand for a specific category of product (as in the case of government requests to reduce the use of water during a drought). The new definition might now read as:

> *The management process that seeks (sometimes unsuccessfully) to match supply and demand in order to create or discourage efficient and satisfying exchanges between producers and customers, whether those customers are those of the marketer or not.*

This definition now suffers from an overly academic tone. It seeks to be precise, in other words, without providing practitioners with a blueprint for what they should be doing on Monday morning. Jillian Farquhar's chapter provided us with another possible thread to include in the final cloth when she discussed selective demarketing. Selective demarketing is the dark side of segmentation and targeting – when we target specific groups of customers, we imply that we do not want to deal with the other segments in the market. Selective demarketing involves deliberate attempts to repel undesirable customers, for whatever reason. The reason is (commonly) that such customers are too expensive or too inconvenient to supply properly, and nowhere is this truer than in service industries. The problem for the would-be selective demarketer is that selective demarketing appears, in some ways, to conflict with corporate social responsibility because it discriminates against some groups of customers, often those who have the least money to spend on the company's products. In the non-profit sector, selective demarketing may result in denying service to some needy groups – as is the case if a hospital emergency department refuses treatment to violent drunks, on the basis that the safety of medical staff is threatened by such patients.

Selective demarketing also creates an ethical problem in the business-to-business arena where refusal to supply some traders might result in their businesses failing altogether, as might happen if a hairdressing wholesaler refuses to supply mobile hairdressers on the grounds that they represent unfair competition for hair salons, who are after all the wholesaler's main customers. Since selective demarketing involves an element of deliberation about discouraging some groups, the word 'active' may need to be included in the definition of segmentation and targeting. Perhaps our definition of marketing needs to be adapted as well, perhaps as follows:

> *The management process that seeks (sometimes unsuccessfully) to match supply and demand in order to create or discourage efficient and satisfying exchanges between producers and customers, whether those customers are those of the marketer or not, through the active encouragement or discouragement of buying behaviour.*

Robin Croft's chapter on ostensible demarketing flags up another problem: that of intent on the part of the marketer. Ostensible demarketing is the act of appearing to remove a product form the market, or deny it to some groups, in order to increase their demand for it. Although there have been many examples of consumer protests at a producer's threat to withdraw a product, few (if any) marketers have ever admitted to doing this deliberately, presumably because there is an implication of deception attached to the practice and this would quite certainly provoke an even bigger, and possibly permanent, backlash against the company and its products.

Ostensible demarketing is therefore indistinguishable from other forms of demarketing, since it relies on understanding the intentions of the marketer. This is one area (of many, it should be said) in which marketing practitioners have a much clearer understanding of what is happening than academic marketers could ever hope to acquire, since practitioners know what they intended to do and academics have no realistic way of researching it.

Croft includes the idea of deliberately having a marketing campaign banned (for example by producing a controversial advertisement) as opposed to simply withdrawing a product. Again, this implies a deliberate intent – some advertising is banned anyway, to the surprise of the marketers who produced it, but few marketers would admit openly to producing an advertisement with the specific intent of being offensive. Although this would not necessarily be regarded as deceptive, it would be regarded as an abuse of the regulatory system, which might affect future decisions by regulators.

Our new definition of marketing, therefore, now has an extra thread to weave in, that of overt versus covert intent. The new thread might make the definition read as follows:

> *The management process that seeks (sometimes unsuccessfully) to match supply and demand in order to create or discourage efficient and satisfying exchanges between producers and customers, whether those customers are those of the marketer or not, through the active encouragement or discouragement of buying behaviour. The process may be carried out using a range of techniques, with the marketer's intentions known or unknown to the customer.*

The complexity of the definition grows, but help is at hand.

Our final conceptual chapter, by Theresa Kirchner, considers the possibility that a marketer might make a damaging mistake. Unintentional demarketing has traditionally been taken to mean a reduction in demand due to a botched attempt to increase demand – as happened early in 2013 when Bic launched a ballpoint pen designed specifically for women. Women, understandably, had not realized that they needed a special type of pen until Bic launched the product, and were scathing about the idea on several social networking sites. The product was ridiculed off the market – a fairly extreme outcome for Bic, who had invested considerable resources in the product, but one that might have been anticipated. Kirchner points out that unintended consequences might accrue from any marketing initiative, not just one intended to increase demand, so she has included the idea that demarketing might also go wrong – resulting in increased demand. This might be indistinguishable (to the outsider) from ostensible demarketing –

which leads us back to the proposition at the beginning of the chapter, that the different types of demarketing need to be defined more rigorously.

Meanwhile, our new definition of marketing has acquired another thread and may need to be restated as follows;

> *The management process that seeks (sometimes unsuccessfully) to match supply and demand in order to create or discourage efficient and satisfying exchanges between producers and customers, whether those customers are those of the marketer or not, through the active encouragement or discouragement of buying behaviour. The process may be carried out using a range of techniques, with the marketer's intentions known or unknown to the customer, and may result in unintended consequences.*

This definition is now extremely cumbersome, and appears to imply that marketers are simply blundering about in the dark, hoping that something will work: in some cases, this may be true, but it does not help a practitioner in terms of the 'what should I be doing on Monday morning?' question. Perhaps the definition could be stated better as:

> *Marketing is the set of activities, overt or otherwise, that are intended to manage supply and encourage or discourage demand in order to create efficient, beneficial exchanges between economic actors.*

This definition allows marketers to judge their actions: will this action encourage or discourage demand in a way that will match it with supply? Will the result be efficient in terms of profit and price, while being beneficial to all parties? Is this action going to result in something that is neither beneficial nor efficient? How can I avoid unintentional demarketing?

Currently, demarketing is one of many areas of marketing that has received little attention. Given that it has the power to influence something as fundamental as the way we define the discipline, demarketing deserves more thought and, dare we say it, research. This book has been an attempt to outline the topic and stimulate debate – the next stage lies with academics and practitioners.

INDEX